Writing Together

Writing Together

Ten Weeks Teaching and Studenting in an Online Writing Course

Scott Warnock
Drexel University

Diana Gasiewski

National Council of Teachers of English
1111 W. Kenyon Road, Urbana, Illinois 61801-1096

Staff Editor: Bonny Graham
Manuscript Editor: Josh Rosenberg
Interior Design: Jenny Jensen Greenleaf
Cover Design: Pat Mayer
Cover Images: nevarpp/iStock/Thinkstock and Blackzheep/iStock/Thinkstock

NCTE Stock Number: 59231; eStock Number: 59248
ISBN 978-0-8141-5923-1; eISBN 978-0-8141-5924-8

It is the policy of NCTE in its journals and other publications to provide a forum for the open discussion of ideas concerning the content and the teaching of English and the language arts. Publicity accorded to any particular point of view does not imply endorsement by the Executive Committee, the Board of Directors, or the membership at large, except in announcements of policy, where such endorsement is clearly specified.

NCTE provides equal employment opportunity (EEO) to all staff members and applicants for employment without regard to race, color, religion, sex, national origin, age, physical, mental or perceived handicap/disability, sexual orientation including gender identity or expression, ancestry, genetic information, marital status, military status, unfavorable discharge from military service, pregnancy, citizenship status, personal appearance, matriculation or political affiliation, or any other protected status under applicable federal, state, and local laws.

Every effort has been made to provide current URLs and email addresses, but because of the rapidly changing nature of the Web, some sites and addresses may no longer be accessible.

Library of Congress Cataloging-in-Publication Data

Names: Warnock, Scott, 1967- author. | Gasiewski, Diana, 1992- author.
Title: Writing together : ten weeks teaching and studenting in an online writing course / Scott Warnock, Drexel University ; Diana Gasiewski, Drexel University.
Description: Urbana, Illinois : National Council of Teachers of English, [2018] | Includes bibliographical references and index.
Identifiers: LCCN 2017052626 (print) | LCCN 2018002767 (ebook) | ISBN 9780814159248 (ebook) | ISBN 9780814159231 (pbk.)
Subjects: LCSH: English language—Composition and exercises—Study and teaching (Higher) | English language—Composition and exercises—Computer-assisted instruction. | English language—Rhetoric—Computer-assisted instruction. | Composition (Language arts)—Computer-assisted instruction.
Classification: LCC PE1404 (ebook) | LCC PE1404 .W275 2018 (print) | DDC 808/.0420785—dc23
LC record available at https://lccn.loc.gov/2017052626

Contents

Acknowledgments

Scott: I would like to thank the many students I have worked with, both in the course described in these pages and in the many other courses I have taught over the past 20+ years.

Diana: I would like to thank every one of my classmates and teachers, all the way back to grammar school, who helped inspire my interest in teaching and learning.

We both hope our book represents one way for student voices to be heard and student experiences—studenting—to be seen more clearly.

Introduction: A Meeting of the Minds

Scott: January 6. *It's the Friday before the winter term begins. I've spent the past month thinking through—based on our program's core syllabus and outcomes—and preparing my online first-year writing course, English 102: Persuasive Writing & Reading. My course site on our university's course learning management system (LMS) is ready to go. I've uploaded the first Weekly Plan of the course. I've added a friendly welcoming announcement the students will see when they have access to the LMS on Monday morning. The overall plan for the course is clear, I hope: the outcomes and learning goals, how the course will flow each week, what the major projects are, when they will be due, what texts we'll be using, and how I will evaluate their work. The fine "content" details? Like any writing course I teach, regardless of modality, I'll work those out as we go in response to what my students are doing. I've been teaching online writing courses (OWCs) for a while. I'm excited to get going.*

Diana: January 8. *I'm back from winter break and about to kick off my second college semester. So far, working out the kinks as a first-year student has gone a lot better than expected; I've embraced the college experience while keeping my grades high, which I've seen is difficult for some, so I'm thankful for that. I also switched my major from physician assistant studies (sorry Dad, the science-thing couldn't last) to public relations, so I'm eager to start working on my communication skills again. Yet, alongside new studies, I have a new course structure to learn. This term I'm taking an exclusively online course for the first time. To be honest, I didn't even know it was online until last week, but it should be convenient since I've maxed out my credits and will appreciate flexibility in my schedule (I mean, I can "go to class" from my couch!). I've heard mixed reviews about online classes from friends and upperclassmen, but since English is one of my favorite subjects I'm not too nervous. I'll log in to the course tomorrow just to make sure I have everything prepared for the week.*

Scott: An Online Writing Teacher

A 2016 report sponsored by the Online Learning Consortium found that more than 5.8 million students have taken at least one online course (Allen, Seaman, Poulin, and Straut). Hundreds of thousands of these learners are taking some type of online *writing* course, and these students are involved in a wide variety of engaging intellectual writing experiences, meeting and working with their teachers and peers in an array of electronic formats and platforms.

I have been involved in extensive work about online writing instruction (OWI) for more than a decade. I have maintained a blog called, aptly enough, *Online Writing Teacher*, since 2005 (2005—more than a decade? How can that be?) and in 2009 published the book *Teaching Writing Online: How and Why*. I have written many articles and chapters about teaching writing online and, more generally, the intersection between writing instruction and learning technologies. From 2011 to 2016, I was co-chair of the Conference on College Composition and Communication Committee for Effective Practices in OWI. Most recently, in 2016, I was part of a group that launched the Global Society of Online Literacy Educators. Over the past decade, I have been involved with faculty and professional development opportunities about OWI with hundreds of colleagues in nearly twenty states.

Many of my activities focus on the pedagogical, practical aspects of OWI. I have made great friends in the field and through my travels have strengthened a fundamental belief in the commitment, skills, and quality of teachers: Everywhere I go, I meet professionals who care deeply about their students. I have tried to do a good job in various professional development roles, yet when reflecting on these activities, I have been struck by a consistent experience: Even after an extensive, multiday workshop, some faculty still voice uncertainty about what the actual experience of an OWC will be like. During our closing conversations, a diligent workshop soul will often ask a version of this: "Okay, Scott, but what will the course *look* like?" Some of these hardworking, well-meaning teachers, who have given up their time to learn to teach an OWC and improve themselves as teachers, still express ambiguity about:

1. What teachers do *each week* that specifically constitutes *an online course.*
2. What teachers do that specifically constitutes *teaching an OWC*, which is fundamentally different from the many content courses that have dominated discussions about online learning.
3. What the student experience will be like in an OWC: *How do students participate and engage in an OWC?*

The final point is interesting but perhaps not surprising when we consider that, based on many conversations I have had, few college teachers have ever themselves taken an online course or engaged in any distance/online learning or professional development experience. A good number have not even conducted a remote meeting except by phone.

This inexperience is worth reflecting on when we examine how people learn to teach. In most cases, university teachers are not trained to teach during their graduate experiences or by the universities that hire them. Inexperienced graduate students are often "thrust into the classroom with little or no pedagogical training," a system that is "a long-running and disturbing national practice," says Leonard Cassuto in the *Chronicle of Higher Education* (Patel, "Training" A8). In a November 2015 *Chronicle* story about a grant-supported effort to help graduate students learn to teach, a student with a recently minted PhD in history said, "I swear, the word 'teaching' was never uttered in my program, much less 'pedagogy,' much less 'student learning'" (Patel, "$3-Million"). Many faculty would no doubt say the same thing. So what is their basis/foundation when they start their first term teaching? They probably work from their own experiences as students. Almost everyone has sat in a classroom, likely in a row of desks. Many college teachers had that experience for nearly twenty years. Something has to stick. But of course those learning experiences would be incredibly subjective, based as they often are on our own narrow school travels. Where else might teachers turn—perhaps to caricatures of school and teaching from our broader culture, such as *Dead Poets Society*; *To Sir, With Love*; or *Lean on Me*? As I often do when seeking insight into human nature, I turn here to *The Simpsons*. In Season 5, Episode 3, when Homer returns to college, he wants to be a "campus hero," so he spikes the punch at an early-term undergraduate mixer. The kids sip the punch and are aghast when they taste alcohol; they are only comforted when someone announces, "Your parents have been called!" Homer grouses about this new generation to his wife: "Marge, someone squeezed all the life out of these kids. And unless movies and TV have lied to me it's a crusty, bitter, old dean." *Simpsons* loyalists will recall that the dean ends up being a cool guy named "Bobby" who is always up for some hacky sack and even played bass for the rock band The Pretenders. The episode lampoons our preconceptions of school, but such strong preconceptions and plain old misperceptions do function for students and parents—and for new teachers too. Without a reliable guide, teachers may either follow what they lived/experienced or what they *think* college teaching is supposed to look like.

This can only be accentuated when a teacher is asked to teach online but has never taken an online course. What do such teachers use as the foundation of their teaching experience in the virtual world? What are the pop culture narratives of teaching online that parallel the many onsite narratives, such as those mentioned above? What student stereotypes are a new teacher's equivalent of the "crusty . . . old dean"? The scarcity of these narratives in pop culture may only be matched by their scarcity in academic literature.

Thinking of it like this is startling: Many people who, by nature, may be nervous about technology, can find themselves in a digital teaching environment that is utterly unfamiliar to them. (Perhaps this is one reason faculty are often warier about online learning than administrators [see, e.g., Elaine Allen and Jeff Seaman's "Conflicted"]). They do not have their own student memories of the clever in-class icebreaker or interesting in-class group activity or even a teacher's style of writing notes on the board from which to draw. To many teachers, going online represents a new teaching frontier. Also, while one could argue that training for OWCs and online in general may be improving,[1] many teachers are still embarking on such instruction with little support and faculty development.

So how, writing teacher, do you know what to do when you begin to teach online?

The Student Voice

Teaching Writing Online: How and Why was well received, probably for the simple reason that it met a demand: Colleagues of mine needed and wanted to know how to teach writing online but did not have specific resources. Soon after its publication, I had envisioned a follow-up project that would, in building on *Teaching Writing Online* and my above-mentioned workshop and conference experiences, provide more specific pedagogical guidance for OWC teachers. But during the planning of that second project, something nagged at me: My experiences in faculty training and at many academic conferences revealed an oft-missing component of conversations about writing pedagogy, online or onsite: *the student voice*. In gatherings, teachers talked, often late into the night, about classroom practices, philosophies, and approaches, but students, the "recipients" of these practices, philosophies, and approaches, were absent.

This absence exists despite a recognition, across disciplines, that students should be more prominent in these conversations. In 1993, in the journal *Studies in Higher Education*, Alan Booth said of history instruction that "any response" to new challenges in such instruction "should begin with a careful consideration of student perceptions and needs" (227). In the sciences, many studies indicate that students' attitudes and interest decline as they proceed through their education; investigating this issue for the journal *Research in Science Education*, Marianne Logan and Keith Skamp followed students for two years, and the process was as important as the results, they said:

> Apart from identifying the teacher's pedagogical approach and classroom environment as two key issues in understanding these students' journeys, the importance of listening to and heeding the students' voice may be an even more critical concern in addressing the decline in students' attitudes and interest in science. (501)

When research does draw on student views, it tends to rely more on quantitative results—such as end-of-course surveys—than deep dives into their experiences. The research on teaching tends to attempt to determine effects based on student surveys or evaluations (e.g., Childers and Berner, 2000).

We do not even have a reliable nomenclature for the student experience. As Mary Louise Pratt famously said, "Teacher-pupil language, for example, tends to be described almost entirely from the point of view of the teacher and teaching, not from the point of view of pupils and pupiling (the word doesn't even exist, though the thing certainly does)" (38). As this thing nagged at me, I wondered if I might more responsibly represent the student experience through a research collaboration. There was support for taking this approach. A *Chronicle of Higher Education* article, "The Human Variable in Teaching," commented that "Every student is a puzzle" (Hoover A28), yet teachers often don't take (or have) the time to solve those puzzles, which may involve listening more closely to students and involving them in our educational research. The Council of Undergraduate Research (CUR) defines undergraduate research as "student-faculty collaboration[s] to examine, increase, and share new knowledge or works in ways commensurate with practices in the discipline" (Wilson 1). The broader approach of "co-research" provides a frame for enabling research participants to see themselves as researchers (e.g., see John Benington and Jean Hartley; Robin Boylorn). And in their introduction to *Undergraduate Research in English Studies*, Laurie Grobman and Joyce Kinkead say undergraduate research has been "slow to grab hold in the humanities, particularly in English Studies" because "we as faculty have not articulated to our students the methodology of inquiry in our fields except as injunctions in our classes to 'write a paper'. . . . As faculty, we need to articulate our methodology, define appropriate tasks for students, and ask for authentic scholarship" (x).

Several winters ago at Drexel, I taught a first-year OWC. Diana was one of the students. She changed majors several times—of course that is common among undergraduates[2]—and ended up pursuing an undergraduate degree in teacher education with a minor in English. She took two other courses with me, one of which was Writing and Peer Tutoring Workshop, Drexel's training course for students who want to work as tutors in our campus writing center. Diana became a tutor (a position at Drexel called peer reader), and while working together in that writing-centric environment, we often discussed our OWC and teaching in general. While continuing to think about the student voice,[3] I approached Diana one day about coauthoring a journal article that would provide a dual-perspective narrative of the experience of that OWC. It would be straightforward but also, I thought, innovative: We would describe specifically what it was like to teach and what it was like to participate as a student in an OWC. At the very start of the drafting process, we hit a pleasant snag. Diana, just with a simple first pass, handed me nearly six thousand words! I stepped back and realized this project might well warrant a more elaborate medium: a book.

Diana: An Online Writing Course Student

So, I wrote six thousand words about my experience in Scott's class. When we initially planned for this exercise, neither of us was expecting what came out of my reflection. I mean, students typically do not put in the effort to pick apart the pedagogy of the course and their subsequent reactions (or, perhaps, they don't have the opportunity to, but we'll elaborate on that point later). When given the chance to provide feedback on a class, my peers often kept their summaries to a brief "It was super easy" (code for they earned an A) or "The professor is a jerk" (code for they didn't earn an A). Sure, a few friends offered more detail on the teacher's style of delivery, charisma, or intelligence, but the rundown mainly consisted of the course difficulty and "coolness" of the professor. What was missing was authentic, detailed, responsive analysis.

To be frank, when would a student have the opportunity to provide such feedback? Course evaluations are conducted and surveys are sent out, but opportunities rarely arise when a college student can sit down and analyze each week, each assignment, and each discussion from a course. Fortunately, I found myself in a scenario where I could produce that exact response. Scott and I realized our professional relationship, classroom experience, and knowledge base on pedagogy could warrant a book, and we plowed forward with enthusiasm.

Despite my bubbling excitement (which was more than justified, considering I was twenty-two years old and could potentially be a published author), I did have incredible self-doubt about my authority on the project. Why would anyone want to hear from me, a newly graduated college student, in the first place? I mean, I earned great grades, but I wasn't a perfect 4.0 student. I was ambitious in my side projects and enjoyed venturing beyond the required work, but I didn't have a story written about me in the school newspaper or anything. I was successful, but there are other young adults who have achieved far more than me at my age. From my perspective, I struggled with my identity within the story. Should I write as the "average student," trying to provide a catch-all perception of an online course? Or should I write as me, Diana, the social, outgoing student who adores writing and is fascinated with the field of OWI?

As I worked through this dilemma, I realized several things were required of me for the project to work:

- Experience as a student
- Decent writing skills
- Base knowledge of pedagogy
- Honesty

The first two aspects are self-explanatory and, for me, easy to meet. The latter two, however, are what pushed me to move forward with my original voice for the project. Having experience as an education major (the major I finally settled on), I would have a somewhat informed idea of what was going on in Scott's mind as he produced work for the course and assessed us. Would I be able to nail his pedagogical reasoning throughout an entire analysis of the course? No, but I would know enough to produce useful feedback on how his course design affected my learning—useful in the sense that I could speak the same educational language as Scott and our primary readers, those who want to teach writing online. I could work as a liaison between students and course instructors, translating both students' reactions and the instructor's intent to help bridge the pedagogical gap between professors and students in higher education, particularly online. This was a role not all students in my position could fulfill.

Education majors are, however, easy to come by. If Scott wanted to, he could have asked any education major (or any student versed in pedagogy) who took his OWC to fill my role, but he didn't. He asked me. So this is where the last requirement of honesty came into play. I have a genuine interest in writing instruction, particularly its role in higher education and online settings. This interest tumbled into my life as I worked in the Drexel Writing Center (DWC), where I frequently provided writing feedback in synchronous, online tutoring sessions. I was already interested in teaching, but once I faced the struggle of communicating with a peer online while trying to provide successful instruction and feedback, I was hooked. Ever since my experience in the DWC, I've focused my studies and coursework largely on OWI, creating a path to eventually work full-time in the field.

So, in all simplicity, I love what we're writing about. Beyond being a student, a communicative student, an education studies student, I have genuine passion for what we can achieve through writing this narrative. Our narrative represents a great opportunity for the field of OWI, and maybe online education in general. While any average student response is useful in providing the generally unheard perspective of "studenting," my unique voice offers so much more: detail, individuality, and honesty.

Scott and Diana: Writing Together

In the coming chapters, the two of us, teacher and student, will chronologically follow the trajectory of a ten-week OWC at Drexel University. The primary goal is to provide our main audience—the many teachers, including graduate students, who teach OWCs or who are in training to do so—with a casebook that describes in detail the teaching and learning perspectives of an OWC. The ten core chapters are filled with specific pedagogical resources to help teachers implement teaching practices that take advantage of the rich, text-based environment of a primarily asynchronous OWC. In those chapters, we describe our strategies, activities, approaches, thoughts, and responses as we moved through a term teaching and *studenting* an OWC. We hope that you will learn detailed approaches about teaching a writing course in a digital environment; you will see specific assignments as well as ways of enacting teaching strategies. Each week, we focus on a particular theme, including offering a brief "Behind the Screen" sidebar of materials and resources relevant to that theme. We include the week's "Weekly Plan" in the beginning, as well as emails and Discussion posts from the class throughout each chapter. In most cases, these are the actual texts from the students and teacher. We created a lot of those words in informal electronic environments, and for this book, Diana and Scott usually chose to leave the writing as it was when it was composed for the course; after-the-fact edits were only made to avoid confusion.

Diana, in some way taking on the role of an ongoing "respondent," will describe how she approached each week's activities. Through that voice, she will aim to lend insight into online student behaviors and practices, and we hope you will understand better how students perceive digitally-facilitated writing courses and how they navigate—and live through—the experience of participating in one. As we mention above, student voices are often absent in conversations about teaching in higher education, and the naturally dispersed nature of an OWC—i.e., the teacher is often not the center of the action—may exacerbate this. While we will demonstrate in the coming chapters how this teaching-learning dynamic is complex, OWC teachers are confronted with some fundamental, challenging questions about students that they perhaps do not think of in onsite courses: *Where* do students do their work? *When* do they do it?

What do they see/perceive when they use their machines to *interface* with the material? How do students perceive teaching *instructions*? How do they develop a sense of *community* in an OWC? How do they handle the *writing and reading load*? In "A Position Statement of Principles and Example Effective Practices for OWI," OWI Principle 1 states, "Online writing instruction should be universally inclusive and accessible" (Conference 7). Diana's perspectives will help you see what students are doing as they access and participate in an OWC. After all, teachers' limited view of students' experiences in higher education may be related to the fact that, in many cases, teachers are unlike those whom they teach.[4] In a broader sense, by following the kind of co-research approach we mention above, we hope we might expand the way other qualitative pedagogical works are created. In our case, the student is not passively being studied but is actively involved in the story- and meaning-making of the experience.

We chose the title *Writing Together* because we interacted almost exclusively in writing through the interface of an LMS and engaged in a writing-based educational journey along with other students in the class. *Writing Together* aims to be an unusually told teaching *story* about an OWC and how the human beings involved on both sides wrote and learned with others who were part of that online learning community one winter. Narrative theorist David Herman said, "Rather than focusing on general, abstract situations or trends, stories are accounts of what happened to particular people—and of what it was like for them to experience what happened—in particular circumstances and with specific consequences" (3). The FYW course we describe is, of course, just one of infinite possibilities for such a course. While we closely follow the syllabus and assignments of the actual course Scott taught that winter, occasionally Scott's narrative brings in learning-teaching experiences from other OWCs; think of it, if you will, as *pedagogical creative nonfiction*. In taking our approach, Scott thinks about the fascinating composition teaching book by William Coles, *The Plural I—and After*. In the introduction, Richard Larson says that Coles's book "shows how one instructional plan was employed at one college in one recent semester by one instructor in his teaching of writing," and

> if reliving, through this dramatic or fictional representation, the experience of this course at that time turns out to illuminate for readers the fundamental experience of teaching [...] as good drama and good fiction illuminate for readers the experiences they represent, I think that William Coles will believe his book to have been worth the writing. (vii–viii)

In our earliest conversations, we felt that the book would be strongest if it had a distinctive voice and flavor from each of us, but we also realized that if the book were too pedagogically and technologically specific, it would be of little use to most instructors.

While the narrative follows a real course, as described in the pre-chapter, not some generalized first-year writing "everycourse," we do generalize the approaches and pedagogies so other teachers might use them in their courses. While the texts and themes will differ significantly from how others might teach, we believe the fundamental pedagogy of having students work together with an instructor in a collaborative, process-driven, writing-centric way is applicable to many teaching situations in which online writing teachers might find themselves. We have only referred to specific assignment texts in which we felt the reader would be interested, or we mentioned those texts because to omit them would be confusing in the context of that week's activities.

A Note about Platforms—and Pedagogy

All that being said, there is of course a pedagogy at work here, and the specifics of it are presented in the pre-chapter that follows. This course was conducted primarily asynchronously, featuring lots of message board work, using a common LMS as a platform. The class involved a significant team project. As a component of a core curriculum, the course focused on rhetorical mode instruction in persuasion/argument, but the strongest informing pedagogy is Writing about Writing (sometimes called Writing Studies) (as described by Doug Downs and Elizabeth Wardle). Scott asked students to engage in a lot of metawriting and reflecting. The final project was a writing portfolio. Scott (as he describes throughout) used a low-stakes grading approach that featured lots of points and many small, graded assignment opportunities for students to earn those points. Of course, these factors all matter and influence the experience and learning of the course. Note too that this was a ten-week course, in line with Drexel's quarter system. Most teachers work in a longer semester system; however, we realized that for a book, ten weeks may be ideal. It made for a succinct book, and one of our concluding arguments is about transfer; the process work surround-

Behind the Screen: In Case You Were Wondering, Online Learning Is Not Going Away

Approach aside, the exigency of this book is real. Thousands of sections of online writing instruction are offered each year in US institutions. According to the National Center for Education Statistics, "In fall 2014, there were 5,750,417 students enrolled in any distance education courses at degree-granting postsecondary institutions" (National). With recent cultural movements in education such as Starbucks' collaboration with Arizona State (Ripley), it is likely that these numbers will grow. Scott's *Teaching Writing Online* continues to sell copies for NCTE even nine years after its publication. In short, OWCs continue to be developed as institutions expand their OWI offerings.

ing Project 1 is transferable to other projects, so in a semester course instructors would develop another, similar round of projects.

Also, nothing pedagogical that we describe is dependent on a specific LMS platform. The experiences Diana relates are mainly about the way she exchanged ideas with colleagues and with her professor using readily available learning technologies. While any good technology scholar knows that a technology invariably influences the experiences (and often thought processes) of its users, we have done our best to write this book from the perspective of being "platform neutral": A teacher with access to basic LMS tools should be able to use teaching strategies similar to those described here.

And a Brief Note about Students

We received Approval of Protocol from Drexel University's Office of Research for this book project. Students whose writings were used in substantive ways explicitly granted us permission to do so. Students had the option to be referred to with a pseudonym throughout our text, and most of the names you encounter in the book are pseudonyms. In any case, we only used the first names of students we interacted with in the course.

Pre-chapter: Scott's Second-Term FYW Course

In this pre-chapter, I provide you with a brief overview of English 102, including showing the syllabus as well as guidelines to help students get acclimated to the all-important Discussions. This chapter should give you an overall understanding of the course's design and goals. This class was the second in Drexel's three-term FYW sequence (we are on the quarter system). At the time, English 102 was named "Persuasive Writing & Reading," although differentiating Drexel's FYW courses by rhetorical mode was fading and has since disappeared, as has happened in many FYW programs. In terms of pedagogy, this course was influenced by two major approaches: (1) a program-wide emphasis on rhetoric, including a touch of classic rhetoric; and (2) an emphasis by me on Writing about Writing (WaW), through which students would learn about *writing as subject/content* and engage in a good amount of metawriting and reflective work. I further expanded/tweaked WaW to what I might call *writing about learning*: Their learning processes were a subject of discussion throughout the term.

This course also stood, as the saying goes, on the shoulders of giants. It was an (ever-evolving) endpoint of decades of teaching and praxis by compositionists. You might refer to Joseph Harris's *A Teaching Subject: Composition since 1966* or Stephen North's *The Making of Knowledge in Composition: Portrait of an Emerging Field* for an overview of the teaching and scholarly perspectives that helped shape my teaching. I was lucky to receive excellent training first at Rutgers University–Camden with Tim Martin and then in a practicum at Temple University with the influential composition scholar who became my dissertation advisor, Eli Goldblatt. My use of computers and digital pedagogies to teach writing would not have evolved to the point that I could write this book without Gail Hawisher and Cynthia Selfe. Throughout the book, I'll cite and refer to influences for specific pedagogical practices, particularly how they manifest themselves in OWCs, but it's important that you know that, well, this teacher didn't just appear out of nowhere.

The syllabus and other material that follow are for your reference; it will help you to see overall what this writing course was about. As mentioned in the introduction, this course was a specific iteration of an FYW course, but many aspects of it will look familiar to those who have taught writing. Note that while I required students to read this syllabus information, we reviewed it together during our synchronous live classroom meeting in Week 1.

Drexel University Department of English & Philosophy
Persuasive Writing and Reading

Prof. Scott Warnock (sjwarnock@drexel.edu; 215.895.0377)
Office: MacAlister 0032 (in the Drexel Writing Center); office hours: T&W 10 to 11:30
Class meeting room: Online only
LMS site direct access: [url]

← I provided my full contact info, including phone, for these online students.

Syllabus Contents

Required Texts	Course Requirements and Grading
First-Year Writing Program Goals and Learning Outcomes	Course Policies
	Major Due Dates
Drexel University Writing Center	Participating in an Online Writing Course

← The syllabus also contained a contents section, which can be internally linked in the document. In line with Guideline 13 of my *Teaching Writing Online*, the syllabus provided "more detail than other syllabi," namely in comparison to onsite courses (46).

Required Texts

[Course writing guide.] This book will help you improve your ability to write and to think about your writing; it includes assignment instructions, guidelines, exercises, and readings.

Stein, Scott, Albert DiBartolomeo, and Kathleen Volk Miller, eds. *The 33rd. The 33rd* is an anthology of writing by Drexel students and faculty.

First-Year Writing Program Goals and Learning Outcomes

The First-Year Writing Program (FWP) at Drexel is a three-course, yearlong writing-intensive sequence. During the year you will learn to

1. Focus on purpose
2. Appreciate and respond to diverse audiences
3. Respond to different kinds of rhetorical situations
4. Use format and structure conventions appropriate to the rhetorical situation
5. Adopt appropriate voice, tone, and level of formality
6. Understand how genres shape writing
7. Write in different genres
8. Use writing and reading for inquiry, thinking, and communicating
9. Integrate your ideas with the ideas of others

← The outcomes for Drexel's entire First-Year Writing program were listed.

10. Use research to develop, support, and enhance your ideas
11. Understand how to develop and document ideas
12. Understand writing as a process
13. Critique your own and others' works
14. Use writing technologies to address a range of audiences
15. Use conventions, including citation methods such as MLA
16. Control mechanics such as syntax, grammar, punctuation, and spelling

Persuasive Writing, the second of these courses, focuses on expanding your understanding of rhetorical aspects of writing through the art of persuasion and by thinking about writing in your discipline/profession. The specific outcomes for Persuasive Writing are listed in the Syllabus Documents and Discussion Guide folder. These outcomes are designed to provide you with a clear roadmap of what you will learn and do in the course.

Drexel University Writing Center

The Drexel Writing Center (DWC) is located in 0032 MacAlister (x1799). Whether you are developing a rough draft or trying to put the finishing touches on a well-developed project, peer and faculty readers will help you evaluate your own writing and determine how to improve it according to your purpose and your audience. The DWC's Web page has more details: [url].

Stop by the DWC—you may find it's one of the best places on campus to help you enhance your writing and thinking.

← The Drexel Writing Center was described right up front. Note that our center provides online appointments.

Course Requirements and Grading

Note: To earn a passing grade, you must complete both projects and the portfolio.

Composition Project 1	200 points	Portfolio and reflective analysis	50 points
Composition Project 2	250 points	Informal writing (ELC work)	350 points
Project 2 Topic Proposal and Research Plan	50 points	Quizzes	50 points
Project 2 Annotated Bibliography	50 points	Participation	+/- 10 or 20 points

Composition Projects

You will have two major composition projects in this course (complete descriptions are in separate documents). These projects, which may integrate writing with other media, should demonstrate the following, in line with the course goals and learning outcomes:

- A clear understanding of *audience* and *purpose*. Your audience members will ask, "So what? Why am I reading this?" Your projects should answer those questions.
- A well-articulated and clear *main point* or *thesis.*
- A commitment to *revising* your project from invention to completion.
- *Research* and *evidence* appropriate for the project, incorporated correctly and cited accurately.

← I used a strategy I call frequent, low-stakes (FLS) grading, in which students receive many small grades. This strategy is important in an OWC, as students work on lots of small writing assignments. FLS grading also helps them learn their way into the environment while avoiding grades serving, as Peter Filene said, as a "pedagogical whip." (A no grading policy wouldn't work well for a school like Drexel, but that's a different conversation.) Overall, the small grades added up to a large portion of the overall course grade.

- Clear *organization.*
- *Grammatical* and *stylistic* clarity appropriate for college-level writing.
- Adherence to the *conventions* and *guidelines* of the project (due dates, length, format).

Writing Portfolio

Keep all of the work you do in this course. At the end of the term, you will select a number of formal and informal compositions you've written in First-Year Writing and develop a portfolio using an electronic portfolio (if you don't have an account, I will help you set one up). You will return to this e-portfolio again in your final FYW course, Analytical Writing & Reading, and later in your Drexel career.

Informal Writing and Discussion

Informal writing and shorter assignments, taken together, are a major component of your grade in this course. Each week, you are required to write the equivalent of several pages in response to the readings, response to my questions, or conversations with your colleagues. Ideally, you will question ideas in the text or brainstorm ideas for the projects. These informal writings will include Discussion threads via our LMS, peer reviews of other students' work, and other short assignments.

← Much like in an onsite syllabus, assignments were described briefly.

Quizzes

We will have a brief reading quiz every week. The quizzes are designed to help you (and your grade): If you complete the readings, you will do well on the quizzes. Quiz rules:

- All quizzes are timed. You will only have a few minutes to complete each quiz, but, if you read, I assure you that you'll find the quizzes quite manageable (and, I daresay, even easy).
- The quizzes will be available for a set period, and then they will no longer be available. There are **no make-ups** for a missed quiz.
- The quizzes are all short answer.
- You may drop one quiz (actually, I will do this for you).

← Each week in this OWC, there would be a quick quiz to help encourage the students to read (see Guideline 20 of *Teaching Writing Online*).

Class Participation

Students who participate at a high level in our online course discussions will be rewarded. Those who frequently miss discussions or who post late may be penalized at my discretion.

Grade Scale

A+: 97-100	B+: 87-89	C+: 77-79	D+: 67-69
A: 93-96	B: 83-86	C: 73-76	D: 63-66
A-: 90-92	B-: 80-82	C-: 70-72	F: below 60

← The grade scale is standard; its appearance here was required by the university.

Course Policies

Academic integrity. All students must abide by Drexel's academic integrity policy. The Drexel *Official Student Handbook* states:

> If an act of academic dishonesty is determined to have occurred, one or more of the following sanctions will be imposed, depending on the severity of the offense:
>
> - Reduction of a course grade
> - An "F" for the assignment or exam
> - Failure for the entire course
> - Other action deemed appropriate by the faculty member
> - Any of the above sanctions with the inability to withdraw
>
> Examples of other action deemed appropriate include, but are not limited to, requiring the student to re-take the exam, re-complete an assignment, or complete an assigned exercise. The decision of the faculty member and the department head shall be reported to the Office of Student Conduct and Community Standards, which is responsible for maintaining student conduct records. The incident will result in an official disciplinary record for the student(s). (128)

A violation of academic integrity is *not limited to* copying a passage from a source word for word. If you acquire specific information from a source, you *must* acknowledge that source, even if you have used your own words and paraphrased that information. You must also refrain from fabricating source material, stealing or buying compositions, or being complicit in a violation of academic integrity (e.g., writing a peer's paper for him/her) (127-128). Please review chapters 19 and 20 of our course textbook for acceptable ways of acknowledging the work of other writers.

According to the Drexel *Official Student Handbook*, a second academic integrity offense may result in "suspension or expulsion, in addition to any sanction issued from the list above" (129). For further questions about Drexel's academic integrity policy, please talk with your instructor, and consult the Drexel *Official Student Handbook*, which may be found here: [url].

← I included a detailed list of policies to help students understand what they were getting into. Again, this was all discussed during our synchronous live classroom meeting in Week 1. I lead off with "Academic Integrity," although I'm not that worried about plagiarism in an OWC: I see tens of thousands of students' words; I get to know the students pretty well!

Accountability. I am here to work with and help you, but you are accountable for your performance in the course. If you are negligent in your duties as a student, I ask that you take responsibility for your actions. *Your accountability starts with your careful reading of this syllabus.*

← I included some comments on "Accountability": I reinforced early and often that this was a hands-on experience that required their direct participation.

Disability. Students with disabilities who request accommodations and services at Drexel need to present a current accommodation verification letter (AVL) to me before accommodations can be made. AVLs are issued by the Office of Disability Services: [url]; 3201 Arch St., Ste. 210, Philadelphia, PA, 19104. [Phone: #]

Assignment submission/File naming conventions. It is your responsibility to ensure that I receive your work. You also should back up all of your work and plan on saving it for some time, especially materials you will use in future portfolios. To help organize the work in the course, please adhere to the following ***file naming conventions***: Name the file with your last name, first initial, assignment name, and a one-word assignment description. *So my first draft of project one would look like this: WarnockSProj1draft fear.doc.*

← File naming might seem like a small thing until you receive fifty projects named "Project1."

Drop/withdraw. Students have until the end of the 2nd week of the term to drop a course without financial responsibility and until the end of the 6th week of the term to withdraw with financial responsibility, according to the University's sliding scale. For details on the sliding scale, see [url].

Late assignments. The learning in this course requires in-depth reading, reflection, writing, discussion, independent work, and team work. To achieve our goals, you must complete your work in a timely manner. Late assignments will be penalized.

Library skills. You must know how to use the library resources. Check out the First-Year Writer's Toolbox: [url].

Technology. Obviously, you need easy access to **our LMS** to participate in this class. You must also have access to some type of media software. If you have trouble accessing our LMS because of your particular computer set-up, you're going to find this course difficult; you will be unhappy. *Important: You need to have back-up technology plans, because a disabled computer will not excuse you from the work in the course.* If you have problems accessing our LMS or using our portfolio software, contact [url] or call the Help Desk at [phone #]. Portfolio support may also be found here: [url]

You must also have an active **Drexel** email account (it is easy to set up your Drexel account to forward mail to another account).

Major Due Dates

Here is a general idea of when projects are due, but the schedule and assignments are subject to change.

Week 3: First draft of Project 1
Week 4: Final draft of Project 1
Week 7: First draft of Project 2
Week 8: Final draft of Project 2
Week 10: Portfolio and reflective analysis

← I wanted some schedule flexibility, so I provided overall project due dates to help students plan their term – but did not lock down every week.

Participating in an Online Writing Course

This may be your first experience in an online course. You'll no doubt find this to be a different experience than that of an onsite class. Following are some things to think about as you begin this online learning experience. I also have prepared a more extensive list of frequently asked questions about online writing courses here: [url].

← I included this extensive final section to provide them with further perspective on what they were about to do in an OWC. I tried to include in this some writing

Follow the Weekly Plans. I create careful Weekly Plans to help you stay organized. If you closely read and follow the Weekly Plans, you significantly increase your chances of success.

Deadlines. It is crucial that you adhere closely to the class deadlines. In fact, you should ask yourself a question: "Am I self-motivated enough to meet these deadlines?" If the answer is "no," then you should probably switch to an onsite section. I have seen too many students stubbornly resist the obvious: They are not good candidates for an online class because they couldn't meet the deadlines on their own. Unfortunately, many of those students have had a poor outcome in the course as a result.

Motivation. When I study the behavior of students in my online courses, I have found a consistent trend: Students who post early on the Discussions have higher grades in the course overall. You can't control everything, but you can control when you get involved in class discussions. Post early—and often!

Contact. You can reach me by phone at the number listed on the Syllabus, but most of our communications will take place via:

Discussions—Discussions will make up the major part of our interaction this quarter, as you can see from the course requirements. See the document "Guidelines for Participating in Discussions."

Email—You need to become familiar with your Drexel email account. That account can easily be forwarded to another account, but I will use your Drexel account to send you mail. We'll do a lot of corresponding that way. Do NOT use our LMS email.

Chat—Sometimes we will correspond via chat, particularly the day before a project is due.

I will spend time checking email and Discussions for course messages each weekday morning (around 9:00 Eastern Standard Time [EST]) and in the afternoon (around 4:00 EST). The day before major projects are due, I will be available at other times. If there is an emergency, do not hesitate to call me.

There is a temptation in an online course for you to think of your professor as a robot who never sleeps. While you are college students, and you may do some of your most productive work at two in the morning, I am an old(ish) man who goes to bed at 10:30. Remember that when you email me in the wee hours of the night and can't understand why I haven't responded to you. The three-dimensional me can be found in MacAlister 0032. My office hours are Tuesday and Wednesday from 10:00 to 11:30, but I am around a lot more than that and will make every effort to be available if you need to see me in person.

personality ("old[ish]") as well as some realistic, tell-it-like-it-is language ("poor outcome").

← I stressed the primary modes of communication.

← I provided a time frame of when I would likely check for messages (although in practice, I had much more availability).

Space. You're working online. Where should you do this work? You need to treat the time you are writing and thinking about the class material as real class time, and therefore you need a quiet work space. In fact, you will have a lot more success in college if you learn to carve out a quiet space when you study. Ask your friends, roommates, and/or family to give you a break during a set time each day, or you'll need to find a good, quiet place on campus or somewhere else where you can study. I know you are probably all skilled multi-taskers, but if you get into bad study habits as a freshman, they will be hard to break later.

← Having a good studying/working space is crucial for online learners. I emphasized that here.

Feeling isolated? Remember, while our class is online, I'm a real-live human being who has an office on campus. If you have concerns, feel free to stop in and talk to me during my office hours or call me. As we progress, if you feel this experience is not for you, you can switch to an onsite section early in the quarter.

← One more time: I'm here to help!

Guidelines for Participating in Discussions

Conversations that we have via **online Discussions** will make up a good part of the work in this course. Whether you are responding to a question or issue I've raised or you are collaborating virtually as a team, we will be working on your thinking—and writing. A few general matters:

- **Read all posts.** Part of your responsibility as a student in this class is to read everything on the Discussions. *All of them*. At the end of the week, you should have *no bold-faced, unread posts.*
- **Check the Discussion boards regularly.** You need to start good habits in Week 1.
- **Sign your name at the end of your post.** We want to know how to respond back to you.
- **Build a conversation.** As I describe below, you will write "primary," "secondary," and "peep" posts. After I read your primary posts, I will post specific questions throughout the term, as will your colleagues. Make sure you look at those questions and respond to them. You'll soon see how this works, but ***do not simply reply over and over again to my initial prompt.***

You will have three types of posts: "primary," "secondary," and "peeps." Each week, I will let you know how many posts are due. "Argument Statements" are slightly more elaborate primary posts.

1. Rules for "primary" posts. These posts should be

- **Essays.** Primary posts should *not be one simple paragraph,* and I expect them to reflect some reasoned thought on your part, beyond what you

← These detailed guidelines, which I refine every time I teach, were designed to help them understand the Discussions. They included specific language about norms I hoped to establish in this crucial learning component of the course. I hoped that just the existence of the guidelines emphasized the importance of this aspect of the course. I start with "general matters"...

might put into a normal email or chat post. My students and I have found that these mini-essays present many excellent opportunities to refine the ability to make a clear, focused point when writing. In other words, these posts are great practice.

- **Detailed.** Each "primary" post must be at least *150 words.* (Note: I'm not as interested in actual word count as I am in the depth of your ideas. Obviously, a post like "Me too!!" doesn't qualify as a "primary" post; it's a "peep"!)
- **Semiformal.** Your posts should contain some degree of formality: spell-checked, organized, etc. However, they will also be part of a dialogue, so in that regard they will differ from major writing projects. I understand that it will take some time for us to reach a mutual understanding of the appropriate level of formality.
- **Referenced.** While you won't always need citations in your posts, you should look for opportunities to build your argument by referencing our readings, other sources, or your colleagues' comments.
- **Courteous.** We don't always have to agree, but no one should resort to flaming attacks.

← . . . then move into the specific types of posts and the "rules" for each.

2. Rules for "secondary" posts. "Secondary" posts are similar to the above, but they can differ from "primary" posts by being

- **Less structured:** Response posts can be one paragraph.
- **Shorter:** Response posts only need to be about *75 words.*

3. Rules for "peeps." "Peeps" are simply very short posts between you and another student. They serve as conversational "glue" in the course. If you post 10 of them during the term, you get 10 points. You cannot make up all peeps at the end of the term. Do one or two a week.

4. Grading. Your Discussion work will be worth 20 to 40 points each week. To evaluate your posts, I will use the rubric below, considering these factors:

- If you complete them in an adequate manner, you will receive Bs.
- If you go above and beyond the basic requirements of the assignments, you will receive As.
- Very good—completed with a great deal of effort and thought—posts will receive full credit (e.g., 10 out of 10). You can also get full credit for posting with great passion or imagination.

← I wanted them right up front to understand how the grading works.

Your Discussion posts will receive a C or below if they

- are too short.
- show little thought (especially if they respond in the same way others have responded).
- are excessively sloppy in terms of grammar, spelling, and mechanics, especially to the point that they are difficult to understand.
- engage in personal attacks or other breaches of common online etiquette.
- are late.

5. Reading. You are responsible for reading all posts in the class.

- Don't *"post and run"*—Once you post, you're *obligated* to see what people say. In some cases, it seems weary students abandon their ideas after they post. More specifically, if someone responds to you, you should follow up with a response, however brief. I must admit that I feel miffed (and sometimes a little lonely) when I post and am ignored.
- Don't *"post ignorant"*—Be original. Don't say the same thing as many other posts on a thread. Read before you post. Part of your job in the class is to "up the ante" with each post.

← Reading, reading, reading—the course experience revolved around literacy (and literacy *diligence*).

6. Shorter posts. In the spirit of keeping the conversation flowing, feel free to post as many shorter, informal comments on the Discussion threads as you like; for instance, writing a quick sentence to clarify a point or to state your agreement with another author's point of view. But remember rules for "primary" and "secondary" posts.

← I emphasized that the goal was to build and sustain dialogue. I wanted to encourage them to post and reward them as much as I could.

7. Staying current. In the Weekly Plan, you will see what posts are due and the deadlines for "primary" and "secondary" posts. One of your responsibilities in taking this course is that you will *check the Discussions frequently* and stay current on the conversations taking place there.

8. Extra credit. Those who are diligent, active Discussion members will find that they will receive a high grade for this part of the course. Excellent posts or posting a number of extra posts in a week can earn ***flair points*** for *extra credit* (some of you may naturally find that you have more to say on some of our topics this term, so I want to reward you).

Other topics

In addition to the specific, graded Discussions about class readings and assignments, I have also created Discussion topics for a few other purposes:

- "Questions about the course" is a Discussion area you can use to ask questions about any work in the class. *Before you email me with questions, post them to this forum.* I will answer many common questions here, and you'll be able to see the kinds of questions your classmates have. These too do not count for your grade, but many of my students have found this Discussion area to be quite useful. We will also use this thread as a place to post anything that seems relevant to the work of the course. Feel free to post here.
- "Writing puzzles" is where I will post specific writing "puzzles" based on the writing in the Discussion posts. I will randomly pick work for us to think about; even my own writing is game for this thread.

← These "other topics" were there to help students build community in the course. "Questions about the course" is often a busy thread in which they help one another.

You will find, I believe, that through these Discussions you will have many opportunities in this course to work on and develop your writing. Make sure you take advantage of those opportunities.

Rubric for Discussion posts

General criteria

Gross mistakes	There are no gross mistakes in the post	There are excessive errors or some other gross mistakes that cause readers to doubt the effort/expertise of the document's creator; these posts score no better than 60%
Ethics	The post appears ethical, including its use of evidence	Some aspects of the post are unethical; for example, it uses inappropriate evidence (including plagiarism), recommends morally questionable practices, attacks others, or uses deceitful data; these posts may fail
Timeliness	The post is on time	Late post; late posts lose 20% of their grade for each week they are late
Length	Post length is appropriate; longer posts are welcomed	Post is too short; short posts lose 20% of their grade; excessively short posts count only as "peeps"

Writing criteria

	A	B	C	D	F
Purpose/Main idea/Focus	Clear main idea that raises an excellent, focused point	Clear main idea that raises an interesting point	Loses focus; main idea is questionable	Why did the writer create this post?; main idea seems uninteresting and perhaps even unreasonable	Main idea is unfocused and unclear; off topic
Organization	Excellent organization; clear topic sentences; transitions between ideas are handled well	Organized effectively but could be refined/tightened a bit (better topic sentences, transitions, etc.)	Adequately organized; needs better division between ideas. Note: One-paragraph primary posts receive a maximum of 8	Disorganized; little coherent structure; confusing	Completely disorganized
Evidence	Relevant, correctly cited evidence; quotes from posts	Relevant evidence; some citing issues	Adequate evidence; citations are wrong	Evidence not used or used incorrectly	No evidence
Audience and context	Clearly connected to other posts and conversations	Relevant to other posts and conversations	Not clearly connected to other posts; unclear if writer read other posts; repetitive; does not build the conversation much	Highly repetitive; not connected to other posts and conversations; may attack other posters; does not build the conversation at all	Irrelevant to conversation; makes no effort to connect with audience; flaming

← The rubric served the role I think a good rubric should: It provided a means of communication between the teacher and students about the expectations of the Discussion posts. It looks like a "regular" writing rubric in many ways, although there are some specific components/categories for asynchronous dialogue, such as four binary criteria and a category about connecting with audience.

Style	Highly engaging, distinct writing style; solid sentences and word choice; may take productive risks	Solid writing style; writer could have written more clearly/ more concisely	Some of the writing is awkward and clumsy; weak word choice or unsophisticated sentence structure	Writing is awkward, repetitive, and/ or wordy; the writing was not engaging	Writing style is inadequate for a college-level assignment
Grammar and mechanics	Few errors, if any; writer shows considerable mastery of the language	Some grammatical/ mechanical errors, but they do not interfere with the reader's understanding of post	Numerous errors that interfered with the reader's understanding of the post	Many errors that made the post difficult to understand; reader questions writer's credibility and skill	Post is filled with errors; reader doubts writer's competency
Originality/ Creativity	Highly original or creative; may take a productive writing risk	Some originality or creativity, but doesn't push the limits	No real originality	Repeats other ideas or posts—reader may not have read other posts	Blatantly copies other posts
Understanding of course material	Clearly demonstrates understanding of course material	Good understanding of course material	Some of the course material details are incorrect	Low understanding of course material	Poor understanding of course material; some errors

← In the spirit of FLS grading and low-risk writing, I wanted them to understand the role of risk in their writing.

← Finally, there were elements of WaW in this course. I wanted them to learn that content too.

Brief Comments about the Readings

Each week, I describe the readings enough so you have some context without overburdening you with too much instructional detail (i.e., as I mention in the introduction, the specific course content here is not what is important, and I know most of you would use different readings and assignments in your own courses). There are a few things to keep in mind about the readings:

- The course support text was a popular guide to writing for first-year programs. It was a required text for English 101 and English 102 at Drexel, and I could assume that many of my students would already have purchased it in the fall. It provided, among other things, a bit of textual-conceptual "glue" for our large program.

- *The 33rd* is an unusual text. From the Drexel Publishing Group's website:

  > *The 33rd* is a multi-genre anthology of interdisciplinary student and faculty writing. It incorporates the winners of the First-Year Writing Contest, the Publishing Group Essay Contest, and the Week of Writing contest. The published pieces include students' personal and research essays, fiction, poetry, non-fiction, humor, and opinion/editorial, along with works by current Drexel University faculty members. (Drexel Publishing Group)

- I used a variety of texts in the spirit of the WaW approach to first-year writing, in which students would study writing as the *subject matter* of the course. Some of these texts were quite challenging pieces from composition and rhetoric scholarship.[1]
- Some "readings" were videos and other multimedia, which Diana comments about later.

1

Week 1: Breaking the Ice in an Online Writing Course

This understanding of how to communicate effectively with peers is crucial for building community among the students—an important feature of OWI.

—Kevin DePew

Scott: Launching a New Course

In any teaching experience, much happens behind the scenes, before students ever enter the class[room]. That preparation work is part of teaching, and it is often difficult for others to see (it's why some people erroneously think teachers have so much time off). I was able to build Persuasive Writing & Reading based on my experience teaching courses like it for about a decade, both onsite and online. Teaching online offers a kind of productive *leveraging*: You have materials, often the literal texts, to put into use in a new context. I never teach a course the same way twice, but as with any teacher in any environment, I had some history to help put the course in motion.

The first thing my students encountered when they "landed" on the course homepage early that January was announcements:

Announcements for Monday, January 9:

- Welcome to our class. I'm looking forward to working with you this term. Note my **contact info** is at the bottom of this page.
- The **Weekly Plan** for Week 1 is now available below. **Start there.** I am loading all the other documents and Discussions over the next few days. Don't hesitate to contact me with questions.
- Remember we will **meet virtually** on Tuesday night at 9:00 PM. See the Weekly Plan.

I have been struck by how many students have told me they didn't know what they were supposed to do at the start of their online courses. Through a simple announcement, I lead them right to the Weekly Plan, which would be crucial to keeping them on track in the course.

Weekly Plans

In *Teaching Writing Online: How and Why*, I said that the way I keep students—and myself—organized is the Weekly Plan: "This simple, yet elegant solution to course organization allows me to provide my students each week with a complete set of activities they must accomplish" (54). My first Weekly Plan is usually the most involved, describing not just the work but trying to establish the course "culture":

Week 1: January 8 to January 14

Each week, I will provide you with a detailed plan of that week's activities. I've taken this approach in an effort to make it as easy as possible for you to stay on track with the work for the course.

Follow the directions in order, from top to bottom. Note that sometimes the deadlines are not rigid (such as "by Wednesday afternoon"). Other times, I ask for a specific deadline/time, such as the quiz's availability this week. When the deadline is specific, make sure that you observe it.

There's a lot of material below in this Weekly Plan, more than in future weeks, but that's because we're getting started. This week, the focus is on getting acquainted (including our Live Classroom meeting on Tuesday night), getting used to this class environment, and launching into our readings.

What do I do?	What are the specific instructions? Where do I find the work or the assignment?	When is it due? (All times ET)
READ	Carefully read the "Syllabus" and "Guidelines for Participating in Discussions" documents, which you can find in the "Syllabus Documents and Discussions Guide" folder on the course Homepage. You might also look over the "Outcomes for Persuasive Writing" document as well.	Read these documents by **Tuesday** evening, January 10, before our Live Classroom meeting (see below).

← The Plan started with overall introductory text. This material, as is the whole Week 1 Plan, is detailed, but, remember, I have text saved from past courses. Onsite teachers have a first-day "spiel," but in an OWC, that textual spiel is preserved; you can modify it for each class. The point: Save everything you write for your OWC!

← The Plan followed a simple three-column design: A "what to do" verb/action, the specifics of the task, and when it was due.

← The first task was to read the course documents "carefully," a word I use repeatedly.

LOGIN and MEET	Occasionally this term I will ask you all to be in the same virtual place at the same time, but most of your work in the course will be *asynchronous*, meaning you will *not* have to be available at a certain time. The purpose of this *synchronous* meeting is to introduce you to the course. **We will meet at 9:00 pm on Tuesday, January 10.** We will finish by 9:45. To participate in the meeting, click on the "Intro to the Course" link on the course Homepage. This takes you to a Live Classroom site. You may have a better experience with this introduction if you have a Webcam, microphone, and headset, but none of these items is required. The first time you click on the link, you will be asked to run through a menu to make sure your computer is compatible with the Live Classroom. If you cannot sign in at 9:00 on Tuesday, please let me know.	**We will meet at 9:00 pm on Tuesday, January 10.**
EMAIL	After you've read the syllabus and participated in our introduction, think about what I'm asking you to do this term in this online writing class. Once you've thought it over, please send an email **memo** to me at sjwarnock@drexel.edu stating you understand the requirements and policies of the course and that you agree with them. Think about what might be an appropriate subject for such an email.	Please send me your email by **Friday**, January 13.
WRITE	Access the course Discussions by clicking on the blue pushpin Discussions tool icon on the left menu of our course management system Homepage. Follow my instructions *carefully* (this will be an early test of your ability to read closely in the class) for the topic "Who are you?" so you can briefly introduce yourself to the class. (This counts as your first "primary" Discussion post, so make sure you read the guidelines for Discussions before you post.)	Please post by the afternoon on **Wednesday**, January 11.

← We would meet synchronously Tuesday in an online space to review the course.

← The "contract" email encouraged students to read the course material. I wanted students to take accountability for the material in the course, but I was also creating a rhetorical opportunity, perhaps particularly relevant to OWC students: Send to your professor an "official" message indicating you have read and thought about the syllabus.

READ and WATCH	Read the following (*Aux*: Auxiliary readings, which are available on our course Website in the Course Readings folder*)*: • *Course textbook*: "Writing to Analyze" 41 pages. • *Aux:* Cicero, "From *On Rhetorical Invention*" 3 pages. • *Aux:* Mastrull, "Pointing Out the Obstacles" 3 pages. • *Aux:* Baron, "The Top Language Stories of the Year" 1 page. • Watch: TED Talk, "Edward Burtynsky on Manufactured Landscapes" 34 minutes.	You'll want to have read by **Thursday** morning, January 12, so you can complete the quiz and start thinking about the Discussions.
TAKE A QUIZ	Quiz 1 can be found in the "Quizzes" folder on the course Homepage. For the quizzes, remember three things: • I am looking for VERY short answers. • The quiz answers can be informal. I don't grade them on spelling, etc. • I am not looking to trick you. If you've read, you should be able to complete the quiz successfully in a few minutes with no problem.	The quiz will be available **Thursday** from 9:30 am to midnight. You will have **5 minutes** to complete it.
SIGN-UP	Again, access the course Discussions by clicking on the blue pushpin Discussions tool on the left menu of your homepage. Please follow the directions in the "Moderator assignments" thread, in the "General threads" area. In that thread, I ask you to sign up for the role of Discussion moderator one week during the term. Note that some weeks there will be more than one moderator.	Make sure you have picked your slot by the **end of this week**.
READ and WRITE	Read all the Discussion topics for Week 1, and then read the following carefully (I know I keep saying "read carefully," but *it really is important for you to read carefully in this online course*): • Post ONE "primary" post to any of the Discussion topics (aside from the "Who are you?" topic). • Post TWO "secondary" posts to any of the Discussion topics (aside from the "Who are you?" topic).	Post your primary posts by **Thursday**. Post your secondary posts by **Saturday**, January 14 at noon.

← In the opening week of this course, I assigned texts and media for students just as in any FYW class.

← As I described in the Pre-chapter, I use weekly quizzes. I migrated my quiz strategy from onsite courses. Quizzes also provide pacing for the course.

← As I describe in Week 2 and throughout this book, I used student moderators each week after Week 1 to encourage discussion.

← The Plan was especially deliberate about how Discussions will work. I'll discuss this much more fully in Week 2.

	Make sure you follow the general rules for Discussion topics, which you should revisit on the syllabus before getting to work here. Perhaps most importantly, and I can't stress this enough, is that you must **post by the deadlines.** If you are late on these posts in the first week of the term, you should seriously reconsider whether an online course is right for you.	After this week, we'll move to a Wednes-day-Friday post dead-line.
READ	Read the assignment instructions for Project 1, which you can find in the Composition Projects folder in the course Homepage. We'll begin talk-ing about this project next week.	Read the instruc-tions by the weekend.

← I wanted students to look ahead to Project 1, encouraging them with a "due" date for reading the instructions.

Diana: Exploring the Online Space

In the winter term of my first year, I discovered a weakness of mine: I'm terrible at scheduling myself. Amid the stress of creating a college schedule for the first time, I had no idea I signed up for Persuasive Writing & Reading, a required English course for first-year students, as an online course. Here I was, only two semesters into my first year at college, and I'm already experimenting with online classes? After a brief panic, I realized I needed to plow forward and begin. After all, it was a freezing afternoon on the first day of winter classes, and I had my dorm room to myself, so it was the perfect time to dive into an online course. I could do this.

I did have an online class in high school for an AP Psychology course. However, it wasn't the same format as the course I was about to begin. In my high school course, the online space was self-guided and the majority of work I produced was done on my own schedule with very little supervision. The only interaction I had with a "professor" was emailing essays to a woman who identified herself as a "retired psychiatrist" every other week. Nevertheless, I earned an A in the course and mostly enjoyed it. While I didn't feel like I was a member of a classroom, that was expected from a course described as "self-guided." What I did love was being in a flexible, online space.

Launching into Professor Warnock's course, I decided to review the course description from the University catalog:

> Teaches terminology and rhetorical strategies of persuasive writing. Advances students' development in the writing process, and promotes their critical evalua-

tion and integration of varied sources as they research complex and open-ended problems. Engages them in the act and study of collaboration, rhetorical awareness of images and design, and an understanding of how genres shape writing. Continues to promote their critical reading of challenging texts. Supports students in ongoing reflective analysis about writing and their development.

Anything that was discussed in this excerpt I was already familiar with or felt I had a handle on from my English instruction in high school and from the previous English 101 course. I was comfortable with the material and didn't have many qualms regarding the course content as I prepared for the first week. I knew this was probably going to be one of my best classes for the term, especially when up against my Chemistry 102 and Biology 102 courses (yuck).

As I opened the syllabus for the first time, I had a brief moment of distraction. I knew I wanted to check one last thing before fully jumping into the course. How have other students reviewed Professor Warnock in past years? I wasn't in a sorority and didn't know any older students, so my only source on the quality of professors would be RateMyProfessor.com. I didn't love the site because of its untrustworthy nature. You can never tell if a review was written by a grumpy, failed student trying to get the last word in against the teacher, or if it's the teacher herself faking a rave review. Nevertheless, what I read were the kind of reviews you would expect about a tough teacher who demanded a lot from his students but would consistently improve their writing by the end of the course. The reviews were overwhelmingly positive, but always followed with a warning that students may not get the A they expect. There were a few negative reviews saying he was too harsh, and I assumed that came with the territory of a tough teacher. Yet, there was one comment that had been written a few years before that convinced me I was in for a treat: *"What a professor should be. If you're looking for a babysitter or someone who doesn't expect you to think, he is not the professor for you. He is an excellent teacher who will improve your writing. I highly recommend seeking out his classes."*

Feeling more assured, I clicked back to the syllabus to finally dive in. The directions for the week instructed us to read the syllabus and guidelines for posting. I thought, "Easy! That'll only take a few minutes or so."

Nope.

The syllabus was nine pages of course description and instructions. I wasn't surprised over the length, because I've had teachers before who have copy and pasted standard guidelines from the university into countless pages of legal jargon. This was totally different. *Paragraphs* were provided on how to post online, not just bullet points. Professor Warnock ran through extensive instructions, providing numerous examples, to clearly explain what he wanted out of us. Was it overwhelming and intimidating? Hell, yes! Yet, what surprised me was the detail and effort that was put into these directions. I knew what to expect for the term, and felt relieved that he clearly intended on that being the case.

However, it still seemed like so much work. For any given week, I identified a set of consistent expectations for us because of weekly expectations referenced multiple times throughout the syllabus:

1. Readings
2. A number of both "Primary" and "Secondary" posts
3. A peep or two
4. A quiz

While the specifics of the readings, Discussion board posts, and topics weren't made clear in the syllabus, I was fine with that. Plenty of information was being thrown at me in this first week, so I didn't need to know the week-to-week specifics, especially since Professor Warnock also outlined the major projects for the course. Depending on where we were throughout the course, I'd probably be working on one of two large composition projects, as well as my portfolio and reflective analysis. Again, I was thankful that I knew about everything ahead of me, but it did come across as daunting.

Once I reached the end of the syllabus, I read a few lines that came as a surprise to me. Under the subheading "Contact," where professors typically list their email, office, and available hours (and, if they're a free-spirited teacher, their cell number), Professor Warnock wrote the following information:

> There is a temptation in an online course for you to think of your professor as a robot who never sleeps. While you are college students, and you may do some of your most productive work at 2 in the morning, I am an old(ish) man who goes to bed at 10:30. Remember that when you email me in the wee hours of the night and can't understand why I haven't responded to you. The three-dimensional me can be found in MacAlister 0032.

While the added information about Professor Warnock's contact schedule was helpful, it wasn't necessarily his specificity that helped calm my nerves. It was the tone in his writing. The natural, conversational voice reminded me there was a human behind the text. I learned that he was an "old(ish) man," would make "every effort to be available" if I needed it, and really encouraged students to contact him with any concerns necessary (mentioning the open door a grand total of five times throughout the syllabus). It was the very first day of the semester, and I already knew more about this teacher behind a screen than I did about my face-to-face (f2f) instructors. Even more, the syllabus was full of advice, not only on how to succeed within the course, but how to succeed in my academic career as well. Some of my favorite lines from his syllabus addressed the experience of being an online student:

- "This may be your first experience in an online course. You'll no doubt find this to be a different experience than that of an onsite class. Following are some things to think about as you begin this online learning experience. I also have prepared a more extensive list of frequently asked questions about online writing courses here: [link]"
- "**Feeling isolated?:** Remember, while our class is online, I'm a real-live human being who has an office on campus. If you have concerns, feel free to stop in and talk to me during my office hours or call me."
- "I know you are probably all skilled multi-taskers, but if you get into bad study habits as a first-year student, they will be hard to break later."

Professor Warnock's apparent effort, care, and thought put toward his students and his work made me feel at ease and secure about the future of the course. I had a clear idea of who he was, what he expected of us, when deadlines should be met, and where I could contact him if need be. Now I just needed to figure out *how* this class would happen online.

Scott: A Virtual, Synchronous Course Introduction

There is a long-running conversation about synchronous vs. asynchronous ways of teaching online, with some weighing in firmly on one side or another.[1] While I believe the method and mode of teaching a course are dependent on factors such as student population, accessibility, and institutional constraints, pedagogically I think asynchronous approaches work very well for writing students. In an asynchronous course, most student work is writing, and writing on message boards has many straightforward, inherently advantageous traits: It is fundamentally open, conversational, semi- or informal, topic-focused, and low-stakes; it is addressed to multiple audiences; it creates a sense of ongoing peer review (see Warnock, "The Low-Stakes"). I'll build my case throughout this book, and we will discuss and demonstrate in particular the role message board writing can play in students' writing development.

Even if, like me, you teach in primarily asynchronous ways, almost all LMSs have synchronous meeting capabilities, and these tools are continually being improved. In the first week of an OWC, for various reasons, I always set up a synchronous meeting to introduce the class and discuss the syllabus. For one, I believe that establishing my teaching persona to the students is crucial; while they will be writing to each other, I remain a key audience for their major projects in the course. I believe that getting to know one another is important in developing classroom community; I'll discuss this idea more in describing the Week 1 icebreaker. Using a synchronous platform also helps them understand that I am a real, engaged person, and they are taking the course with other real people.

As most OWCs are, our course was scheduled in Drexel's catalog as fully online with no meeting time; students were not expected to be in the same place at the same time. An institution *could* block off meeting times for availability, but since scheduling flexibility is a big draw for online learning, most do not. So I scheduled a meeting for Tuesday night at 9:00 p.m. In the Weekly Plan, I made it clear I did not expect everyone to be there but they should drop in if possible. Our LMS enabled a recording of the meeting, so it wasn't a problem if students could not attend—they could always view the recording. One student posted our first post to "Questions about the course" expressing concern about a conflict:

Author: Alan	**Topic:** Questions about the course
Subject: Late due to previous class	**Date:** January 10, 12:36 AM

I have a film class that extends a little bit after 9 pm. And we are supposed to meet at 9 pm, correct?

Being the first week, this might not be a problem but it will be a consistent issue for both of us in the later weeks. Unfortunately, the other possible film classes are full as of now so rescheduling isn't going to be easy. Is there something you can suggest?

Reply

Students often compose this kind of unsure writing early in a course: They act as if I am going to bite their heads off for missing something. Taking advantage of this opportunity to continue developing my teaching persona (and to calm the student!), I assured Alan about the recording in a Discussion post: "We are not going to meet at 9:00 on Tuesday every week—in fact, we're only going to meet all together like this a few times this term—so you shouldn't have any future conflicts."

The meeting's purpose, as described in the Weekly Plan, was "to introduce you to the course." Using screenshare capabilities in our meeting software, I displayed the course site, Weekly Plan, syllabus, and "Guidelines for Participating in Discussions." Students used either voice or chat to ask questions. Although most were silent, they could use an emoji function to give me a thumbs-up or smile so I had a sense that they were tuned in. We had a minor initial glitch, as some students had trouble logging in; a couple others said they were "kicked out" and had to re-log in. In the chat, I did provide my phone number, which one student called mid meeting. I sent an email at 10:00 p.m. immediately after the meeting to apologize for some of the technical glitches.

I felt in our forty-five-minute meeting that they got to know me better and to understand the expectations and opportunities of the course, as they would in any first-class orientation.

Diana: Virtual Meeting

On the first Tuesday of the term, the class met with Professor Warnock online. Everyone had a choice to use their webcam so we could see one another, but Professor Warnock was the only one who decided to do so; regardless, everyone could communicate via instant messaging. Professor Warnock talked primarily about the basics of the course, repeated some of what was said on the syllabus, and gave us a tour of the online space. What was most useful, however, was interacting with a talking, living person. A picture of your professor is better than nothing when taking a course online, but you can never put too much trust in a school-issued photo (mine certainly never turned out great, no matter how much preparation I put into the shot). Hearing and seeing my professor speak to me made a world of a difference.

He warned us that he was speaking to us from home, so we shouldn't be alarmed if we saw a little boy, his son Zachary, run across the background. This was such a small aside, probably something impromptu and insignificant to Professor Warnock, but it mattered to me. We could see his life outside of the classroom. It sounds silly, but I now felt more accountable for producing work for him. In fact, this was the most I had learned about a professor so early in a course—I was in his living room, after all.

During the actual synchronous video experience, students had an option to chat to the whole group and have Professor Warnock respond. One student dominated the question-asking, avidly making sure he understood everything perfectly. I'm sure it was helpful to others who felt anxiety about the course, but it was funny how this was already beginning to mirror an f2f course: One student was dominating the conversation, most students were complacent, and some (or maybe just me) were peeved that the student was being unnecessarily vocal. Nevertheless, the online meeting was useful in preparing myself for the course, organizationally and emotionally. I connected with my professor and my classmates in a communal setting, while receiving useful, focused information regarding the future of the course.

Behind the Screen: Getting Acclimated with Icebreakers

In a *Chronicle of Higher Education* article, "The Absolute Worst Way to Start the Semester," Prof. Kevin Gannon says:

> At my university—as was the case at other institutions where I've taught—students call the first day of class "Syllabus Day." Their expectation is that they'll show up, the professor will hand out the syllabus, go through maybe 10 minutes' worth of housekeeping stuff, and then turn them loose until the course really starts later in the week.

Students often do think day one, even week one, is a kind of throwaway. But in distance learning (DL) in general and OWI specifically, the first few days are incredibly valuable. In particular, you want to use that time to have students meet each other and you—their *audience(s)* for the writing they will do over the next few months. In *Teaching Writing Online*, Guideline 6 suggests starting class with an icebreaker; I said, "Just as you might in an onsite class, you can start getting to know your students, and shaping yourself to them, with introductory icebreakers. . . . The 'black box' of audience can be a problem for students in an onsite class, so imagine how this might be exacerbated when they never see the instructor" (6–7). I also note that I can use my own writing style and voice in icebreakers to "demonstrate the type of persona I wish to take in the course" (8).

As Lisa Meloncon and Heidi Harris point out, icebreakers can be a major way to "inspire online community" (427). In providing a good review of articles about engaging online learners to reduce class attrition, Lorraine Angelino, Frankie Williams, and Deborah Natvig said, "In using the learner-centered approach, educators should open lines of communication with students as early as possible," getting "to know their students and assess each student's pre-existing knowledge, cultural perspectives, and comfort level with technology." Students, they add, "need the opportunity to get to know each other and feel comfortable before learning can take place," and "Virtual icebreakers" are a key part of such strategies (7). In *A Position Statement of Principles and Example Effective Practices for Online Writing Instruction* (Conference), Online Writing Instruction Principle 11 states, "Online writing teachers and their institutions should develop personalized and interpersonal online communities to foster student success"; OWI Principle 11's Effective Practice 11.2 focuses that recommendation: "OWC teachers should develop course community early by employing 'icebreakers' and other activities that make use of the LMS and that engage student writing" (23).

With a good icebreaker, students can learn about each other and make person-to-person connections while also becoming familiar with the course interface. It is worth noting such pre- and early-term efforts can help all students, but Michael Gos points out the specific value such efforts have in assisting nontraditional students.

Scott: The All-Important OWI Discussion Icebreaker

In the Weekly Plan, I asked students to provide me with a "contract" email. I received a range of contract responses, allowing me to encourage students with a personal "Looking forward to working with you"–type response. (My brief responses, by the way, also automatically added their emails into my address book.) Perhaps most important, this exchange provided me with a clear opportunity to see students who were not participating. I checked in with those who hadn't sent me a message at all, so I did not have to wait long to discover seven students had not read the Weekly Plan.

The first week of an OWC always presents opportunities I can capitalize on with a good icebreaker. An icebreaker/introduction activity can help in any course, but it's particularly valuable in an OWC where it can be integral to constructing the writer-reader relationships that will drive the course; as I mentioned, students need to learn quickly who their *audience* (including me) will be over the next few months. Icebreakers also provide students with an early low-stakes opportunity to develop their writing voices and identities: Who are they in this online course? Even simple things like how they sign off on this initial post can help create the personalities the rest of the class will "see" and interact with. Icebreakers also give me an opportunity to develop my voice and to model message board behavior. I posted this:

Author: Scott Warnock **Topic**: Who are you?
Subject: Who are you? **Date**: January 5, 4:53 PM

Dear members of English 102,
Make sure you READ AND FOLLOW the directions below carefully.

I'd like to get to know you a bit and, perhaps more importantly, for you to get to know each other. So, could you please let us know a few things about yourself?:

-Tell us who you are and where you're from.

-What is your major? What are you interested in pursuing as a career?

-Describe one thing—and it can be anything—that you have that helps demonstrate an important aspect of you. Think of it this way: if we were in a face-to-face classroom and I asked you to bring something that demonstrates an important aspect of you, what would you bring and why?

-What are some topics that you like to debate or that you have strong feelings about? (Note: You don't even have to reveal which side you're on; just tell us what the topic/subject is.)

← I addressed them directly, emphasizing, with a rare ALL CAPS, the importance of following directions.

← This list may not be unusual for any course icebreaker, except I asked them to describe what they might bring to an onsite class.

Please provide your email address, and sign this post the way you would like us to address you (i.e., do you go by a nickname?).

Feel free to reply back to each other on this Discussion thread, and please note that this thread is separate from your other Discussion requirements this week.

Looking forward to hearing about you,
Prof. Warnock

Reply

← I gave a little more information about how to proceed.

← As a further way to connect with them, I used a welcoming complimentary closing.

While of course I wanted students to introduce themselves, I also hoped that by responding to each other they would start to build connections and develop early a sense of community, which I felt they did in many instances:

- To Diana, who mentioned her recipe book, Parinda replied that she had a similar book of "passed down family recipes."
- Alexa said she wanted to pursue pediatric oncology because of having experienced cancer throughout her life. Both Alan and I empathized by briefly describing our own experiences.
- Lisa revealed a learning disability—in Week 1!—and Donald said, "I think its great you try your best and keep going. Good luck to you during this course."
- Parinda said she would bring her wedding ring, as she was recently married! Several students congratulated her.
- Alexa said to Rio, "Nice to meet you. I think It's great how you've come from another country especially the Philippines! My parents are from there as well, so I guess we have that common background."

In addition, several students asked each other questions about their choice of major.

I responded to every post, trying to find common ground while also building myself as an audience for these students:

- Karen wrote a lengthy introduction but said she would bring her "mentality." Responding, I mildly chastised her for bending "the rules a wee little bit."

- Lisa said she was interested in a job as a "personal shopper," to which I quipped, "now that is one job I would be terrible at."
- Jennifer said she lived in Ocean City, New Jersey, and I shared with her that I lived there in college as well, working as a lifeguard.
- Donald said he aspired to be a physician's assistant, and I informed him my cousin was a PA "and he does very well for himself."
- Arthur expressed a love of the Red Sox and said he'd bring either a playoff ticket or a jersey. He not only loves them, he said, but they are also "a connection I share with my father." I said, "I love that your interest in the team is a link between you and your dad; I'm trying to get my kids to root for the Eagles, but so far they're lukewarm about it at best. They love soccer!"
- Alan said his mother considers him "older," mainly because of his "preference to music," and I asked him more specifically what type of music he liked.
- Ethan said he was a business major, and I was able to say how much I liked and respected the faculty in Drexel's LeBow College of Business, several of whom were my friends.
- In terms of his argument preferences, Deryck said, "If there's a debate with two sides, one side representing a logical standpoint, the other representing an emotional standpoint; I tend to choose the logical standpoint," allowing me to offer this early glimpse into the rhetorical backbone of the course: "Well, it seems you enjoy appeals to *logos* over *pathos*, yes?"
- Jackie has a twin, and I described to her my twin niece and nephew.
- Some students posted similar comments. There were several nursing students, a few students who said they would bring an art or sketchbook, and a couple video game designers. I "aggregated" those results later in the week in an effort to make those connections explicit.

Again, the icebreaker post was required, so students would also get a sense of how the low-stakes course grading would work, as I described in the prechapter.

Week 1 was labor-intensive for me, as I responded to every student's icebreaker post, mostly on Thursday and Friday, in line with Guideline 32 of *Teaching Writing Online*: "Respond a lot, especially early in the term" (124). As I was establishing myself, in this textual environment, as a real, engaged person, I was also modeling how to engage in Discussions. The early, low-stakes icebreaker also helped emphasize the importance of following directions: Eight students did not do what I asked of them in describing something they would bring to class, and I drew attention to that.[2] You cannot help them enough in the first two weeks to acclimate to the norms of online learning. A few posts were late, drifting into Week 2, but I still responded to each one. Matt (who didn't last long in the course) posted late and incompletely, and I had to write directly to him, "You would do well to review the directions for this introductory post again."

Diana: Breaking Into the Online Conversation

Here we go. My first impression to my classmates. In an f2f class I always enjoyed icebreakers, regardless of how nervous I was. I don't mind getting up in front of strangers, blushed face or not, and improvising my way through a mini speech about myself. Maybe it's an only child confidence thing, or maybe I just like the limelight. Either way, I've always found it energizing to introduce myself to new peers and to learn about them as well. For my summary, I discussed my hometown, career ambitions, and favorite topics of discussion.

Author: Diana Gasiewski **Topic**: Who are you?
Subject: Who are you? **Date**: January 10, 10:40 PM

Hi everyone,

My name is Diana Gasiewski, and I'm from New Hope in Bucks County, Pennsylvania. Currently, I'm a Communications major in the accelerated Public Relations track. If we are discussing dream jobs, I would do anything to work as a well esteemed food critic in newspapers or culinary magazines; however, I'm content in pursuing any executive public relations position in the culinary field.

With that said, my recipe book would outline my passions brilliantly. It's unfortunate you all can't see this thing—a binder, three inches wide, filled with recipes, cooking tips, and restaurant reviews ripped from newspapers, magazines, cookbooks, and even my grandmother's own collection. Not only does it show my enthusiasm for this hobby, it demonstrates the care and diligence I put towards any work in my life.

← Summing up yourself in a few sentences is always difficult, because you don't want to overshare or come across as too bland, so I stuck with the basics, but sprinkled in the "fun fact" of my food interests.

To switch gears, I have often found the education system, government, and food industry to be fascinating topics of discussion. Interestingly enough, they frequently play off each other to dramatically affect each citizen's mind, health, and spirit. Yet, in and of themselves, they are interesting topics nonetheless.

I look forward to possibly discussing these topics with you all, and I am eager to hear your interests as well. If in need of ever having to reach me, my email is dmg329@drexel.edu.

Best regards,
Diana

Reply

← Why "Best regards"? I know this is an academic class, so I should still be formal. Right?

After posting my icebreaker, I experienced a sense of writer's remorse. Why did I focus on so many boring things like cooking, topics of discussion, and career pursuits? I used the words *fascinating* and *government* in the same sentence. Ugh! I mean, I do like all those things, but they're definitely not the only things I love and do. I explore tiny neighborhoods in Philadelphia, plan mini vacations with my friends, hold lengthy discussions about the best comedians, and deeply love my family; I came across as a cold, business-oriented geek in my icebreaker, and I'm not like that at all. Now my classmates are going to think I'm some stuck-up person who only cares about being successful. What's worse, the icebreaker is permanent. Unlike icebreakers in an f2f course that are fleeting and breezed through on the first day of class, this little summary of myself can be referenced throughout the term by anyone who cares to go back to Week 1 and see what I thought of myself. I'm going to have to do a better job at properly representing who I am in the weeks to come.

At least, that's what I thought until I read my classmates' posts. It seems they were just as quirky as mine. Jackie wrote a memorable post about her twin:

Author: Jackie **Topic**: Who are you?
Subject: Who are you? **Date**: January 12, 10:28 PM

Hello everyone! I am Jackie. I am a tiny Asian girl who was accidentally born in Canada when her mother was visiting a relative.

My current major is Computer Engineering, but I am thinking about switching to Computer science. Ever since I was little, I've always had a fascination with building things and playing on the computer. So, when it came to choosing a major for college I ended up choosing computer engineering (on whim). The reason why I am thinking about switching majors is because I would like to do something that incorporates art. So, I am currently looking into Game Design.

I do not know what I would bring in for "something that describes" me. But if I could, I would bring in my younger twin sister. She is very important to me because in a sense, I am her and she is me. We have a very strong bond and we have the "twin sense" where we can tell when something is wrong with each other. We are very similar yet different. Everything I do/have is the opposite of what she does/has. It's like looking into a mirror but seeing your reflection in different colors. So, in a sense, I feel that she is the definition of me.

Feel free to ask me anything you want. Awkward questions won't phase me.
-Jackie

Reply

Alexa and Alan had this interesting exchange:

Author: Alexa
Subject: Who are you?
Topic: Who are you?
Date: January 11, 12:22 AM

Hey guys,

My name is Alexa, and I'm from New Jersey. My current major is Health Sciences and I plan on pursuing a career in Physical Therapy. I hope to specialize in either pediatric oncology or intensive rehabilitation. I'm still unsure of which direction I want to follow, but as of right now I'm swaying more towards pediatric oncology. I've been around cancer my whole life, from growing up with both of my grandmothers suffering from this disease, to several of my aunts having it, followed by my own mom as well. So, cancer is something very important to me and I hope to work with kids dealing with the effects of this disease.

While I chose to pursue a healthcare related field, I have a deep appreciation for the arts. With that being said, I feel that my art pad filled with paintings and drawings, and my notebook from my senior art history class would demonstrate a unique aspect of who I am. It shows the diversity of interests I possess, and demonstrates my imagination, creativity, and expression, as well as the cultural and historical understandings I have obtained. Somehow, I plan to incorporate my artistic abilities into what I plan to do for a career.

As for topics of debate, for some reason I'm really fascinated about the level of decency of the education system here in our country compared to that of other nations. I feel that the level of American education is way below the belt than what it should be. Not only do Americans lack in the level of skill in mathematics or science, but also in other capabilities in which students in other countries seem to acquire, such as reasoning and a wide view of perspectives as well as a global awareness of current and past situations. It's an interesting thought to explore and think about how different things would be if education was different, being that it does play a major role in people's lives. I'm always up for a good debate about any topic.

-Alexa

Reply

Oh man. Poor Alexa. I mean, from this post I don't know much about her unfortunate familiarity with cancer, but it's nice she's channeled that into a fantastic career path. Alan chose to respond.

Author: Alan
Topic: Who are you?
Subject: Who are you?
Date: January 12, 6:14 PM

Cancer huh? Actually, my aunt passed away due to a terminal case of lung cancer. She succumbed just a few weeks before. I'm not so personally grieved as I am more concerned for her two daughters. My mother told me that they and my uncle would move back to Hong Kong to live with the aunt's family. It's not comforting to hear but . . .

Reply

Oh dear, oh dear, Alan. After reading these few submissions from my classmates, I realized the awkward transition some may have to the online format. Of course, quirky classroom comments will always exist. Whether they're coming from the perpetually socially awkward, those who have the inevitable brain fart, or from a conversation that went completely off the rails, off-color comments are inescapable. The new risk that is posed online, however, is that these comments are undeletable and preserved for the remainder of the course—this was a hurdle I wasn't expecting to encounter.

Scott: Week 1 Discussions

The pedagogical pillar of our asynchronous course that term was written Discussion board work. As I said, I believe asynchronous Discussions, humble as they are to use, are a powerful teaching tool. Discussions requirements varied each week, and I will describe the pedagogy in detail in Week 2. In addition to the icebreaker, I created four threads this week, and the Weekly Plan outlined the specific posting requirements.

As they could most weeks, students could distribute their posts in any way they liked. I wanted to establish that they could build conversations organically based on their interests. There was a flexibility here that they would grow accustomed to in the coming weeks; in fact, I have never had an issue with students not getting into the groove. Some students do overachieve in Week 1, thinking they are required to post a primary and secondary post on *every* thread. I make it clear this isn't the case, but even across the ether I can sense the relief when I let them know that they have been doing *too much work* at the start.

I did get some questions as they became acclimated: some via email and some via the "Questions about the course" forum. I had this brief exchange with a student named Diana:

Author: Diana Gasiewski
Topic: Questions about the course
Subject: How do I properly post discussions?
Date: January 10, 10:53 PM

Hi Prof. Warnock,

As I get a feel of how discussion posts work in this environment, I've noticed there are two ways to post on a particular topic. For instance, the "Who are you?" discussion has posts that were added by clicking the 'Create Message' button on the main page of the discussion. While on the contrary, the "Moderator Assignments" discussion has your main post, titled "Moderator Slots," with all additional posts added by clicked reply on your previously mentioned message. In what fashion would you like us to post our discussions?

Thank you for your time,
Diana

Reply

Author: Scott Warnock
Topic: Questions about the course
Subject: Re: How do I properly post discussions?
Date: January 11, 9:09 AM

Hi Diana,

This is a great question. Mainly, your decision is based on how you want your post to function: Do you want to respond back to something I or someone else said, or do you want to start your own thread/idea?

One good tip is that it's a good idea to change the message subject, unless you are directly responding to another student or me.

You will quickly see how to operate in this environment—everyone just has to plunge in and get going!

Let me know if this helps,
ProfW

Reply

Author: Diana Gasiewski
Topic: Questions about the course
Subject: Re:How do I properly post discussions?
Date: January 11, 10:50 PM

Thank you very much for your feedback. I'm sure I will catch on once things get started.

Best,
Diana

Reply

"Catch on"? Students who show this kind of volition normally do catch on to the norms of an OWC—and soar. I was confident Diana would be okay.

Late Monday morning of that first week, I posted the four prompts to get them started. The first thread was designed to get them talking about Project 1:

Author: Scott Warnock | **Topic**: Burtynsky and sustainability
Subject: Burtynsky and sustainability | **Date**: January 9, 10:55 AM

Hi folks,

We're going to start talking about Project 1 very soon; in fact, you can look at the instructions now in the Composition Projects folder.

← This "content' topic was focused on sustainability.

First of all, what is "sustainability"? Now, how does Burtynsky's photography speak to the issue of sustainability? What does he say he hopes to achieve with his photographs and ideas? What did you think of the effectiveness of the argument that he attempts to build through his images?

← I provided four straightforward questions directly from the reading.

To respond to this thread, you may want to look again closely at [our textbook], "Writing a Visual Analysis."

← I direct them back to our text.

Looking forward to your responses,
Prof. Warnock

← I sign off in a way I hoped was friendly and welcoming.

Reply

The course I was teaching, working from the core syllabus in our FYW Program, stressed rhetoric, and our FWP director, Professor Rebecca Ingalls, had expertise in classical rhetoric and a good vision of incorporating such material into a first-year curriculum. The next thread, based on our short Cicero reading, was prompted like this:

Author: Scott Warnock | **Topic**: Cicero
Subject: Cicero | **Date**: January 9, 10:52 AM

Hi everyone,

I asked you to look at a brief excerpt from the classical rhetorician Cicero. Why does he say that exordium is so important? What are the five rhetorical causes? What are some strategies that speakers can use to gain/increase an audience's goodwill? How do Cicero's strategies help to prepare us to address specific audiences?

Looking forward to your responses,
Prof. Warnock

Reply

← This too was content-driven. I wanted them to work together to show understanding of key ideas. A prompt like this would probably not work as a requirement for a whole class: Responses would become repetitive.

The other two threads that week were also the kind of straightforward threads that can drive an OWC (again, I describe these prompt categories more next week): You ask students, with just a bit of framing/contextualizing, to respond to a particular reading. The threads had similar subject lines: "Writing to analyze, thinking about _____," and I filled in the blank with that reading's author. I asked direct questions in short prompts for each:

- What was the main point of the reading?
- In our textbook readings, the authors discussed trying to "have some emotional distance" from a topic—do the authors we were analyzing do that?
- How effectively have the authors used "evidence and support"?
- Did the qualities of analytical writing, as manifested in our textbook, appear in these readings?
- Finally, no reading is value neutral, of course, and, because this was a persuasive writing course, I asked them to weigh in at the end of their post on the argument being made.

The students, even in the newness of Week 1, did a good job diving in and writing in response to these four prompts. In later weeks, we will describe/narrate in several different, specific ways how students worked on the Discussion threads.

Diana: First Run at Discussions

The first series of Discussion prompts seemed reasonable enough and fairly expected. Professor Warnock had us introduce ourselves to the class and respond to the readings and assignments for the week. It seemed rudimentary, and I didn't have any problems finding words to fill the word requirement for the primary and secondary posts. Then again, it was the first week, so maybe he was going easy on us.

What I found interesting was how long I spent reading my classmates' posts about themselves and their responses to the readings. I'm independent, play solo sports, hold a small friend group—I'm not one to seek out strangers' opinions. And yet, there I was, spending an extra half hour on the Discussion boards reading classmates' posts with no grade "reimbursement." Perhaps competitiveness got the best of me, and I just wanted to see how I stacked up against the rest of the class. Or maybe I was genuinely interested in reading everyone's stories to see if I we had any similarities or if they had any fun facts.

I rarely do this in an f2f class, seek to learn about my classmates, but snap judgment may be responsible for my interest, or the lack thereof. If I'm sitting next to a kid and he always wears lacrosse shorts, a Drexel shirt, brings a lacrosse stick, he's probably on the lacrosse team. I don't share too much in common there so I probably won't reach out. If the girl who sits next to me wears different old school, classic rock T-shirts every day and brings a tote bag from the local jazz club, I'm probably going to chat her up. Because my peers' physical presences and participation frequency can reveal information about their personalities or interests, I don't feel the need to fish for information in an f2f class. But in this online environment where all I have is a name to go by, so much is left to be discovered. Are they my age? Are they shy or outgoing? What are their interests? Would they be easy group partners? And last, how would I even begin to notice all this in an online format? The anonymity fascinated me, and I was eager to read more posts from these new classmates of mine.

As I prepared for my posts, I chose to respond to the Cicero prompt. Out of the three posts, I was most familiar with that content since I covered ancient rhetoric in my senior year of high school. For my post, I constructed a succinct summary of rhetorical clauses, referenced President Obama as a skilled rhetorician, and closed with several strategies successful rhetoricians use to address diverse audiences. After a good handful of other posts were submitted, Professor Warnock wrote the following message:

Author: Scott Warnock **Topic**: Cicero
Subject: Follow-up: Cicero **Date**: January 13, 8:31 PM

Hi all,

You wrote some thoughtful pieces about an article that, while not long, was a little complex. It's funny how some of this may appear common knowledge, but, as Alan says, "The etiquette was maybe revolutionary for his time."

Diana uses a superb example, including that Obama had to address many different audiences. Could you provide another example? Can you also elaborate on some of the many ways that Cicero suggests orators/rhetoricians bring their audiences around to their cause?

Let us know,
ProfW

Reply

First things first, the professor said I had a "superb example." I'll just give myself a little pat on the back for that. Second, oh crap. The professor is going to be reading, responding to, *and* referencing all our posts? Yikes. Now there's a lot of pressure to produce quality work knowing Professor Warnock, "ProfW," can pull out my text and repeat it for the rest of the class to read. But then again, it was pretty cool that I was certain he would read every one of our posts and hold us accountable for our content. I responded to his question:

Author: Diana Gasiewski	**Topic**: Cicero
Subject: Re:Follow-up: Cicero	**Date**: January 14, 2:59 PM

To follow up with your suggestion, I don't have to look far for another example. You, Professor Warnock, and all other teachers are superb examples of speakers having to address myriad audience clauses. It is understood that educators have to attract auditory, kinesthetic, and visual learners, but considering Cicero's five clauses, they must also appeal to various opinions. There will always be students who agree, disagree, or simply cannot decide on a given lecture point, and as many of us must know, there will always be those who are ignorant or passive as well.

Reply

Well, that was a bit of a bumbling response. Though, it was my first stab at holding a discussion in an online classroom, as opposed to making initial primary posts. I'll have to find a line between writing a response that's educated and professional while also reading as natural and "flow-worthy" for a discussion. It will be a quirky process transferring proper classroom dialogue to an online format, but I think I'll get my voice down eventually.

Reading and Taking a Quiz

Reading worked the same as an f2f course. I would complete the readings on my own schedule in accordance to the rest of my responsibilities, which meant usually early in the week. I was surprised that the quiz was so easy and straightforward. Then again, I had read my assignment for the week, and I was able to reference the texts if needed. At first I thought, "Oof, does this guy know I can totally just skip the readings for the week, and when it comes to quiz time just pop open the texts and reference them?" But no, he was one step ahead of us. The five-minute limit would make it difficult to take the quiz blind while referencing the material.

While I didn't get to choose from a series of multiple choice questions and instead had to formulate my own short answer, I still felt that the short-answer quiz was easy enough to complete. In fact, I felt more comfortable being able to elaborate through my own words rather than select a multiple-choice answer written by someone else. This was helpful in an English course, when grading is occasionally associated with opinion and bias. After completing the quiz and receiving a 100 percent, I held the impression these quizzes would be "reading checks" as I moved forward in the course.

Scott: Starting "Composition Project 1" and Moving through the Week

In an OWC, you have to get things moving in Week 1: At the end of the week, I asked students to review composition Project 1. This project's goals lined up with those of my institution and its FYW program: "This first project invites you to *analyze, evaluate,* and *develop an evidence-based argument* about a sustainability campaign that interests you." The project description is available in the appendix. I know this assignment will not be in line with the teaching style and interests of many of you. Remember, the supporting pedagogy and course narrative are our book's focus, not assignment details, and I will describe the process-oriented way in which we moved through Project 1 while keeping specifics in the background.

Course Announcements to Help Students Keep Pace

I updated the announcements Wednesday and Friday. On Wednesday, I reiterated some start-of-the-week messages:

Announcements for Wednesday, January 11:

- Again, welcome to our class. Note my **contact info** is at the bottom of this page.
- The **Weekly Plan** for Week 1 is now available below. **Start there.**
- I'm sorry about the confusion re: our **virtual meeting.** Thanks for your patience.
- Don't hesitate to contact me with **questions.**

On Friday, I gave them info about the following week, including the key piece of information that the new Weekly Plan was available, which it always would be on Friday:

Announcements for Friday, January 13:

- **Weekly Plans:** The Week 2 Weekly Plan is now available.
- **84 posts.** We're off to a strong start on the Discussions, with 84 posts. Nice job.

- **Make sure you follow directions!** Some of you did not follow the directions for the intro thread. Thanks to those who went back and re-posted, but make sure you **read carefully during this course.**
- Our **half hour introduction-to-the-course meeting** is **archived and available**. Click on the "Introduction to the Course" link below. You'll see a list of "recorded archives." Click on January 10, and you'll be able to view and listen to the course intro session.

Availability and Emails

As with any class, I had to anticipate first-week issues and snags. While I hoped they would use the "Questions about the course" thread, students also emailed me. Deryck asked, "Please let me know if none of my answers show up" on the quiz; he was concerned he clicked "submit" too early. I emailed that he was fine. Katie emailed with a question about secondary posts, and then after I replied, she texted me that her computer crashed and her posts would be late. She followed with an email, to which I replied, "As I said via text, I appreciate that you let me know. This is certainly not a big deal." While I did send Katie a response late on Sunday evening, almost every other email I sent was during "normal business" hours.

In Retrospect: Getting Going in an Online Course

We both realize that too often teaching and learning online are exoticized: seen as hopelessly cutting edge (to an overworked teacher) or extraordinarily different (to an unfamiliar student). As a foundation of *Teaching Writing Online*, Scott described an approach and philosophy of *migration* (xvii) to help direct teachers away from the idea that an OWC was a bizarre, unfamiliar teaching and learning environment. While, in his first of forty-one guidelines, he writes, "Teaching writing online offers you new ways to apply theoretical and pedagogical concepts about writing" (xiii), in Guideline 2 he says teachers should "think about what [they] do well, and then think about how [they] can use various resources to *translate* those skills to the OWcourse" (xvii). Through that translational experience, OWI can push teachers to be better in general.

That first week, especially day one, can be carefree in onsite courses. We both found Week 1 quite different. The students and the teacher had a lot to do, but much of it was to set up the rest of the term so the students were learning to *write,* not learning how to navigate the interface, and the teacher was focusing on *writing instruction,* not on tech support. In general, Scott wants that first week to be a good indicator of the requirements, expectations, and workload so students can *succeed.* Retention is an ongoing issue in online courses of all kinds—and universities and colleges in general—and at least some of the problem is because students are simply not prepared for the self-driven work, no matter how involved the professor is, of an online course.

With this first week finished, we were both ready to go, and that was important, because next week we would be moving right into topic ideas for Composition Project 1—and seeing who would step up as the first student moderator.

An OWC is about writing. We start from there. If it's all based in writing, then students are presented with a wide array of new literacy opportunities, but, to perhaps best (and most quickly) capitalize on those opportunities, students need to get comfortable in the writing environment and even community of the course. It's worth it. As Joan Tornow said twenty years ago in *Link/Age: Composing in the Online Classroom,* composing in online environments provides great opportunities for community, and this digital compositional environment might enable new ideas about literacy. We were ready for Week 2.

2

Week 2: Discussions: The Online Writing/Interacting Environment

Many of our theoretical assumptions about audience are predicated on [the print model], and on the (in practical, physical terms) unidirectional flow of text from author to audience.

—Rebecca Lucy Busker

Scott: Some Tips and Advice

This group was really smart! The first week went well, and I said so in the Weekly Plan:

Week 2: January 15 to January 21

Again, please simply follow the directions in order, from top to bottom.

Okay, I'm impressed. This group got off to a strong start in Week 1. I'm excited about the prospects for this term.

This week, the focus is on topics for Project 1 and doing some reading and writing about evaluative writing and how to conduct a rhetorical analysis.

You'll note that if you wait too long on the readings and Discussions that you could have a lot of work to do at one time.

What do I do?	What are the specific instructions? Where do I find the work or the assignment?	When is it due? (All times EST)
READ and WATCH	Read the following: • *Course textbook*: "Writing to Evaluate" 43 pages. • *Aux:* Benoit and Harthcock, "Attacking the Tobacco Industry: A Rhetorical	You'll want to have read and watched by **Tuesday**, January 17 so you can complete the

← At the top of the Weekly Plan, I was overtly encouraging.

← I assigned a good amount of reading/watching this week. The Benoit & Harthcock article, whose title describes it quite well,

	Analysis of Advertisements by the Campaign for Tobacco-Free Kids" 16 pages. • *33rd*: Biemiller, "Odd Girl Out" 82-88. • Watch on *YouTube*: "In Defense of Rhetoric" Professional Communication, Clemson University. 14 minutes.	quiz and get to work on the Discussion topics.
TAKE a QUIZ	Quiz 2 can be found in the Quizzes folder on the Course Homepage. Again, remember that for the quizzes: 1. I am looking for VERY short answers. 2. The quiz answers can be informal. I don't grade them on spelling, etc. 3. I am not looking to trick you. If you've read and watched the materials for this week, you should be able to complete the quiz successfully in a few minutes with no problem.	The quiz will be available **Tuesday** from 9:30 am to midnight. You will have **five minutes** to complete it. If you miss the quiz, there are no make-ups. I will drop one quiz though.
WRITE and READ	You did a solid job in Week 1, but please review the Discussion guidelines on the syllabus before you start on this week's work; it'll all become habit soon enough: • **Project 1 topic Discussion**: Follow the instructions on the Discussion thread "Project 1 topics." I am asking you to propose a topic as **ONE** primary post, and then you will write **ONE** secondary post in response to one of your colleague's topics. • **Reading Discussions**: You will have several reading Discussion options this week. You will post **ONE** primary and **ONE** secondary post on our reading Discussions. Don't forget to stay current on the Discussions, and make sure you *read* through everything on the message boards.	Post your primary reading posts by **Wednesday** night, January 18. (I know some of you are night owls, and while I don't want to encourage procrastination, you can post as late as you like on Wednesday night/Thursday wee morning.) Post your secondary post by **Friday**, January 20, at 4:00 pm. **This is a hard deadline.** Complete all your posts for the "Project 1 topics" thread by **Thursday** evening, January 19.

was accessible through our LMS. (As always, I gave students the page count, 16 pages, so they would have a sense of the work involved.)

← Accompanying this material was our second five-minute quiz. I provided some detailed reminders about how the quizzes worked.

← They did well in Week 1, and I reinforced that, but I again directed them to the instructions for Discussions. After the Week 1 toe-dip, I felt they were ready to dive in, and I tried to steer them away from procrastination. Note that everyone had to post to the Project 1 topic thread, both a primary and secondary post.

MODERATE (one of you)	This week our moderator will be the courageous John. I will be in touch with John, and then he will serve as moderator for some of our Discussions this week. He will be an active voice in encouraging conversation, and he will provide a summary at the end of the week. Thanks to John for his bravery in going first here.	--

← The first moderator was ready to go. I gave some compliments and encouragement to spur him on.

While they were doing well, I wanted to reinforce the importance of Discussions, so I had a post prepared to help those who were straggling a little or were confused. (I have a file of such posts that I can tweak for a particular class.) I posted this in the "Tips Advice Resources" Forum:

Author: Scott Warnock
Subject: Discussions
Topic: Tips advice resources
Date: January 18, 9:14 AM

Hi everyone,

You did a good job in week one on the Discussion message boards. There were a few things I want to comment about.

First, your job as a student—right?—is to challenge yourself. Many of you did not post to the thread about invitational rhetoric, making me wonder if you read that piece. Sure, that was the toughest read and posting there would have been a challenge for you, but *that's what you're here to do.*

Basically, make sure **you spread your posts out** among the different threads.

Second, all term we are practicing the difficult skill of **using evidence.** You did a fantastic job of using evidence this week, and I hope you continue to use evidence to support every one of your points. Draw on quotes from our readings, from each other's posts, and from my posts. When you use a text, cite a page number.

Third, we started really strong last week and then the conversations fizzled. This may be a result of the fact that it was week one and that the deadline was a Saturday, but the secondary post conversations are crucial. Make sure you look for my "summary" posts each week on the threads and build your conversations during the second half of the week from those posts.

Your goal each week with the Discussions should be: **No bold by the weekend.** (Discussions are marked in bold until you open them.) You should have no bold-faced Discussions by the end of the week. If you do, you've fallen behind here, because remember I am expecting that you will read all of the posts.

Also, you probably discovered something this week. If you wait until last minute, you're faced with many unread posts. People here posted early, often and well.

A few other things to help you: Please DO:

- Re-read the Discussion guidelines.
- Check the Discussions regularly to see the flow of the conversations taking place.
- Change the subject of the thread.
- Use your secondary posts to answer questions posed by me or others. Those questions are there for you to build the conversation. Also, I hate to be ignored . . .
- Sign your posts, so we know what to call you when we respond.
- Build a conversation—as part of that goal, ask questions that we can think about.

Please DO NOT:

- Answer my initial question over and over again. As you imagine, that quickly gets boring.
- Post blindly without reading. Remember, I expect you to read ALL the Discussions. It's noticeable if you have made a point that another student already made.
- Feel compelled to always agree. Intelligent argument is part of the course.

Again, solid work in week one, folks. You kept me hoppin'.

Let me know if you have questions,
Prof. Warnock

Reply

Also, in the spirit of constructive *redundancy* (see Guideline 17 of *Teaching Writing Online* 56), I posted this on the homepage announcements:

Announcements for Monday, January 16:

- Your materials are up for **Week 2.** Follow the **Weekly Plan.** Remember the **quiz** is tomorrow.
- Your **grades** for Week 1 are posted. Note that your current "Peeps" grade is a *running total:* When you write your 10 short Peeps for the term, you get 10 out of 10 (easy) points.
- See the "Tips advice resources" thread about **using evidence** in your posts.

Initial Moderator

For many reasons, I think student moderators are important to successful asynchronous OWC conversations. The strategy of using student moderators to lead the knowledge creation in a class is not new, of course; for example, Matt Bower and John Hedberg said online teachers should "consider student-led strategies if a student focus on the content is to be encouraged" (477). Moderation creates pedagogical opportunities to teach students to work with other students' writing, and they offer, especially for time-strapped teachers, a great way to leverage time by having the students help manage the conversations. In Week 2, the first moderator (or as I described him in the Plan, the "courageous" John), volunteered. I had emailed John on Friday of Week 1, providing him with straightforward moderator instructions:

> **From:** Scott Warnock
> **Sent:** Friday, January 13 2:26 PM
> **To:** John
> **Subject:** English102: Moderating in Week 2
>
> Hi John,
> Thank you very much for stepping up and being our first moderator in the course. Moderating is not difficult, but it does take some extra work for the moderator that week.
>
> As moderator, please do NOT start a new thread. Simply post **early** in the week in one of the existing threads – but not the Project thread: I'll be working in that one – letting everyone know that you will be moderating that thread. If you have any doubts or questions, please contact me before you post.
>
> You can moderate the conversation in any way you like, but please do the following:
> - As I said, write a short post letting everyone know that you'll be moderating the conversation on your thread. Do this early in the week.
> - Keep up with what's being written.
> - Try to move the conversation forward with questions and new ideas. Basically, your goal is to build the conversation on the thread.
> - At the end of the week, please post a message **summarizing** the activity on your thread and your participation on it as moderator.
>
> Please note that moderating is a 15-point grade and that your moderator posts are separate from your other graded Discussion posts this week.
>
> Again, if you have any questions, please let me know.
> Thanks again,
> Prof. Warnock

So, as moderator, John's first job was to choose one of the threads to moderate in the Week 2 Forum. As with almost all work in our course, moderating was worth an informal grade, which I hoped productively encouraged students to do a good job.

A New Student

My long experience teaching in different modalities has indicated that there is more student "movement" (i.e., drops and adds) in my online courses than in other modalities. This makes sense for a lot of reasons. Tuesday afternoon of Week 2, I received this pleasant message:

> **From:** Artan
> **Sent:** Tuesday, January 17 2:56 PM
> **To:** Scott Warnock
> **Subject:** New Student to English 102-901
>
> Hi Mr. Warnock,
> I am a new student to English 102-901 as of today. I have a few question regarding this course. I have read the syllabus and documents for this course. First off I wanted to ask you if I need or can make-up anything that was discussed/done in week 1. I see that there was a quiz taken in week 1, will I be able to make that up? Also do I have to know anything about this course other than that on the syllabus? I want to get caught up and know what I'm doing for this course because this is my first online course. If you could answer these questions it would be great. I will be waiting for your reply.
>
> Thanks,
> Artan [Student ID#]

In replying, I used my "big bark" teacher voice, sternly cautioning—but all with the student's best interests in mind!:

> **From:** Scott Warnock
> **Sent:** Tuesday, January 17 4:34 PM
> **To:** Artan
> **Subject:** RE: New Student to English 102-901
>
> Dear Artan,
> First and foremost, as your teacher, I am here to work with you and to help you have success in this course.
>
> However, I'm concerned that you're entering this course so late, especially as it's your first online course. My long experience teaching online has shown me that students who enter this late tend not to have a good outcome. That being said, if you are committed to getting caught up in the course, I am here to work with you.
>
> You should immediately read the Weekly Plan for week one, which is in a folder on the Home Page. I will drop the quiz from week 1, but you will need to get cracking to make up the other work from last week and get on track for this week.

You may want to call me, and you're welcome to do that at the work number below.

Please don't hesitate to ask me any questions,
Prof. Warnock

I even provided my cellphone number. Artan and I communicated via email about the course requirements throughout the week (as it turned out, he would be a good member of the course and do quite well, contrary to both my cautions—and many similar experiences!).

Diana: Still Feeling Out the Course

Working from the library this week to see if it was a better "class space" for my online class, I opened the course homepage and read the schedule for the week. While, at times, the schedule could come across as daunting (I mean, the instructions for the week alone were 565 words, and I saw I had to read sixty-two pages on top of that, not including reading my peers' posts and responding to them), it was helpful nonetheless. What was particularly useful was the language ProfW used in the instructions: "You'll want to have read and watched by Tuesday"; "I know some of you are night owls"; "While I don't want to encourage procrastination, you can post as late as you like on Wed." This use of "you" and "I" personalized the professor-student interaction for me. Regardless of when ProfW had written these Week 2 guidelines, I felt like he was there, on my screen, telling me exactly how to succeed in the course. The announcements continued this theme:

Announcements for Wednesday, January 18:

- Good job getting started on the **Discussions** this week. Make sure you spend time writing a **good topic** and responding to your colleagues with a good secondary post.
- See the "Tips Advice Resources" thread about **using evidence** in your posts.

What appeared to be created specifically for our course, however, were ProfW's feelings regarding our first week's worth of work. He wrote, "Okay, I'm impressed. This group got off to a strong start in Week 1. I'm excited about the prospects for this term." I thought, "Wow! He likes us! And wait a minute, he actually told us what he thought about our work? As early as the second week?" That was rare coming from a professor so early in a course. But here we were, already getting *feedback* on our work. On a similar note, this feedback was much different from the individual, one-on-one reviews I usually received from professors. Never have I received a progress review lumped together with the rest of my classmates (unless we did something bad, that is). It was interesting to have the perspective of working together online. My classmates weren't directly responsible for my grade, and I wasn't responsible for theirs, but we did need to work together to create an enjoyable class environment online.

Readings

This was the second week we got to watch a video along with readings. Cool! Anyone who was a student knows that reading "Watch the clip ______" in an assignment list is always a relief. Was this going to be a usual trend in the course? Of course, I couldn't know for sure yet, but it felt nice knowing the coursework might be diverse. I could tell these weren't lazy placeholders of content, but rather a conscious attempt from ProfW to mix up the coursework for us. I know my classmates and I could really tell in high school if teachers were tired that day or forgot to plan a lesson when out of nowhere they'd have us watch a movie loosely related to the content we were covering in class. I once watched *Back to the Future* in a physics course because we were talking about Einstein's "twin paradox." Sure, that could be discussed, but there were more distractions from that film than educational lessons. Instead, ProfW incorporated many themes in the video that linked with our Discussion prompts and focus throughout the week.

The narrative accounts from our additional readings posted on our LMS, as well as the readings from *The 33rd*, were all interesting and engaging, but the material from the textbook for the course was already beginning to drag. While I wasn't an English or writing major and certainly wasn't a professional by any means, I was comfortable with the skill of writing. This book seemed elementary to me, and I already started skimming it only two weeks into the course. I knew enough to keep it near me for the quiz, in case I forget anything last-minute, but I was starting to lag in the readings. Perhaps the text was useful for other students, and I guess that imbalance of writing experience is what's to be expected in a first-year writing course.

Speaking of the Quiz

Great. I'm only two weeks into the course and I already messed up a quiz. For some reason, I submitted before saving my answers. I emailed ProfW about the issue, adding, "A pop up window informed me that I needed to save my answers before hitting submit but before I had time to do so, the quiz stopped because time had run out. I would greatly appreciate it if you could let me know if my answers were in fact saved." ProfW emailed back only an hour later:

> **From:** Scott Warnock
> **Sent:** Tuesday, January 17 12:13 PM
> **To:** Diana Gasiewski
> **Subject:** Re: Eng 102:901 Quiz 2 Concern-Diana Gasiewski
>
> Hi Diana,
>
> I just checked, and your answers were not saved. I reset the attempt, so you can quickly re-take the quiz.
>
> Let me know if this works for you,
>
> ProfW

Thank god. I retook the quiz (and got a 5!) and wrote back, "Thank you very much. I was able to retake the quiz and properly save my answers."

Scott: Getting the Discussions Going

Much of our course was structured around asynchronous, written conversations on course Discussions. This environment, which uses a simple, ubiquitous learning technology, provides a platform on/through which students *write* in rhetorically rich ways to accomplish almost everything in the course. As a teacher with many years of experience, I feel good about my ability to moderate/facilitate onsite conversations.[1] Online, this experience can often be better, with students writing their way to good ideas while everyone participates. A big objective of this book is to *show* you how these conversations worked in the course, and we will use several different methods of summarizing and describing the Discussions in the coming weeks, including visual representations of the nodes and connections of a few selected threads. Our goal is not to provide in-depth discourse analysis of the dynamics of these conversations—that is another project!—either through specific visual representation tools/approaches (see Lucas and Moreira or Hansen, Shneiderman, and Smith) or even at the level of discourse precision of, say, Jefferson's Transcript Notation (see Atkinson and Heritage); instead we want to provide perspectives on how these conversations operated in terms of pedagogy, knowledge-building, and course community.

In Week 1, students had begun to acclimate themselves to the writing environment. While I provided instruction and hands-on guidance, I think it is important to reiterate that in an OWC I don't expect them to get it all in Week 1, and there is no pressure, grades or otherwise, for them to demonstrate mastery of the online writing Discussion environment right away. Some instructors struggle because they raise the stakes too high too early, not only for the students but for themselves: They are afraid that everything has to be running smoothly from the start.

Discussion Work Schedule

Each week, as Diana mentioned in Week 1, students would have two levels of response: primary posts and secondary posts. In Week 2, I settled into the Discussions teaching schedule that I would use all term—for both the students and me:

- On *Monday* I would post prompts. Monday of Week 2 happened to be Martin Luther King Jr. Day, and I worked at home, posting all the Discussion prompts by the end of the day. My prompts are within a thread, just like the students' posts: I like to be part of the action. In some LMS systems, the instructor's prompt can serve as a kind of title or header, but I want my prompts to be part of the threads.
- After Week 1, posting deadlines are consistent for most weeks: *Wednesdays* for primary posts and *Fridays* for secondary posts. I would check in on Discussions briefly on *Tuesdays* and *Wednesdays*.
- On *Thursdays*, usually in the morning, I would set aside two hours of dedicated time to read and respond to Discussions. I conceived of this as "teaching" time, and I would actually set a timer to help me allot my time properly. The issue usually would not be spending enough time, but spending, early in the term, too *much* time in the text- and idea-rich Discussions. Many weeks, I would also think about their overall work on a thread and, largely attempting to use one of the moderating roles described so well by George Collison and his coauthors (see "Behind the Screen" for this week), I would provide *synthesis* posts designed to push the conversation forward: I'm teaching on these boards!
- I set aside a one-hour block of dedicated time on *Fridays*, as their secondary posts were appearing, to continue reading and responding.

It is important to note that the three hours of time I dedicated to Discussions corresponds to in-class teaching time for a three-credit course. If I was doing other *teaching*—not course prep, not evaluating—work that week, I would dedicate less time to Discussions, and posting requirements would likewise be less for students.

I think, based on students' posting behaviors through the years, that a primary post and two secondary posts is about a class worth of work time for students. Remember, not only are they composing 300 to 500 words, but they are also spending time reading so their posts are anchored in conversations; I specifically ask for such context in the Discussion post rubric (see the pre-chapter).

Behind the Screen: Using Discussions in an OWC

Much has been written about asynchronous writing tools, and writing teachers have long considered the potential of a fundamentally writing-rich learning environment. In 1990, Lester Faigley looked at student work in these environments and saw much promise, including in how instructors take on a participatory, student-like role and potential shifts in identity. Jim Cody, in 2003, observed that asynchronous online discussion forums can enhance learning—specifically for community college students. In 2005, Kristine Blair said of message board writing for students: "The practice they receive through writing to communicate with their instructor and peers can be as influential to their writing skills as major essay assignments" (sect. 2, para. 5). Many of these teachers and scholars influenced me, and recently, in "Teaching the OWI Course," I wrote, "Again, a great—and perhaps revolutionary—thing in OWI is that students will engage in most course interactions via writing" (162); in "The Low-Stakes, Risk-Friendly Message-Board Text," I wrote, "Facilitated by digital tools, these asynchronous student texts have several traits that allow them to fall somewhere between the personalized informal writing students might do . . . and the formal material in larger course writing projects" (97). This writing-centric environment presents many opportunities for student learning.

It also presents infinite opportunities for teaching, whether for matching your onsite style or exploring new ways of instruction. For instance, in "Two Roads Diverged in a Wood: Productive Digression in Asynchronous Discussion," Joseph Ugoretz said instructors should *encourage* digression in message boards. In an article in the *Journal of Educators Online*, Katrina Meyer explored how a method of having students evaluate each other's posts can influence a class. Vanessa Paz Dennen looked at nine quite different classes in "From Message Posting to Learning Dialogues: Factors Affecting Learner Participation in Asynchronous Discussion" to determine factors online teachers might consider in using message boards.

There are also numerous texts to help you moderate digital conversations. One of my favorites is George Collison et al.'s *Facilitating Online Learning: Effective Strategies for Moderators;* these authors describe a variety of roles that are particularly helpful in pushing student thinking on Discussion boards (I try to use these roles when I create my midweek "synthesis" posts):

- *Generative guide*: Provide range of positions to indicate different lines of questioning.
- *Conceptual facilitator*: Like a lecturer, but build from posts as well as course texts.
- *Reflective guide*: Re-state elements of student posts.
- *Personal muse*: Offer personal insight.
- *Mediator*: Uncover students' unstated reasons for their comments.
- *Role play*: Take on the role of different characters/voices (106–117).

If you do a little exploring, you can tap into a wide variety of resources to match—and enhance—your creativity in teaching in discussion-based environments.

Types of Prompts

There were five threads in Week 2. In this book, you will see that I use a variety of prompt types, and they fall into loose categories, based on *purpose. The prompt is designed to help students*

1. Have a conversation about assigned texts/media.
2. Write-to-learn about specific content (and in WaW, that content is often writing itself).
3. Work on/explore a specific aspect of writing.
4. Generate ideas for writing projects.
5. Metawrite:
    a. About their own texts: Write about their own writing.
    b. About texts (usually Discussions, but sometimes projects) composed by other students.
    c. About the course itself.
6. Argue about a topic.
7. Reflect.
8. Develop course community/meet one another.
9. Understand/work through course logistics.

These categories have blurry edges that reflect the blurred edges of teaching. For instance, a thread may start in a course text and then lead to dialogue focusing on metawriting or on a rhetorical mode. A thread about a course text may be connected to project topics.

Elements of Prompts

You will see several types of prompts this week, and Diana and I will dissect example posts throughout the book, but as with the types of prompts, there are certain characteristics that I have found that help make prompts effective:

1. Clear, succinct subject line.
2. Clear, direct language (think about OWI Principle 3 Effective Practice 3.1: "When text is the primary medium, OWI teachers should use written language that is readable and comprehensible" [Conference 12]).

3. Salutation/greeting (sometimes you may be welcoming, friendly, or even playful).
4. Context: How does this thread fit into what is happening in the course?
5. Overt goal or objective.
6. Instruction: What are they to do in this thread?
7. Minimal number of questions (teachers can get into trouble here: they overdo it with complexity and length, forgetting that both they and other students will build the conversation as it goes; you don't need to frontload everything).
8. Further anchoring of prompt to material in course/other texts.
9. Possible broadening of topic (e.g., students may be analyzing an argument, but you can also ask their stances on the argument's topic).
10. Complimentary closing, perhaps inviting questions and comments.
11. Work(s) cited, if appropriate.

Naturally, not every characteristic will be in every prompt, nor are they always in this order.

Thread: A Few Powerful Little Engines

This week students proposed topics for Project 1 on the Discussions. This is a "generate ideas for writing projects" thread, but I provided additional structure by introducing them to one of my favorite approaches to invention, Joseph Williams's thinking "engines":

Author: Scott Warnock **Topic**: A few powerful little engines
Subject: Powerful little engines **Date**: January 16, 2:42 PM

Dear students,

I'd like to introduce you to an incredibly powerful little "engine" to help you generate good topics for your writing projects—in all classes. Ready?:

← A brief introduction to the "content."

1. "Most people believe that ___, but a closer look will show that ___."

Seems pretty humble, but this type of thinking has given birth to many of the great ideas of our time. If you can find a topic that fits those blanks, you are perhaps on your way to a good piece of writing. This little "engine" has several siblings:

← A quick sentence to emphasize the goal.

2. I am analyzing/comparing ____ so that I can explain/understand ____. 3. If we (do not) understand ___, we will (not) understand ___. 4. What we know about ____ is that ____; what we don't know is ____.

These "engines" can help you generate an approach to address the ultimate question your reader will want answered: "So what?"

Looking at one of the readings in chapter 89 of [our textbook] or *The 33rd*, how does the author's work fit one of these engines? How does that help to make the argument more effective—or does it not?

These engines are discussed in some detail by Joseph Williams in his book, *The Little Red Schoolhouse.*

Let us know,
Prof. Warnock

Reply

← Their specific instructions for this thread.

This was a low-traffic thread. There were only eight posts (really, nine, but one student reposted because of formatting woes), and four were by me. By Tuesday afternoon, Diana had posted a lengthy post about one of the essays, changing the subject to "Biemiller's Use of a Little Engine." She and I had a brief but useful exchange.

When teaching in an asynchronous discussion format, OWC teachers will need to get used to a surprising class dynamic: It can be easier for them to be ignored than it is onsite! Katie wrote a good primary post analyzing a reading titled "Breast or Bottle?" She framed her comments using the engines, writing: The author "uses the engine 'I am comparing breastfeeding to bottle feeding so that I can understand why women choose to do either while also persuading the reader.'" I replied asking why she chose this particular essay, but she never replied back! Similarly, Michael described how another essay writer uses a "little engine," but he misunderstood the prompt or simply didn't read closely. I asked him to elaborate, and he too did not respond! It was early in the term, and students were not revisiting the boards, I suspected.

Thread: Defending Rhetoric: John as Moderator

"Courageous" John chose to moderate a thread about rhetoric:

Author: Scott Warnock
Subject: Defending rhetoric

Topic: Defending rhetoric
Date: January 16, 2:51 PM

Hi all,

You probably encountered the term "rhetoric" a lot last term (or you should have!). Be honest: What did the term mean for you? Did it have a negative connotation?

How do the grad students from Clemson describe/defend rhetoric? Why did rhetoric fall out of favor both as an academic subject and more broadly? How do we use rhetoric in our everyday decision making? Why is rhetoric useful, particularly now? How is rhetoric especially important in terms of the technologies we use to communicate?

Yours in rhetoric,
Prof. Warnock

Reply

← This prompt connects overtly with last term.

← This prompt is idiosyncratic to our course and overall program, but it develops a series of questions based on a short video.

I think largely due to his presence—John wrote eleven posts himself—this was an active thread, with thirty posts from eleven different students and lots of back-and-forth dialogue among students. I contributed only three posts to this thread. In fact, on Thursday morning of that week, during my dedicated time on the boards, I wrote, "I'm almost reluctant to jump in here because I think John is doing such a good job." The students were also mindful here of citing, which of course was one of my goals; I wanted them in the *low-stakes environment of the message board* to use research and consider how to cite properly. We provide a representation of their interactions in Figure 1. Each "node" is time-stamped and includes the postword count after the author's name.

Thread: Evaluating Evaluative Arguments

As I said, teachers often overcomplicate Discussion prompts. Many onsite courses are framed around a straightforward pedagogical model: Students read a text and walk into a room and discuss it. The course, in many ways, depends on the teacher's ability to manage the student conversations. That model can be replicated in online learning, but I think a key is not to be too fancy with initial posts, recognizing that the conversation will develop: As an analogy, imagine a teacher starting an onsite class by immediately asking the complex final exam question. In Week 2, I again created a straightforward text-based prompt that drew from readings:

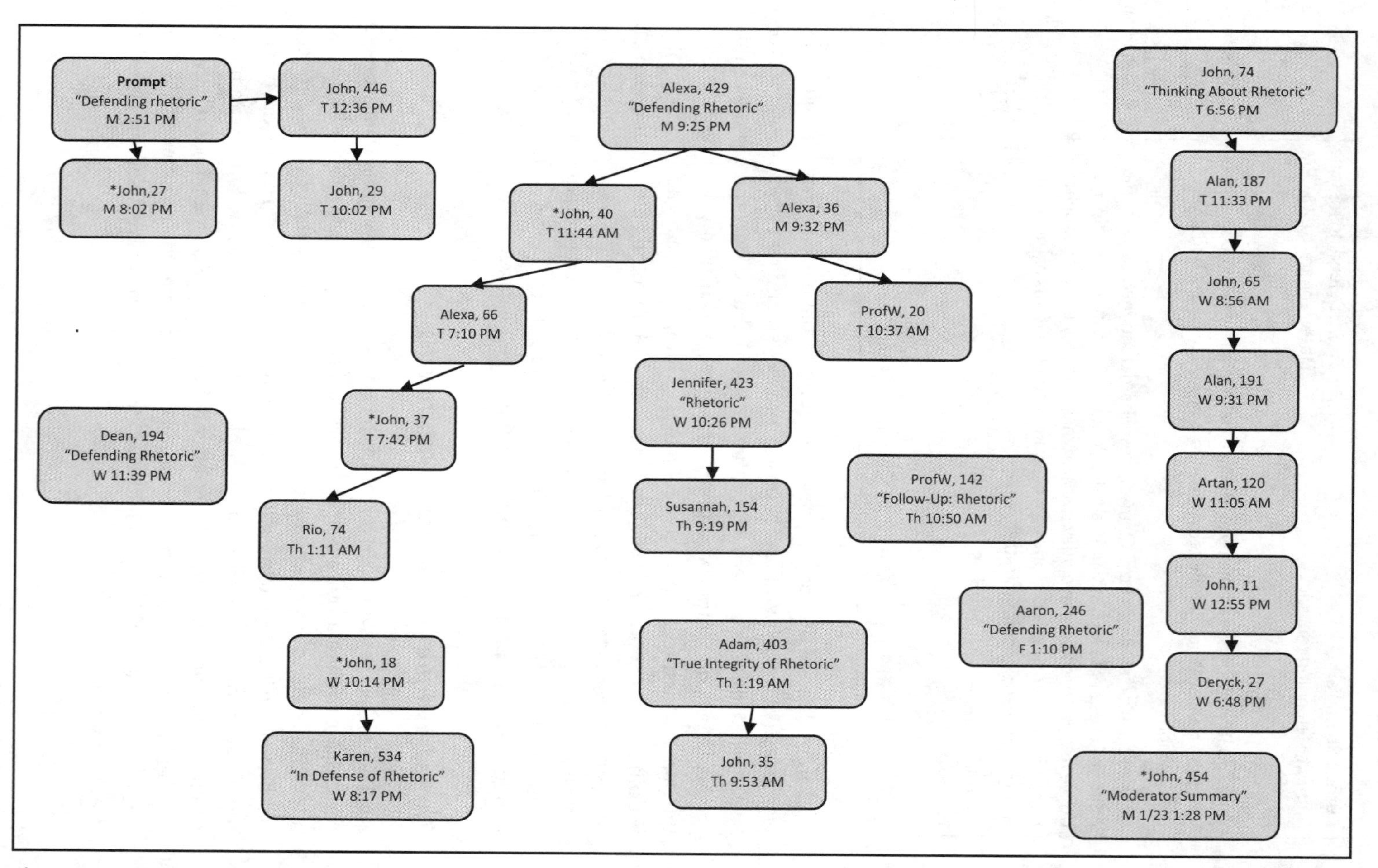

Figure 1. Week 2 thread: defending rhetoric.

*Moderator post.

Author: Scott Warnock
Subject: Evaluating evaluative arguments
Topic: Evaluative arguments
Date: January 16, 2:30 PM

Dear students,

Looking at any of the essays we read this week (Mohler, Burr, Bradshaw, or Lawrence from our textbook or Biemiller from *The 33rd*), how do the authors go about trying to not just make a judgment but to "convince [the] reader to agree"? How effectively do they outline the criteria by which they make their evaluation? Make sure you use your text(s).

Perhaps the best thing to do here is to start separate threads based on the essays you choose to discuss.

Let me know if you have any questions,
Prof. Warnock

Reply

← This prompt works directly from our course texts while providing some choice. (If students are going to read a course text, I am committed to using it and discussing it.)

There were eighteen posts by eight students (one of the posts was an accidental blank—the student clicked "Reply" too early, I supposed!). Four of the posts were by me.

Thread: Rhetorical Analysis of Anti-Tobacco Campaigns

Sometimes, you do too much, and that was probably the case this week, as I put a fifth thread (including the topic thread) in front of the students. I did this mainly because of the core syllabus; although I wasn't clear how to make use of the fairly chunky core syllabus rhetorical analysis of anti-tobacco campaigns, I felt that, as I always do, if I assign a reading, I should do something with it. Going against my own advice of keeping prompts short and direct, this sprawling prompt posed sixteen questions. Unsurprisingly, this thread had light traffic.

Thread: A Writing "Puzzle"!

The role of grammar instruction in FYW has been much discussed and debated.[2] An OWC provides lots of opportunities to write, but some may want to know, "How do you *teach* grammar in this environment?" I believe the writing that takes place throughout the term provides strong opportunities to create sentence- and mechanical-level awareness among students. The thousands of multiaudience words allow me to work with all levels of writing. However, I also want students, again, informed by a WaW pedagogy, to talk about grammar and mechanics. One way I have done this is through what I call "Writing Puzzles." I use (what I hope) are nonthreatening "puzzles" in a forum about specific grammar and mechanics questions, and I periodically mine the message boards for common issues. I'm not looking for embarrassing typos; I'm seeking more complex yet shared issues and then I ask students to identify and discuss the "puzzle" (see Warnock, "Message Board Prompts . . ."). On Friday, I posted this on the "Puzzles" forum:

Author: Scott Warnock
Subject: Writing puzzle #1
Topic: Writing puzzle #1
Date: January 20, 11:16 AM

Hi folks,

Periodically I will put up here some "writing puzzles," derived from what I see on the Discussion boards. If you like, see if you can identify the grammar/mechanical error/mistake. Here's one:

"A person's educational level determines their earning power, so a person should value higher education because it provides them with a better chance of earning a high income."

Reply

Over the next three days, ranging across the weekend, Alan, Diana, and Rio had a seven-post conversation with me, discussing pronouns, gender-based language, and even whether the sentence was a comma splice!

Diana: Working through Uncertainty in Discussions

I understood that I was to post in two different Discussion threads, one on our first project and one on the course readings, but the deadlines for these posts took me a while to figure out.

WRITE and READ	You did a solid job in Week 1, but please review the Discussion guidelines on the syllabus before you start on this week's HLC work; it'll all become habit soon enough: • **Project 1 topic Discussion**: Follow the instructions on the Discussion thread "Project 1 topics." I am asking you to propose a topic as **ONE** primary post, and then you will write **ONE**	Post your primary reading posts by **Wednesday** night, January 18. (I know some of you are night owls, and while I don't want to encourage procrastination, you can post as

← The listing of the deadlines for each of the assignments for this week were out of order. Just from glancing at the deadlines quickly, I saw I needed to post something on Wednesday, then something on Friday, then something on Thursday? While the ordering wasn't

	secondary post in response to one of your colleague's topics. • **Reading Discussions**: You will have several reading Discussion options this week. You will post **ONE** primary and **ONE** secondary post on our reading Discussions. Don't forget to stay current on the Discussions, and make sure you *read* through everything on the message boards.	late as you like on Wednesday night/ Thursday wee morning.) Post your secondary post by **Friday**, January 20, at 4:00 pm. **This is a hard deadline.** Complete all your posts for the "Project 1 topics" thread by **Thursday** evening, January 19.	that difficult, it was still a bit odd, so I needed to really focus to see what was due each day.

If I compared the deadline order to the order of the material in the instructions, it was reversed. The parallel listing between the assignment box and due date box was confusing. The vague language surrounding the Project 1 Discussions also left me perplexed. I combated this by posting everything as soon as possible, then responding to my peers once I saw I had someone to respond to.

When it came to producing content, it felt simple enough. I'm like a fish to water when given the opportunity to write, so producing the primary posts just felt like mini-essays in response to the content provided to me. I felt like it was something I had done before, both verbally and through writing. But when it came to responding to my peers, I still felt a tad hazy on how my style and voice should come across. I understood this was an academic setting, but *how* academic should I be in these secondary posts? Should I mirror how I speak in an in-class setting? Let's say I was in an f2f class and someone had just presented a graded, academic five-minute speech (sort of like the primary posts) and the class was able to discuss her presentation afterward (similar to the secondary posts). We would all speak casually. However, this class is online, and it's a writing course. Should I continue to write as I would in essays? What does essay writing even look like? As you can see, I was beginning to go down the rabbit hole. To save myself from muddling my voice further, I went ahead and wrote my submission, but I made sure to read many of my peers' posts to see what other students were doing. If I felt like my writing was different from my peers, I would work on it in the following weeks.

If I truly felt lost or overwhelmed by the instructions from this week, I could get ahold of ProfW. He made it clear last week that he was easily accessible by email, phone, or even f2f, so if the confusion was significant I wouldn't have had a problem reaching him. But the problem wasn't that big. I just needed to plug along. In any exchange of information, some messages are going to get a little hazy along the way. Rather than slow things down by asking tiny questions or thinking too much about the issue, it was best to have some faith that everything would work out and simply move forward.

Scott: Topics for Project 1

When my students have a major project, I spend a significant amount of dedicated course time at the topic stage. Onsite, I've honed approaches that I think work well. Online, this process can be even better; by requiring all students to both post a topic and respond to a classmate's topic, the students' proposals and the dialogue about them happen within a writing-to-learn framework. In general, this approach leads to open dialogue, and I can abstract general comments about topics, both strengths and weaknesses, and synthesize those thoughts into one post that they can refer to as much as they like. I created just such a synthesis post this time: The subject read: "PLEASE READ: Many proposals are off topic." I emphasized key aspects of the assignment instructions, including that they were having trouble focusing on the rhetorical goals of the project, and I ended on this encouraging, but stern, note: "Finally, this type of problem is a natural part of the topic process, although I admit I wish some of you had spent more time reading the project instructions (and perhaps annotating them). We will work it out."

Diana: What Am I Going to Write about for Project 1?

Because ProfW advised us in the week's announcement to push ourselves and dive into threads we were the least comfortable with, I directed most of my writing efforts to the thread on Project 1 Topics:

Author: Scott Warnock	**Topic**: Project 1 topics
Subject: What are you going to write about?	**Date**: January 16, 2:28 PM

Hi everybody,

In memo form (see p. 379 of our textbook for memo headings)—addressed to me and the rest of the class—post at least one potential idea for Project 1 by Wednesday. (Remember, this memo counts as a primary post.) If possible, you might frame your idea in the words of one of the thinking engines, such as "While most people believe _, a closer look reveals _."

Describe your thoughts in some detail; certainly, the more detail you provide, the more help your colleagues and I can provide. You can include questions for us, and you can describe the sources you might use.

You are not committed to the initial topic you discuss here. Your thinking can change based on the input you receive.

After you post your idea(s), I am asking you to post at least one secondary post in response to someone else's topic idea by Thursday as well. When looking at your colleagues' topics, you might address the following questions: Is the topic clear? Is it a good topic? Is the author's main point/argument clear? What would you like to see addressed in the project? What sources might be good? You can keep your comments brief, but try to think of something constructive to say that will help the person.

It would certainly be useful to ask questions here. Your colleagues and I will do our best to provide answers. If you have a good question about the project in general, start a new thread.

Thanks,
Prof. Warnock

Reply

There was quite a bit to cover here. I needed to figure out what memo form was, closely read the requirements for Project 1 again, come up with a decent project idea, summarize it for my classmates, and then respond to someone else's post even though I wasn't 100 percent sure what I was even doing? It's okay. I could figure this out. I dipped my toe in the water by first reading the few initial posts from my classmates. Artan wrote a lengthy summary of his Project 1 idea on sustainability and wildlife. He described the overall problem of sustainability, specifically how polar bears are affected by carbon emissions, and closed by discussing his project plan: to attract attention to the issue, discuss various organizations that help the cause, and close with offering ways others can get involved to help. While the topic was a great start, it seemed broad, but Karen and Alan jumped in to help him. They both suggested he focus on one aspect of preserving wildlife, like a specific organization or species that's in decline. ProfW then offered his feedback:

Author: Scott Warnock
Subject: Re: Sustainability and Wildlife
Topic: Project 1 topics
Date: January 20, 10:41 AM

Hi Artan,

You get some good comments about the scope of this project, and Karen is even more focused, but there is a larger problem, in that you're off track in terms of the project PURPOSE. You write, "For this project I want promote the sustainability of the wildlife by attracting more attention to the factors that enable this to happen." See the post at the top of this thread and look at the project instructions again.

We'll figure it out,
ProfW

Reply

Oh, duh. That's where the problem was. Artan not only forgot to put his post in memo form, but he was also off-track on the overall project requirement. It was really nice to see my classmates work to help him out and to see how gracious and helpful ProfW was in pointing out his error. Even though all of this was out in the open for anyone to read, I didn't feel embarrassed for Artan. The way the Discussions were set up, we were all working together to figure out the requirements of this class. There was a firm sense of community, even as early as the second week of the course, in that we were all here to make mistakes and learn together. Maybe I'd be the one missing the boat later, and my classmates would learn from my mistakes.

Artan certainly wasn't the only one who was foggy on the requirements. Several students needed a refresher on what was required. After receiving feedback on what he missed, Donald wrote a follow-up post:

Author: Donald
Subject: California water conservation and sustainability
Topic: Project 1 topics
Date: January 21, 3:04 PM

I misunderstood the focus of the project. I reread the guidelines again and I will instead address water conservation efforts in California. Since I am from Southern California and understand this situation very well, I fell that this would be a much greater campaign to evaluate than my old topic. This topic will be more effective in that it concerns one of our nation's top producers of agriculture. This subject is very well researched and I should be able to find a lot of information. Example campaign would be the California Water Awareness Campaign.

http://www.wateraware.org/

Reply

ProfW responded to Donald:

Author: Scott Warnock
Subject: Re:California water conservation and sustainability
Topic: Project 1 topics
Date: January 21, 3:34 PM

Hi Donald,

I very much appreciate your straightforward response here. As I said, that's why we talk about topics!

I know water conservation efforts have been a big part of SoCal for a long time, so I think your analysis of campaigns in that area could yield a great project, and one that is relevant to you.

Let me know if you have further questions,
ProfW

Reply

Watching my classmates feel out the very discussion that I was nervous about was super reassuring, as was ProfW's support throughout the whole conversation. It was also helpful to see my classmates work through providing the appropriate advice to each other. Before jumping onto the post, I was nervous about coming across as too preachy, too all-knowing, or not providing enough advice. After reading through a few posts, I realized I wasn't the only one. Alan wrote a constructive response to John regarding the specifics of his topic, but he was modest in his suggestion:

Author: Alan
Subject: Re:Lead build up at outside shooting ranges
Topic: Project 1 topics
Date: January 18, 10:31 PM

I'm not good in giving critique or suggestions so don't take my word for it but I don't think you clarified how CO2 is worse than Pb? Are there more ways than one that CO2 is less threatening than Pb? Not sure where I intend to go with that one but it should be given some thought. Are there alternative bullets that can be used instead of lead type bullets that are less baneful to the faculty or wildlife? What is the respective lethal dose for CO2 and Pb and does the lead build-up amount results in more casualties than say air pollution resulting from CO2 build-up? Like I said, don't take my word for it but I feel as if you are claiming that lead is the greater threat than carbon dioxide. Granted, they're major problems confronting this generation today but it seems you're prioritizing what worse. Sorry if it feels judgmental.

Reply

John was modest in his reply to Alan.

Author: John
Subject: Re:Lead build up at outside shooting ranges
Topic: Project 1 topics
Date: January 19, 9:47 AM

No no, it's not judgmental. I was trying to say that despite the notion that CO_2 is going to kill us all, lead in fact is more deadly to children. You asked some good questions that I think I could have elaborated on a little more; check back when the drafts are posted, I'll make sure to stick them in there.

Thanks for the input.
John

Reply

These two, I felt, did a fantastic job providing feedback to one another that promoted helpful discussion on the progression of their topics. They also set the stage for how to provide advice without being afraid of coming off as, in Alan's words, "too judgmental."

I now felt ready to take a stab at my project proposal. I made sure to provide a thorough overview of the general topic I planned to discuss while also offering multiple options for a specific campaign I could focus on. That way my peers would have different options to provide insight on and direct me down the best path.

Author: Diana Gasiewski
Subject: The Farm-to-Table Movement
Topic: Project 1 topics
Date: January 17, 1:30 PM

TO: Prof. Warnock and Eng 102:901 Class

FROM: Diana Gasiewski DG

SUBJ: Farm To Table: Topic 1 Proposal

DATE: January 17

Our country desperately needs to consider going on a diet. Not just a health-conscious diet—though that is in serious need of order—but a farm-to-table diet. The average plate of food in America travels an average of 1,500 miles from grower to consumer (Halweil). Instead of buying from a local farmer, businesses have found it more cost-effective to buy from mass distributors. These business owners, however, do not realize the unsustainability of their choices. Over-traveled, mass produced foods increase greenhouse gas emissions, consume unnecessary amounts of fuel, and inhibit small farmers (Halweil).

To promote buying local, the Farm-to-Table campaign is working to endorse slow and sustainable food. While this practice is slightly more cost effective, the campaign has established an honorable and promising image to engage readers in the movement. They have successfully pointed out the harmful practices of alternative methods of food distribution, and have proven the outweighing benefits of the slow-food practice.

Therefore, I believe the Farm-to-Table movement would be the perfect sustainability campaign to analyze, evaluate and support for my first project in English 102. I do have some concerns, however, for what ads I will actually evaluate. What is unique about the Farm-to-Table movement is that it has come about in a non-advertised manner, and rather through inspiration of various authors and leaders in the food industry. Many actual campaigns have arisen throughout the country in response to this movement, such as PhillyHomeGrown and SlowFoodUtah; however, no collective, national campaign has evolved. How do you all suggest I go about actually observing advertisements in the Farm-to-Table Movement? Should I analyze the movement as a whole, or should I focus on one actual campaign, such as PhillyHomeGrown?

Thank you for your time and input,
DG

Reply

Katie was the first to respond with helpful advice:

Author: Katie
Subject: Re:The Farm-to-Table Movement
Topic: Project 1 topics
Date: January 18, 11:49 AM

Diana,

I think the farm to table movement is a great topic to discuss. I am a supporter of this movement as I grew up in a rural area of Pennsylvania and always ate fresh grown fruits and vegetables. I do, however, think that you should focus on one specific campaign to narrow down this broad topic. Make sure to also consider the fact of the amount of preservative and pesticides sprayed on certain grown foods. You should also consider campaigns that support organic industries.

Good Luck!
Katie

Reply

Then ProfW jumped in:

Author: Scott Warnock
Subject: Re:The Farm-to-Table Movement
Topic: Project 1 topics
Date: January 18, 12:35 PM

First off, Diana, this is a very good topic proposal. Nice job.

I agree with Katie. I think you should focus on the local movement, as I think that will make the task more manageable, especially because of the seemingly decentralized methods of the overall movement.

I'm excited about this project. I think it will be interesting to see how this national movement appears in a local market—and how successful its efforts are.

Let me know if you have questions,
ProfW

Reply

After initial worry and hesitation, extensive reading of my peers' posts and responses, and careful construction of my own, I successfully tackled a difficult thread I was nervous about. My peers were beginning to show how helpful and personable they are, and ProfW was still just as helpful as the first day of the course. After this thread, I felt more confident not only about my first project but about Discussions as a whole.

Scott: Moving into Week 3

On Friday, I posted the Week 3 Weekly Plan, which said at the top, "The focus this week is on the first draft of Project 1. We'll complete peer reviews. We'll also discuss argument strategies." In a new paragraph, I wrote, "Check Tuesday this week. It's a busy day, especially if you wait until the last minute to complete your readings." The Friday announcement reinforced all this:

Announcements for Friday, January 20:

- See the **Project 1 Topic** thread. Many of you wrote proposals **that are off topic.** We will work this out, and I am here to help you, but please see that thread.
- The Week 3 **Weekly Plan** is available. Note that your **first draft of Project 1** is due **Tuesday night**.

In Retrospect: Topics and Other Discussion Writings

It's worth thinking for a moment about what would have happened this week in a similar onsite course. At the end of the week, it's likely students would have achieved the same general *outcomes*: They would have discussed the readings, including some complex rhetoric-based readings. They could have learned about Williams's engines. They then, in some form or another, might have launched into conversations about topics for their first projects. The conversations could have been helpful—in fact, they could have been fantastic. But in our OWC, they did all of this same work using writing. Some of the writing, to hearken back to what James Britton and his coauthors called it, would be expressive and some would be transactional, but the students would be developing it all in writing.

This is a major difference, and it's a way of thinking differently about how to conduct FYW courses in any modality. Moderators, topic Discussions, course lessons—students are put under productive pressure to turn/express thoughts into/as writing.

The teacher must design the experience effectively: Really, what the teacher must do is *teach.* Teachers should design straightforward prompts and then participate, that is, moderate, and build the dialogue. But they should help students engage in student-to-student dialogue. The experience also should be worth something in the context of the course, whether by grade or something else. The informal writing, the smaller, low-stakes assignments, should be designed to build into the bigger projects; this is a challenge and opportunity not just in OWCs or hybrids but in using low-stakes writing in general.

The topic thread provides a specific, useful example of this. Students were able to communicate about topics for a complex writing project in a productive way, as Diana describes, due to the design of the Discussions. In an onsite course, students may have broken into small groups and discussed project ideas and provided feedback; they may have even worked in pairs. However, the benefits of those exchanges would be limited to the small group and would certainly be limited to those who were there that day. Online, every student's work on the project topic and subsequent conversations on how to improve the topics were available for all to see and comment on. From this, they could learn from early missteps of their peers where their own topics may have been off track, while also learning how to provide better feedback.

The Discussions can drive an OWC, and perhaps they *should* as well.

3

Week 3: Rough Drafts, Peer Review, and Response

...in a typical peer review session, students would ideally develop the thinking skills necessary to effectively evaluate a paper, as well as practice using feedback they receive from their peers.

—KRISTI LUNDSTROM AND WENDY BAKER

Scott: Process for Their First Drafts

As I wound up Week 2, I found myself scrambling to have everything ready for the following week. On Friday, I had two committee meetings in the afternoon and an allergy shot in the morning: Life, it stays with you. At about noon that day, I had gone through everything from Week 2 and was ready to upload the Week 3 Weekly Plan.

Week 3: January 22 to January 28

The focus this week is on the first draft of Project 1. We'll complete peer reviews. We'll also discuss argument strategies.

Check Tuesday this week. It's a busy day, especially if you wait until the last minute to complete your readings.

What do I do?	What are the specific instructions? Where do I find the work or the assignment?	When is it due? (All times EST)
WRITE	The first draft of Project 1. **Attach your completed draft to the Project 1 topic in this week's Discussions.**	The draft is due by **10:00 pm on Tuesday**, January 24. That's a firm deadline.

← At the top of the Plan, as usual, I expressed our primary goals (and concerns) for that week.

← I gave explicit instructions for submitting Project 1 drafts, but even my

	Make sure you give your file the proper name; see the Policies on the Syllabus. Several of your classmates will review your draft (see below).	Please don't be late. Aside from being penalized for missing the deadline, you will also disrupt our peer review process. I don't like unnecessary disruptions.
PEER REVIEW	I have set all of you up into peer review groups that you can access via the Discussions. As I've mentioned, you will post your draft of Project 1 on your peer review group topic. Then each of you will follow the peer review directions and comment on **each** project that has been submitted.	Please complete all peer reviews by the **weekend**. Make sure you spend some time on each review, and, much like our normal Discussions, *be sure that when possible your review complements/adds to/critiques the other reviews in your group.* Your peer reviews altogether count for a 20-point grade.
READ	• *Course textbook:* "Using Strategies for Argument" 30 pages. • *Review in course textbook* chapter about documenting sources 10 pages. • *Aux*: Jones, "Finding the Good Argument OR Why Bother with Logic?" 24 pages. • *The 33rd*: Sherlock, "No Such Thing as a Free Lunch" 115-29.	You'll want to have read by **Tuesday**, January 24 so you can complete the quiz and work on the Discussion topics.
TAKE a QUIZ	Quiz 3 can be found in the "Quizzes" folder on the Course Homepage.	The quiz will be available **Tuesday** from 9:30 am to midnight. You will have five minutes to complete it.
READ and WRITE	Read all the Discussion topics for Week 3. Note that the requirements below are separate from the peer review work: 1. Post ONE primary post to any of the Discussion topics.	Post your primary post by **Wednesday** night, January 25. Post your secondary post by **Friday**, January 27, at 4:00 pm.

reference to the syllabus didn't prevent students from making file naming errors . . .

← A big part of this week's work was the peer reviews; to help reinforce their importance, I graded them as a "double strength" primary post.

← I assigned a variety of readings this week.

← I hoped they were on track now, and the course tasks were mapped out on certain days to encourage *pacing* and *predictability* (see Guideline 35 from *Teaching Writing Online*).

	2. Post ONE secondary post to any of the Discussion topics. Don't forget the "Peeps" requirement for the Discussions this term.	
MODERATE (two of you)	This week our moderators will be Alan and Diana. I will be in touch with them, and then they will moderate some of our Discussions this week. They will be active voices in encouraging conversation, and they will provide a summary of their assigned topics at the end of the week. Thanks to Alan and Diana for moderating here.	If you have not signed up for a moderator slot, you need to take care of this on our Discussions.

← Now the moderators were getting rolling…

Yes, this week students would be submitting rough drafts for their first writing projects. That is always a big, red-letter week for writing teachers. For some, that's because they picture themselves shackled to student drafts for dozens or even scores of hours. Indeed, the scholarship of response is infused with a longstanding stream of negativity, going back to Nancy Sommers's observations about the often "mean-spiritedness" (149) of teacher comments. For others, it's a big week not just because of workload but because of the opportunity to delve into their students' thinking through a larger writing project.

My plan was that drafts were going to arrive by 10:00 p.m. on Tuesday night. In the past, I had often created deadlines like 6:00 p.m. or some similar early evening time, but the reality is that I work a pretty standard 8:30 or so to 5:30 or so workday. If I did not see the drafts at 5:30, I wasn't going to see them until the next day. So why not give students more time? Teaching online has changed my view of time, as I have realized that my clock life does not have to line up with my students' clock lives. That being said, I have sometimes stretched a deadline way into the wee hours of the night, but I then thought that kind of deadline might encourage unproductive and perhaps even unhealthy student behaviors: I don't want them staying up until 4:00 a.m. doing work for my course. Ten p.m. or 11:00 p.m. seem like good compromise times. I posted this announcement to reinforce the schedule that week—and to provide a comment about how some of them needed to circle back to the Discussion conversations:

Announcements for Monday, January 23:

- Your latest **Discussion questions and grades** are available.
- You are doing a good job as a group on the **Discussions**, but remember that this is a **conversation** that you must follow all week. I've posed questions to a few of you on the boards, and I was greeted with silence....
- Remember the **first draft of Project 1** is due **Tuesday night**.
- I am still missing **emails from *five* of you about the course policies**. That email was due in Week 1, so please get it to me. (See the Week 1 Weekly Plan.)

Scott: Question about a Grade—and Why I Use FLS Grading

I have mentioned my grading philosophy: frequent, low-stakes (FLS) grading, which I use for a variety of pedagogical and learning reasons. Especially when teaching online (although I use FLS grading in almost all my courses), I use grades as a way to communicate with students: They receive many small, low-stakes grades from me as a form of feedback, and those low-stakes numerical grades provide a mechanism for students to see how they are faring and then talk to me about their progress in the course. FLS grading also allows me to have a class structure in which students can write a great deal, but they don't have to wait for me to read and respond in length to everything: *I am not the bottleneck in the system* (as I reinforce in Guideline 25 of *Teaching Writing Online*). This is particularly valuable in the multiaudience environment of asynchronous discussions. As I'll describe in the next few chapters, I still provided detailed response on major writing projects, but, and I always think about what I am doing in the context of other faculty who teach scores of students, I was leveraging my time as a teacher with FLS grading.

Midweek, I had a brief email exchange with Alexa that demonstrated how FLS grading can be used as a platform for conversation:

From: Alexa
Sent: Tuesday, January 24 7:25 PM
To: Scott Warnock
Subject: English 102 - Grades

Prof W,

Its Alexa from your online english 102 course, and I had a problem with the quiz for today. While I was on my 4th question, dragonfly 3 wireless shutdown but then it came back on and I thought it would be enough time to complete it, but I guess time ran out by the time I clicked finish, but I'm not sure if the internet connection shut down affected my completion of the quiz.

Also, I just had a question regarding my grades. I haven't been doing as well as I would like these past two weeks and I was just wondering what I was doing wrong and how I could improve my weekly grades.

Thanks again for your time!
Sincerely,
Alexa

> **From:** Scott Warnock
> **Sent:** Wednesday, January 25 10:19 AM
> **To:** Alexa
> **Subject:** RE: English 102 - Grades
>
> Hi Alexa,
>
> Your quiz did come through, so it was okay.
>
> I'm glad you asked about the grades. In Week 1, I recorded that you missed a secondary post. In Week 2, I recorded that you missed a primary post. Those are the primary reasons your weekly grades are so low, because otherwise your work has been strong. If you believe that I made an error and missed a post, please let me know. You can also post late, which will give you reduced credit but would be better, of course, than a zero.
>
> Let me know – I'm happy to talk about grades,
> ProfW
>
>> **From:** Alexa
>> **Sent:** Wednesday, January 25 10:45 AM
>> **To:** Scott Warnock
>> **Subject:** RE: English 102 - Grades
>>
>> Hi professor!
>>
>> Thanks so much for getting back to me. Week 1 makes sense, as I seem to have missed a secondary post so I will complete that and turn it in late for some credit. As for Week 2, my primary post was on "Defending Rhetoric" which I posted on January 16. If that didn't count as a primary post, I apologize and will complete one for late credit as well. Thanks again for taking the time to go over this with me! I appreciate it!
>>
>> Alexa

From: Scott Warnock
Sent: Wednesday, January 25 4:12 PM
To: Alexa
Subject: RE: English 102 - Grades

Hi Alexa,

This is why we have these conversations. I read that post but neglected to record a grade. Your grades have been updated.
Sorry for the inconvenience,

ProfW

FLS grading helped make these easy issues to discuss—and fix.

A Student Says Goodbye

Online courses are not for everyone. During the first few weeks of the term, students were deciding to drop; again, my hope is that their decisions would be informed by the many small grades they were receiving. Some of these students simply vanish. But sometimes they send a brief message, as Ellen did on Thursday, writing to me in an email, "Hello, I think that withdrawing from this course would be best for me as I have never taken an online course and it is very difficult for me. How can I do this?" I do not want to persuade a student to remain in a class that is not working for them, but, as an online teacher, I do not want them to drop because they feel isolated or out of touch with their instructor:

From: Scott Warnock
Sent: Thursday, January 26 1:40 PM
To: Ellen
Subject: RE: Class Withdraw

Hi Ellen,

You would talk to your advisor. While I support your decision, I do want to know if there is anything I can do to support you in the class. It seems you are having trouble meeting the deadlines, but when you do, your work has been good. I just reviewed your rough draft, and while it needs some revision, you are not alone.

You should feel free to call me if you want to talk this over, but, again, if you do believe that withdrawing is your best option, please talk to your advisor.

I wish you the best either way,
Prof. Warnock

Ellen did not remain in the course, as it turned out.

Diana: Creating/Designing a Personal Schedule

As I prepared for Week 3 I found the mini "blurb" at the top of the Weekly Plan extremely helpful. It read, "The focus this week is on the first draft of Project 1." While this line seems simple and expected from a professor, it was surprising to realize how infrequently I received a heads-up like this in college courses.

General focus points are particularly absent from many of my f2f courses. I am guessing this is because of the day-to-day flow with many small-picture goals that distract professors (and students) from the larger picture. Alternatively, the format of an online class allows professors to provide instructions more easily for their students since the material is all in one place. In my case, that material was in a Weekly Plans tab on my course homepage. This focus point helped me narrow my homework plan to one specific goal, which helped to minimize the workload from my perspective.

ProfW provided another useful note in the Weekly Plan, writing "Check Tuesday this week. It's a busy day." It wasn't the heads-up that was most helpful—it was the declaration of Tuesday being a specific day of *work* in the course. This was an approach I had never considered at this point in the course. Deadlines were just that: deadlines. Any time before that was independent time for me to get the work done free of any consistent scheduling. Up until this point, if three things were due on Thursday at 10:00 p.m., I'd begin the night prior at 10:00 p.m. Working late into the night, usually until 2:00 to 3:00 a.m., I used the final day for editing or last-minute work. I chose this schedule because I typically completed other coursework immediately after the associated class during the day. In f2f courses, attending class to complete lectures or discussions was as much a part of the weekly schedule as were deadlines for papers or quizzes. This evened out stress and responsibility. Yet the unique pace of the online course offered the luxury of independence. In my mind, I gave myself plenty of time because I've always been a strong student, but that twenty-four-hour turnaround was a tough time restraint to put on myself. In ProfW's online course, however, this independence came with a risk. I was not preparing myself for problems that could occur during this last-minute, overnight scheduling.

The only places to work on material this late at night at a city campus were the library, a common space in my residential hall, or my dorm room. The library wouldn't work because walking through West Philadelphia late at night was not always the safest option, even with public safety and a very courteous boyfriend. The shared space in my residential hall also wouldn't work, considering it was reserved for any activities sleeping roommates would be upset about (gaming, chatting, flirting). So I resorted to working quietly in my dorm room, fighting the urge to sleep or watch TV.

Therefore, after reading ProfW's note about Tuesday being a "busy day," I realized my current schedule would not keep up with the demands of the coursework. I acknowledged my responsibility to create reasonable writing sessions in accordance with the deadlines and scheduled a logical work week, placing my rough draft at the top of the to-do list so my peer reviewers had plenty of time to respond.

Scott: Peer Review and Online Writers' Groups

The submission for their Project 1 first drafts would not be through an assignment link in our LMS. Instead, as I announced in the Weekly Plan, I set the students up into three-person peer review groups on the Discussion board (following a long lineage of writing researchers and teachers like James Berlin and Peter Elbow, I am a staunch believer in the value of peer review). Technology-wise, this was easy to do, and it allowed me to put them into smaller subsets in the class, basically online writers' groups. These groups have a variety of advantages, but a primary one is this: I ask, in these asynchronous peer reviews, for reviewers not only to respond to the draft they are reviewing but to *account for a previous reviewer's comments in their response.* What this means is that the first student to provide a review only needs to focus on the draft, but the subsequent reviewer must synthesize previous comments into the review. This is a potentially much richer rhetorical and reviewing (and reading) environment, I think, facilitated by the OWC. (I have also used four-person groups for this purpose.)

I provided complete peer review instructions via a post in each group thread:

Author: Scott Warnock **Topic**: Week 3 - Proj1 Peer Review 1
Subject: Peer review of Project 1 **Date**: January 23, 11:42 AM

Dear members of Group 1:

Please post your first draft of Project 1 here as an **attachment** to a post. Only your group members have access to this thread; each person in the class belongs to one group.

← A small detail, but the greeting was specific to that group.

After the first drafts have been posted, **each** member of the group will review each draft (so all of you will write two peer reviews). I think it would be ideal organization-wise if each draft has its own thread, but you can work that out amongst yourselves.

Please follow the peer review instructions below, but also make sure that if you are not the first reviewer that **you take into account what the other reviewer said before you write your review; in other words, I don't want the author to get obviously redundant comments.** Post your review as a response to the author on this Discussion topic.

The criteria:

In a **150-word memo to the author**, please review the project, framing your comments around these areas (do NOT simply answer these questions—and don't feel obligated to address every question):

Does the project fulfill the assignment (look at the assignment directions again)? Why or why not?

What's the writer's purpose?

Is this a good topic?

Does the writer account for audience effectively?

Is the analysis clear and effective?

Does the writer successfully use techniques of persuasion and argument in evaluating the effectiveness of the campaign? Can you suggest sources?

Is there anything else the writer should have used?

Comment on the grammar and mechanics. Do recurring, glaring errors interfere with the project's message?

Name two main strengths. If this were your project, name two ways you would improve it.

Remember, reviews must be wrapped up by the weekend. And while I don't want you to be mean, a common flaw with peer reviews, especially the first time around, is that they are too nice.

Please let me know if you have questions,
Prof. Warnock

Reply

← Instructions here were explicit. I wanted them focused on reviewing, not figuring out the review process.

← A key piece of instruction was in bold: Take into account what the other reviewer had said.

← I tried to make the "genre" expectations explicit, including length. Why not help them learn to write a memo in the process?

← As with any peer review, I provided considerable detail about the parameters.

← My closing comment reinforced the value of this activity.

I do participate in the peer review threads, mainly challenging students, particularly those who, despite my emphasis in the instructions, simply run through and answer the questions. I also have to manage the logistics, starting with basics. As I mentioned in the pre-chapter, in order to keep things straight, I provide straightforward file naming instructions. Alas, despite reinforcing this in the Weekly Plan and elsewhere, nine of the eighteen students did not name the draft file correctly (it seems that 50 percent has held firm throughout time, no matter what I do), so I had to reply with a simple post saying something like "your file is not named properly. Please refer to the Syllabus policies and resubmit." Sometimes, despite my best efforts, I have to go even further (not even using a pleasant greeting!):

Author: Scott Warnock
Subject: Re:Proj1draft Bulb
Topic: Week 3 - Proj1 Peer Review 4
Date: January 26, 1:02 PM

[Student],

I'm sorry to seem like a nag, but I'm asking all of you to do something rather simple: Name the file correctly. Please review the syllabus policies for file naming and re-name your file appropriately. This one still is not correct.

Thanks,
ProfW

Reply

Students also asked questions about the review process. For instance, Diana asked on Thursday on her peer review thread, because she had Word's review capabilities, "Would it be okay if I made corrections on my group members' drafts through that method and sent the papers back to them?" I responded, "Good question. You can use the review comments to some degree, but I would actually prefer if you don't focus on editorial-type comments and instead think about the project as a whole and write back to your colleagues." She replied, "Yes, I completely understand. I'll work on my memos shortly."

I think that—and often say this overtly to students, regardless of modality—the peer reviews may be the most "real" writing students do in class: Writing to a real audience for a genuine purpose: to help another student's writing improve. I want them to have this kind of conversational exchange, which I think, following from observations of other teachers like Kristi Lundstrom and Wendy Baker, is not only of value to the reviewee *but to the reviewer as well.*

Diana: How to Provide Feedback (and Tough Love)

Late at night, with a lot of uneasiness, I started the peer review requirement. I normally wouldn't start a project so late in the week, but the anxiety I had about the assignment resulted in a late start. Classmates and friends in high school frequently asked me to review papers, application essays, letters, and speeches, but what I typically provided was a copy edit of sorts, not a "big picture review" that ProfW was asking of us. To be fair, I loved giving advice to others since I never had a younger sibling to take under my wing, and I especially loved giving writing advice since writing is one of my strong suits and peers of mine seemed to enjoy my reviews as well.

However, moving this interchange online seemed to strip away all the ease I normally had when giving feedback f2f. In person, I would have no problem saying the following to a peer: "I would seriously reevaluate your use of quotes in the second paragraph. You did a great job grabbing your audience's attention in the introduction, but I'm afraid you may lose some with a paragraph composed of 80 percent quotes." I said something similar to this in my first peer review for the course. My group member really did have a main body paragraph with five sentences, only one of which was in her own words. She needed to be told this. But for some reason, in this online setting, my words seemed to take on an air of pretentiousness.

At first I thought my discomfort stemmed from not knowing my classmate personally; however, while my college was much larger than my high school, I had comfortably provided writing advice to unfamiliar peers in earlier years. Then I assumed my rise in academia was the source of uneasiness. Maybe I was supposed to give hard-hitting feedback to my peers as a college student, and I simply had to get used to the awkward shift in content. And yet, that was not quite it either, considering this was the same tone in advice I had given all along.

Then it hit me. I had no way of knowing her first impressions of my review. Sure, I might eventually receive a thank you message explaining how useful my feedback was, but I had no way of reading her facial expressions or body language in real time or being able to answer clarifying questions if she had any. My advice was now more of a letter than an f2f discussion, and it did not sit well with me. As it turned out, my group member wound up appreciating my advice, writing: "You made me realize how problematic my second paragraph was with the amount of quotes I use. Without that specific critique, I would have probably overlooked the problems in that paragraph and it would have never gotten changed and revised."

I should have felt rewarded for my feedback, but as I concluded this week's activities, I was conflicted about the impression I was making on my classmates. Interestingly, I realized I do not spend a great deal of time worrying about this in f2f classes.

Scott: Cultivating Approaches to Argument

Because of the peer review and drafts—I thought about the peer review as an activity that would take up a full class onsite—I scaled down the Discussion work in Week 3. They had only one primary and one secondary Discussion post due, mainly based on our readings. I created three thread options. In the first, they worked from the course textbook and a student essay in *The 33rd*. The second thread offered another approach to the same readings, this time contextualized around political issues. Finally, I offered a thread about something I enjoy teaching: logical fallacies. I used a few passages from a political commentator's book that is filled with such fallacies.

On Friday of Week 2, I had again emailed students who had signed up to serve as moderators. One was a student who had so far been a strong presence in the course: Diana.

Diana: Keeping the Conversation Going

I was excited to act as a moderator in Week 3, so early in the term. Not only was the task of leading a conversation among my peers totally in my wheelhouse, it was also an opportunity to tackle a difficult assignment early in the course without heavy judgment. While I was not completely confident about how to approach my responsibility, I knew being one of the first moderators would come with more lenient grading.

While I prepared to take the initiative of simply asking questions to direct the conversation in a focused, academic manner, I realized the underlying difficulty of leading an online class in discussion. The trouble did not stem from producing content, but from eliciting quality responses out of others. I had many friends who expressed frustration about this aspect of their online courses: They warned me that online discussions were capable of becoming bland and fruitless. My peers described initial motivation to submit thorough, well-written responses early in their online courses, but they said they would lose this motivation later in the term. Why? Because their posts were not acknowledged with quality responses. My friends referenced simple, one-sentence-long responses saying, "Good idea!" or "Cool!" that failed to stimulate conversation. Or, in the worst cases, some of my friends' posts would go completely unnoticed without a single response. I asked my peers how their own responses compared to others in their classes. They explained that their initial attempts were short yet insightful responses to their classmates, but they admitted to writing similar bland posts by the end of the course because "no one was reading them anyway." While I didn't see that assumption demonstrated exactly in our Discussions quite yet, I knew what my friends might be talking about. The majority of my classmates wrote concise yet detailed posts that related to the posts their peers had submitted, but there were a few stragglers who would jump in last-minute with a "Yeah, I agree" post that was obviously lazy and forced. These were easy to observe because of their irregular timing. I had a feeling these students wouldn't last long in the course or, at the very least, wouldn't be deeply involved in future Discussions.

Still heeding my friends' warnings, however, I prepared for my role as moderator while considering the possibility of low peer involvement. I realized that this breakdown in quality, academic discussion was not exclusive to the online classroom. Students are fully capable of arriving unprepared or unwilling to participate in f2f classrooms as well. I remember debating this point with peers while discussing Paulo Freire's "Banking Concept" of education in another course. A majority of the class was in agreement that teachers should engage students, provoking thought and discussion to reach understanding rather than delivering information in a linear, trickle-down fashion from teacher to student. I was surprised, however, to realize I was in the minority who believed students share equal responsibility in this educational theory. I explained my frustration with students who routinely blame professors for leading an uninteresting class but fail to create engaging content themselves. I frequently saw students who were seemingly comfortable with "banking" education—reluctant to participate in discussion, ask questions, or stimulate their peers—while they purported to desire a different type of lecturing entirely.

While I understood many students had a propensity for disengagement and passivity in all classroom formats, I observed an additional challenge in our online course: asynchronous attendance. If students are simultaneously present in a course, in both f2f and online classrooms, and Student A asks a direct question to Students B and C, it is unlikely Student A's question would go unanswered. Perhaps the other students could initially respond with a shrug or "I don't know," but Student A would have the ability to ask an immediate follow-up question or provide instant clarification to further discussion. However, in an asynchronous, online classroom such as mine, receiving direct responses is a totally different battle. Students may log on early in the week, produce their minimum requirement of three posts, and fail to log on and join classroom conversation for the remaining days because, frankly, they do not need to. Later, the remaining students log on and submit primary and secondary posts that receive little to no feedback because the majority of the class has already produced their content and logged out (virtually and metaphorically) for the rest of the week. What does not help is that our LMS's discussion technology does not notify students when replies have been made to their posts. All major social media platforms have included this feature since their inception, so it blew my mind that our big-time / school-sponsored LMS still neglected to incorporate this obvious need.

Therefore, as an early moderator of an asynchronous discussion board, my dilemma was twofold: I needed to (1) counteract my peers' tendencies to learn passively and (2) get them back online to engage in discussion. Thinking back to previous f2f courses that had quality, ongoing discussion, I realized the majority of them incorporated and promoted frequent argumentation. Not disagreement, not yes / no answers, but detailed, informed, specific argumentation. While my peers (and I!) can be content with a bland circulation of "I agree / disagree" comments that fill the minimum word requirement for the sake of easy conversation, we are perfectly capable of engaging in quality conversation if there is enough to argue about. I know people love to talk about two things: themselves and what they believe in. So, if I could create lines of conversation that promoted conversation in these two areas, my peers would be more inclined to log back on and respond productively to others' posts.

Fortunately, I realized this spark for online discussion in the same week we had an intriguing read on Rush Limbaugh's methods of rhetoric:

Author: Scott Warnock **Topic**: Logical fallacies & rule breakers
Subject: Logical fallacies & rule breakers **Date**: January 23, 11:51 AM

Hello all,

Please look over the PDF document "Logical fallacies," which you can find in Course Materials. This material is taken from Rush Limbaugh's book *The Way Things Ought to Be*.

Note that the pages are not continuous, and that I've bracketed and numbered specific areas that I want you to look over.

Pick at least two of the numbered areas (there are eight total), and do one of two things: Either identify a few logical fallacies (as described on pp. 475-78 of [our textbook]) OR identify how the text violates one or more of the "rules of argumentation" as described by Jones.

Describe why you consider a passage to contain a fallacy or to be a violation of a rule. How might Limbaugh bend the rules of logic to advance his argument? Is what he is doing effective?

Read the material about fallacies and the rules CLOSELY, and think carefully before you identify a fallacy. Also, make certain that you clearly describe the context and the fallacy at work (quote if you need to).

I can assure you that there is plenty to work with here.

Have fun,
Prof. Warnock

Reply

Perhaps ProfW was way ahead of me and knew to pick engaging, controversial reads ripe for argumentation. Early posts on this thread reflected this assumption and consisted of thoughtful and supported summaries of Limbaugh's logical fallacies. However, they were not that difficult to argue with because, surprise, everyone agreed Limbaugh used a lot of fallacies. Therefore, I created the following post to spark deeper conversation:

Author: Diana Gasiewski
Subject: Follow up: Logical Fallacies
Topic: Logical fallacies and rule breakers
Date: January 26, 10:35 AM

Hi everyone,

I think we have all thoroughly established that Rush Limbaugh isn't the greatest rhetorician. Yet, consider that he is still one of the highest rated radio talk show hosts, and is a bestselling author of two books. In spite of his constant usage of logical fallacies, he is still hitting home with a whole lot of people.

Why do you think this is so? Do you think his audience is blind to his poor argumentation? Or rather, do you think they are aware of his fallacies, and listen to him because of the ridiculousness of it all?

Looking forward to hearing your responses.

–Diana

Reply

What followed was a collection of sparking comments:

- "How can something so base and stupid thrive; this is what draws people to Limbaugh."
- "People are just attracted to very lame and stupid media."
- "Reminds me of Jersey Shore, people being paid a lot to be jerks haha."
- "It's hard for me to not look over at the right and wonder if it's all an act or not."
- "But to my dismay, and to answer your question, I believe that their audiences believe every word that pours from their mouths."

- "I think a lot of Rush's fans are old, conservative men who are stuck in their ways (I know a few)."
- "What many individuals need to realize is the whole point is to 'shock' the person listening, watching or reading. If you can 'shock' someone into agreeing with you it can be very difficult to persuade them otherwise."

Now, I will be the first to admit that these comments did not align perfectly with our educational discussion. What these comments did, however, was bring my peers back to the Discussion board. This was something easy and relatable they could comment on that would start an extension of their discussion. Once back to the boards, they were present to respond to other questions. For instance, I needed clarification in another peer's post and asked him to elaborate on specific sections. This student, who I had not seen much of in prior weeks, responded to my question and other classmates' comments not once or twice, but three times. Even though I was bringing my peers back to the Discussions with a slightly off-topic question, they were present. They were there to then answer other questions, ask questions, and engage in dialogue.

Perhaps the answer to my initial concerns was the same solution for all discussion anxieties—if one understands her audience and asks the right questions, conversation will roll along. I just needed to understand the unique demands of my new audience, online millennials, who required relatable topics with the opportunity for a variety of argumentative points. Once I understood what they *wanted* to talk about, getting them back online was not the issue I anticipated.

I summarized my feelings about the discussion with the following post (these end-of-week "summary" posts were also part of the requirement of being a moderator):

Author: Diana Gasiewski
Subject: Moderator summary
Topic: Logical fallacies and rule breakers
Date: January 28, 11:06 PM

Hi everyone,

When first analyzing the prompt, I worried our discussion would be fairly one dimensional. Limbaugh obviously isn't the greatest rhetorician; therefore, I was predicting simple listing of his logical fallacies and not much else. Now, I am happy to say I was proven wrong. Not only did everyone properly point out Limbaugh's fallacies, but most of us made an effort to analyze his motivation for using such poor rhetoric. We hit it on the head when observing his necessity to entertain his audience. Then, when discussing how the public reacts to his rhetoric (or lack there of), we were able to see why he has been able to succeed. From that, I'm sure we could have started a whole new discussion on the Jersey Shore, and related trash entertainment, but that's a topic for another day.

Overall, great job everyone, and remember: a good post answers the question, but a great post answers, deepens, and propels the question.

Keep up the hard work.
Diana

Reply

Scott: Pushing Students in Week 3 Discussions

As I have mentioned, student moderating is not only valuable in terms of the course learning, as I believe Diana demonstrated above, but it is also a great time-leveraging pedagogy for OWC instructors. Diana was busy carrying the moderating weight for one thread and Alan on another. Although the students were busy with their drafts and the peer reviews, there were still vigorous written conversations taking place. As it was still early in the term, I continued to push them about *how* to work in this written learning environment, as I did in the "Approaches to argument" thread during my Thursday morning Discussion work, when I posted this:

Author: Scott Warnock
Subject: READ PLEASE: Conversation on these boards
Topic: Approaches to argument
Date: January 26, 11:20 AM

Hi folks (this post is re-posted in "Tips advice resources"),

As I mentioned, you are doing a good job on the Discussions, but we need to work harder on building a conversation. Karen started the Sherlock thread. Then three other people re-started threads about Sherlock. That's not the way it should work. Those other posts about Sherlock need to incorporate what has already been said on the Discussions, following from Karen's post; that's the type of conversation we are looking to build.

Please don't take this too critically. I just want you to build a more organic conversation, and, of course, that means you have to do one of the key tasks required in this course: Read each other's posts carefully.

Let me know if you have questions,

Prof. Warnock

Reply

This post was drawn from my mini library, allowing me to reduce keystrokes while still, with only slight customization, being a positive, encouraging, and regular presence.

Thread: Approaches to Argument

My prompt on the first argument thread was this:

> **Author**: Scott Warnock **Topic**: Approaches to argument
> **Subject**: Approaches to argument **Date**: January 23, 11:50 AM
>
> Hi folks,
>
> You may find the approaches to argument described by our text starting on p. 461 quite useful in your own argumentative and persuasive efforts.
>
> Why? They can help you peel away the structure of persuasion, seeing why certain tactics work. Note, of course, that there is sometimes substantial overlap among these approaches.
>
> Take a look at either Sherlock's piece in The 33rd or one of the essays in chapter 13 of the textbook (you can start different threads to discuss these pieces). What appeals, approaches, and strategies do these pieces use to make their points? Are the arguments ultimately effective?
>
> Thanks,
> Prof. Warnock
>
> Reply

← I started off with a clear connection to our book and how knowing *about* writing might help them *with* writing (a major theme for me).

← Then I provided clear instructions and questions.

This prompt combined elements of a straightforward "work from the text" prompt while asking students to explore a specific aspect of writing. I'll describe some of the activity on this thread. By 5:00 p.m. Monday, Karen had started off a subthread writing a 500-word post analyzing one of our textbook readings, ultimately concluding it was successfully crafted. Her post received seven replies, beginning later Monday evening when Alexa agreed with her "evaluation" of the argument: "I find it interesting how you brought up that refutation, if used correctly, strengthens your argument." Students agreed with what I found to be a thoughtful analysis, although one student, Nate, wrote that the author "does have a powerful piece and it did educate me about this topic but it did not fully persuade me."

I participated a few times in this subthread, mainly pushing Karen, who wrote a good, long post, but I wanted to provide her with a "furthering question" (working from the ideas of Collison et al. that I described in Week 2) based on her statement that the claim in the essay wasn't explicit:

Author: Scott Warnock	**Topic**: Approaches to argument
Subject: Sherlock's Claim?	**Date**: January 26, 11:29 AM

Hi folks,

Good posts, but, Karen, I do think that Sherlock states her claim overtly. Where is it? Is the issue in finding it perhaps because of her approach: Is this an inductive or deductive essay?

Think it over,

ProfW

Reply

She and I had a brief exchange, although I am not sure we got far in terms of induction and deduction.

As the week progressed, several students started subthreads with long, detailed posts, such as Lisa's 600-plus-word post providing a close, paragraph-by-paragraph read of another textbook essay. Working with Alan—this thread's moderator—I used that post to spur a conversation about conclusions. I wrote about one essay, "Conclusions are incredibly difficult! What is the value of ending with a striking note, like the author does here?" Two students followed up on this idea, while Donald, Nate, Karen, and Lisa also discussed Lisa's initial post.

Alexa wrote a 360-word post tackling how another essay in our textbook used a Toulmin approach. Others explored this essay as well, including Karen, who started off by saying, "Because Alexa already gave a summary of Fish's article, I won't repeat her too much." While we were primarily *analyzing* the readings, the essay Alexa addressed, written by Stanley Fish, argued that a southern state legislature should apologize for slavery, so my Thursday post moved directly into Fish's argument. I asked a straightforward, one-line question: "Do you agree with Fish? Why or why not?" Four students posted their opinions; all of them, including the moderator, explained their stance in some detail.

One textbook essay was about food, and moderator Alan used "Progress thus far (I think . . .)" as a Subject in asking this: "Already asked Donald, but give this a thought: any idea how the government or farmers could feel incentivized to grow healthier crops?" This question prompted a twelve-post debate that included a wide variety of evidentiary material.

Another subthread involved a conversation about an essay focused on a campaign to fight malaria. The initial post, by Susannah, analyzed the essay through a Rogerian lens, which we had read about: an argument approach that seeks common ground or goals. Several students responded with good points, including John: "I can also see a downside to this. I believe it's called the Bystander

Effect (don't quote me on that). With the 'group' aspect coming into play, it's easy for someone to think 'well, if everyone else is helping, I really don't need to.'" Several students then commented about the "Bystander Effect."

This was an active thread. Even one student, who posted late, on Saturday, still wrote a 400-plus-word post analyzing a reading, and another student responded. Alan, who had posted ten times as the moderator, wrote a long summary post to close his moderation responsibilities.

Thread: Rogerian, Collaborative Approaches

Another thread was asking them to write to learn about specific content:

> **Author**: Scott Warnock **Topic**: Rogerian, collaborative approaches
> **Subject**: Rogerian, collaborative approaches **Date**: January 23, 11:49 AM
>
> Hi folks,
>
> I'm going to ask you kind of a hard question here because this is a political year and the arguments are getting revved up out there. Can we look at our political conversations in terms of Rogerian argument (again, our textbook 471-2) or perhaps as "argument as collaboration" (Jones 157)? Is there an opportunity in our culture to take a more Rogerian, collaborative approach to some of the divisive issues of our time? If so, how might that work?
>
> Think it over,
> Prof. Warnock
>
> Reply

Nine posts followed my prompt post on this thread. The first post, by Ethan, was a lengthy, interesting look at the election debates; Ethan made this observation: "In terms of the Rogerian argument within these republican debates, each candidate has to find a way to separate themselves from the others because they are coming from the Republican Party." I pushed for more research and depth, and while two other good-sized initial posts were posted on this thread, the students did not explore this topic as much as I had hoped.

Thread: Logical Fallacies

Perhaps spurred by my own interest, my students have often really dug into discussing fallacies, and this term was no different. This thread ended up generating thirty-two posts, including eleven by Diana, the moderator. I only posted four times on this thread, largely because Diana was so active and effective—which, of course, is exactly what I was going for in using moderators.

Students appeared to indeed "have fun" with this thread, pouncing on it and combing through the brief selections of text to find fallacies. There were some good conversational exchanges and some good wordplay, with Diana, to the appreciation of her classmates, using "Rush-ian" to play off "Rogerian." There was a lot of material generated on this thread. Midway through the week, I was able to comment on their fallacies work:

Author: Scott Warnock **Topic**: Rogerian, collaborative approaches
Subject: Follow-up posts **Date**: January 25, 11:23 AM

Hi folks,

I'm glad some of you enjoyed looking at the fallacies. You've done well. My personal favorite fallacy, by the way, is *ad hominem*, or attacking the opponent's character.

It would be good if some of you went back for secondary posts and looked to see what each other has done. I too will comment on these interesting interpretations of the fallacies in this text.

Nice work,
Prof. Warnock

Reply

This was an instructional thread, basically designed to teach them content. To do that, we had to have a socially constructive, communicative environment in which students read each other's posts. About half the class contributed to this thread. Of course, some conversation ranged into politics and even some Rush-bashing (creating a few logical fallacies of their own along the way . . .), but students did a good job focusing on analysis. As Diana said above, she was able to move the conversation into a productive direction Thursday morning with her "Follow up" post, which asked them to ponder why Rush was "still hitting home with a whole lot of people."

Diana: A Discussion Debate

After coming out of my moderating work in the "Rogerian" thread, I was proud of the conversation my classmates and I built. After writing many posts in that thread, I really wasn't looking to contribute much more to the Discussions that week, but knew I had to pop into one more thread to receive full credit that week. I opened the "Approaches to Argument" thread and saw a great moderating post from Alan from the night before.

Author: Alan
Subject: Progress thus far (I think…)
Topic: Approaches to Argument
Date: January 25, 8:46 PM

Already asked Deryck, but give this a thought: any idea how the government or farmers could feel incentivized to grow more healthier crops?

You would think that the government would care about health since how committed the FDA, USDA, and EPA are. But ultimately, money is a flame that draws moths in the wrong places. If they cared less about money and more about their duties then perhaps money would go into more nutritional feeding. Actually, the government should reconsider their hunger campaign and focus not getting rid of hunger but malnutrition. What do you think?

Reply

No one had responded to Alan yet, so I decided to help him out and ask a question of my own to stoke the fire.

Author: Diana
Subject: Re:Progress thus far (I think…)
Topic: Approaches to Argument
Date: January 26, 10:52 AM

Has anyone stopped to consider why the government is giving more subsidies to farmers of less healthy foods (meat, dairy, corn and soy beans) rather than to farmers of fruits and vegetables? Like Alan said, you would think the nutrition organizations of the government would be invested in our national health. Perhaps they have ulterior motives? Such as monetary investments in the corn, meat, and dairy industries.

Just a thought

Reply

Again, I was really not looking to get into another long conversation, but being that I was a co-moderator this week, I wanted to help Alan. John responded:

Author: John
Subject: Re:Progress thus far (I think…)
Topic: Approaches to Argument
Date: January 26, 1:37 PM

I don't believe there are ulterior motives. Meat is just as good for you as fruits and vegetables; why else would there be a concern for protein intake with vegans or vegetarians? I just think priorities are not in order when it comes to distribution of funds among farmers of any kind.

Reply

Huh. That wasn't the kind of response I was expecting. I didn't agree with much of what John said, but maybe I hadn't explained myself clearly in my previous comment. I decided to respond:

Author: Diana | **Topic**: Approaches to Argument
Subject: Re:Progress thus far (I think…) | **Date**: January 26, 2:30 PM

Humans do not need meat in their diet in order to be healthy individuals. Therefore, it is outrageous that the government gives 73.80% of federal subsidies for food production to the meat and dairy producers, and a mere 0.37% to vegetable and fruit farmers. This is why a salad from a local market costs more than Chicken Nuggets at McDonalds ("Health vs. Pork …"). It seems contradictory that the USDA would suggest vegetables and fruits to make up more than a third of an individual's diet, while providing very little relief to the farmers who produce this food ("The New Food Pyramid").

When you consider, however, that there has always been a revolving door between the meat and dairy industries and the government, it may not come to a surprise at all. During the Bush administration, the chief of staff at the USDA was the former chief lobbyist for the beef industry in Washington, and the head of the FDA was the former executive VP of the National Food Processors Association ("Food Inc."). You would think they would want the best for their former companies, right?

Works Cited

Food Inc. Dir. Robert Kenner. Prod. Elise Pearlstein. Perf. Eric Schlosser and Michael Pollan. Magnolia Pictures, 2009. Online.
"Health vs. Pork: Congress Debates the Farm Bill." PCRM.org. Web. 26 Jan. 2012.
"The New Food Pyramid." Washingtonpost.com. The Washington Post Company. Web. 26 Jan. 2012.

Reply

I guess the stubborn part of me couldn't help but argue my point of view. I was hoping that would have settled things for the time being, but John responded back within a half-hour.

Author: John | **Topic**: Approaches to Argument
Subject: Re:Progress thus far (I think…) | **Date**: January 26, 2:51 PM

Only 3.2% of the US population are vegetarians. What of the other 96.8%? Do you honestly feel that the government should provide equal funds among these groups, even though there are 32x the density?

Reply

Okay. Was John doing this on purpose at this point? After my next response, John and I had an exchange over five more posts, each around 150 words. We referenced several sources each, constructed thorough arguments, and stayed active on the Discussions, significantly exceeding our required work for that week—all for the sake of debate! ProfW closed the conversation with a small but encouraging post:

Author: Scott Warnock	**Topic**: Approaches to Argument
Subject: Re:Progress thus far (I think…)	**Date**: January 27, 4:11 PM

Wow. I really enjoyed this thoughtful, researched debate.

ProfW

Reply

I left this conversation with mixed emotions. I was happy to contribute as a moderator, help Alan with his thread, defend my argument, and receive praise from ProfW. On the other hand, I was worried about how I would come across to my classmates after this debate. Would they think I was too headstrong? Too much of an overachiever? Cocky, even? The good news was, debates like this weren't as disruptive in an online space as they would be in an f2f classroom. We've all been in a situation—whether at the family dinner table, a meeting, or a college course —when two people are going at it and exclude the rest of the group. While it can certainly be entertaining, prolonged two-way debates can disrupt the flow of group conversation. Online, this debate between John and me could be totally ignored if someone wasn't interested.

Scott: Responding to Drafts

I feel like this chapter is almost built on a trick premise, because its title implies there might be big differences in how teachers manage the drafting process in OWCs. For teachers who use digital technologies, their own response process may not vary much regardless of modality. In our class, the group peer reviews carried much of the process weight this week. The peer reviews were for the most part strong and I believe helped both the writers *and the readers* of the drafts. Students did make use of the group aspect of the reviews, with reviewers contextualizing comments in light of what others had said, although they did not engage in this accretive process as robustly as they might have (and as students have in other courses of mine). Mostly, their additive comments were straightforward; e.g., "Your second paragraph needs some work, perhaps you could just follow what Karen said in her post" or "Other than what I've said and what Jennifer has said. . . ." (The following week, I would ask students to respond to their reviewers, so we added to the review feedback "loop" in that way.) The peer reviews, as I believe good peer reviews should, did help me in my responses to students about their drafts.

I was also aided by response technologies. I think the pressure on teachers that stems from providing written response can be significantly alleviated through smart use of teaching technologies. These technologies are not exclusive to OWI, but digital environments are perhaps conducive to exploring such tools: Since teachers are already online, they may be more open to seeking tools to replace pen-and-paper/coffee shop response (Guideline 31 of *Teaching Writing Online* makes a similar suggestion: "Technologies of response can help you rethink the way you provide feedback to your students about their writing" [Warnock 121]). For response to rough drafts, in my peer review thread prompts, I offered choices; each student could either:

1. Meet me, virtually or onsite, one-to-one to discuss the draft.
2. Receive written feedback.
3. Receive feedback via audiovisual (AV) tools.

For the most part, students chose a one-to-one conference. The onsite meetings provided an interesting dynamic. Some of my colleagues walk into the first day of their onsite classes with a copied list of students' names and pictures. I don't do that, but I do take a peek at my photo class list online to see what my students look like before meeting them for the first time onsite. Among other things, what I'm struck with is how little they resemble those small ID photos, when they are often hesitant first-year students just getting started. Even four months later, they have a different demeanor and sometimes look (maybe having dyed their hair neon green at that point!). This dynamic is more fascinating in an online course, as at the point I meet them in person I have seen thousands of words of their writing and have a distinct sense of their intellectual selves.

The peer reviews were being completed that weekend between Weeks 3 and 4, so at the end of Week 3 and beginning of Week 4 (I wanted to read the reviews first) I blocked off fifteen-minute slots for those who wanted to meet me; students signed up for those meetings on the Discussions. I cleared out a few days on my calendar, and, because this was an OWC, I wanted to be sure students knew that these conferences could take place over the phone. The second most popular method of receiving response was AV. AV response can be provided through

Behind the Screen: Technologies of Response

Writing instructors and researchers have long been interested in the practice and theory of responding to student writing. Response, at all levels of writing instruction, is one of the most important things that writing teachers do. Technologies have provided new ways to facilitate traditional written response, which often involves stacks of papers (and red pens). Using technologies to respond to student writing is not inherently connected to OWI: Much response work has always been virtual, in the sense that it happens when teachers and students are not together. However, because OWI takes place digitally, teachers may be more apt to try new approaches and tools for response. Among other advantages, digital tools might make responding easier on the body—written response can be physically taxing.

Voice. Instructors have been using voice since well before online learning—all the way back to the 1950s, in fact. Jeff Sommers, an early proponent of voice response, has offered many insights into how spoken response might provide feedback that not only differs in quantity but also in depth from written response. In "Response Rethought . . . Again: Exploring Recorded Comments and the Teacher-Student Bond," he provides clear-cut ideas about how to provide spoken response. Sommers also wrote, with his former student Cheryl Mellen, about how audio response made him seem more human (Mellen and Sommers). And in "Response 2.0 . . . ," he said that providing commentary in an audio recording, versus only written remarks, can improve the quality and depth of responses, strengthen the rapport between student and teacher, and encourage students to be more actively engaged in understanding and applying feedback.[1] Chris Anson ("Talking"), Noreen Moore and Michelle Filling, and I ("Responding") have also described specific voice response strategies.

Rubrics. Digital response can introduce teachers to the variety of rubric tools, both freestanding applications and quite good rubrics built into LMS systems. While a robust literature cautions about using rubrics to sleepwalk through response, smart rubrics can save typing time and allow teachers to spend more time thinking about what to write to students on their drafts.

Commenting tools. Commenting tools often work with rubrics, providing ways of delivering packaged comments to students. Specific tools like Annotate Pro can provide comment libraries to save keystrokes, allowing you, ideally, to focus your creative writing energy on specific parts of your students' projects.

Strategies. Aside from the technologies themselves, response in digital environments lends itself to different and perhaps new approaches. Beth Hewett has done a great deal of work thinking through writing response strategies for digital environments. In particular, see her *The Online Writing Conference: A Guide for Teachers and Tutors.*

screen capture software such as Jing or Camtasia (TurnItIn's Grademark also includes an easy way to record three-minute audio clips). The software records your screen, including any mouse or cursor movements, as well as your voice-over comments. The trickiest part is often providing students with access to the video, but technologies like Jing make it easy, as all you do is send the students a unique URL.

Using AV software to provide spoken or spoken/video feedback has been discussed in detail by many people, and I say more about it in this week's "Behind the Screen" sidebar. However, response technologies speed up more than just the process. They can also, and this is more significant for those who teach many students, lessen the psychological malaise/pressure that accompanies trying to provide smart, useful writing advice *in writing* to all your students.

Some students still like written comments; that is usually about a quarter of the class, and that held true this term. I was happy to oblige. In Word, I wrote back to those students using Track Changes. I wrote comments within the text, mostly questions, and then wrote a global comment at the beginning.

Returning drafts to students was a function of modality. If I met students in conference, after the meeting I would email them the draft with the comments. Those who wanted only written comments also received an email with that marked-up draft. For AV response, I sent students a link to the video, and the comments and paper were thus meshed together (keep in mind, though, that I had been thinking and writing about AV for some time by the time I had taught this class, so I did not face a tech learning curve).

I had to budget my time to respond to student drafts, much like any FYW teacher, in any modality, would have to do. However, because I was dividing up my mode of response in three ways, I felt, as I usually do, that responding to student writing was not the grind that so many teachers have written about in the composition literature.

Diana: Rough Draft Response

Wait. A professor actually reads my essays thoroughly and extensively responds to them so I can get a better grade? Until this class, I had the preconception that college professors were evaluated on how hard their classes were to pass. I don't know if it's the movies painting the picture of a senior, pantsuit-wearing professor beginning her class by shaming a student who isn't prepared (I'm referring to *Legally Blonde* here, when the Harvard Law professor asks the main character about a class reading and, when that character says she hasn't received her books yet, gets kicked out of class) or if it's the hype of entering academia, but I entered college thinking that was the norm. Yet, here I am, in a first-year writing course, receiving feedback like this:

> Hi Diana,
>
> This is a good draft, and, as I've noticed all term, you write extremely well. You have a good topic, and after reading your comments at the bottom, I believe we can turn this into a strong final draft.
>
> Your reviewers are encouraging and provide some good advice, including Susannah's interesting idea for a conclusion.
>
> You have a good idea for the analysis part of the project, especially in your use of rhetorical tools and terms, but I think you want to organize that section much more clearly, thinking specifically about your topic sentences. You also, as you note, want

to describe the campaign more clearly. You might think about the old writing advice, "Show, don't tell." Show us campaign examples, probably using visuals.

Then you'll want to evaluate and then persuade us whether the campaign is effective or not. You say it is "extremely effective." Why? How do you know that? You have a good sense of how to use evidence in your writing—a demanding skill—and you'll want to think about how to evaluate the campaign, based on any evidence you find and on the success of the rhetorical tools.

This is a little clunky, but it demonstrates that you definitely understand what to do with this project: "Through an analysis of the farm-to-table campaign, observation of the rhetorical strategies used and the public's response will reveal the persuasiveness of the campaign." Let's flesh out the analysis and that will enable you to think about the evaluation.

I'm not worried at all if you go over the word count, even if it's by a lot.

We will have a workshop next week to revise these rough drafts, so you will have plenty of opportunities to make this better.

If you have any questions, please let me know,
Prof. Warnock

Diana Gasiewski
Prof. Scott Warnock
English 102

[Insert Witty Title Here] **I think you're up to the task!**

A man takes his seat in a cozy, dimly lit restaurant. Waiters are in a graceful rush as the float around the dinning room, balancing trays filled with beautiful dishes, breezing past the man and his wife, leaving behind delicious aromas. As the couple scans over the menu, analyzing each dish with careful consideration, they see several of the menu items have tiny tractor icons next to a dinner selection. Referencing the bottom of the menu, they realize those selections feature locally sourced ingredients from farms in the greater Philadelphia area. White Dog Café, the restaurant this couple is dining at, happens to be one of the many restaurants in Philadelphia participating in the farm-to-table movement ("About Us"). **Nice start. Great writing.**

← Aw. Well, that made me feel good knowing the professor thought what I had to say was interesting.

Is it likely that this couple picked White Dog Café solely for its support of local farmers? Are they more prone to choosing the "tractor" items over the non-local items, or does it even faze them? Farm-to-table restaurants and the practice of locally sourced foods are definite trends in the modern culinary world. Yet, is this movement just that, a trend, or does it have lasting power? Through an analysis of the farm-to-table campaign, observation of the rhetorical strategies used and the public's response will reveal the persuasiveness of the campaign. **Okay, let's see about refining this purpose statement, but it's a good way to propel you through this draft.**

The farm-to-table campaign has been in existence for nearly twenty-five years in Philadelphia. Ever since the boom of mass agricultural production, small local farms have been underutilized across the nation. Because of the discount bigger distributers promise, restaurateurs generally look . . .

← ProfW complimented me while giving me a push to try harder, and I wasn't even mad about it.

After receiving this feedback, I realized that my perception of college professors was all wrong. They weren't there to catch me making a rookie mistake, they weren't there to weed out the dummies who shouldn't be in college, and they definitely weren't there to try to kick me out. They cared. After ProfW demonstrated this kind of teaching at a higher academic level, I gained trust in the future of my academic journey. While he was the first professor to give me detailed feedback on an essay, I was sure he wouldn't be the last.

In Retrospect: Reviewing and Responding to Writing

Week 3 was a demanding week for both of us. Responding to students' drafts is where the main teaching of a writing course often happens, with texts building upon texts. Again, much of the work of writing teachers has always been "virtual" in that it takes place away from students, with a teacher reading and then thinking about writing. OWI changes that only in that it opens up digital ways of communicating with students about their writing. Digital tools can alleviate some of the time and psychological pressures of responding to student writing, while also providing better response. The now-common platforms to provide voice comments can alter the response process considerably for teachers, to the considerable benefit of their students.

Time is always a consideration in writing instruction. In a week like Week 3, a teacher of an OWC will be working with drafts. Students in the course are doing a considerable amount of reading and responding to each other about drafts of their writing projects. For teachers, the draft process itself can be streamlined and arguably improved through good peer review coupled with the use of response technologies. By using student moderators and simply lessening some of the expectations of one's own participation in the discussions, teachers can engage in a sensible and appropriate amount of work. For students, a week like this will be writing heavy/intensive, but the exchange of ideas, of critiques, happens all in writing—which seems thoroughly appropriate for the overall goals of a writing course.

Entering Week 4, we would be moving through the final drafting of Project 1.

4

Week 4: Revision and Focusing on Final Drafts

...the medium shapes not only talk, but revision itself.

—Beth Hewett in her dissertation, *"The Characteristics and Effects of Oral and Computer-Mediated Peer Group Talk on the Argumentative Writing Process"*

Scott: Helping Them through the Final Stages of Project 1

The primary, front-and-center assignment for students in Week 4 was to write the final draft of Project 1. I slowed everything else down so students could focus on this significant course task:

Week 4: January 29 to February 4

The focus this week is on the final draft of Project 1. We will also refine our thinking about persuasive writing and introduce Project 2.

What do I do?	What are the specific instructions? Where do I find the work or the assignment?	When is it due? (All times EST)
READ	• *Course textbook*: "Writing to Convince" 43 pages; "Strategies for Collaboration" 5 pages. • *Aux:* Ingalls, "Writing 'Eyeball to Eye-ball'" 18 pages.	You'll want to have read by **Tuesday**, January 31 so you can complete the quiz and get to work on the Discussions and the citation exercise.

← I was succinct in the introduction comments: I wanted them to focus on the final drafts.

PARTICIPATE	Please log into our live classroom via the link on the Homepage at 9:15 pm on Tuesday night. We will run through an approximately 45-minute workshop on the Project 1 drafts in which I will ask you to spend some serious thought time with your draft. If you take this seriously and block out distractions, every second of this workshop should help you in writing your final draft. After the workshop, please submit your worked-up draft of Project 1 based on the workshop to the "Project 1 Workshop dropbox" in the "Other Assignments" folder. See the thread "Workshop times" in this week's Discussions. I could move the workshop to a more convenient time if 9:15 on Tuesday doesn't work.	We will meet in the live classroom at 9:15 pm on **Tuesday.** If you have a conflict, a recording of the workshop will be available, and you can self-pace through the workshop.
SUBMIT	Again, after you have taken part in the workshop above, please submit your worked-up draft in the Project 1 Workshop dropbox in the Other Assignments folder. This draft should include all of your notes and any other drafting work; in other words, it doesn't need to look nice. This process is worth 15 points.	You must submit this work before you hand in your final draft on **Saturday**.
TAKE a QUIZ	Quiz 4 can be found in the "Quizzes" folder.	As usual, the quiz will be available **Tuesday,** January 31 from 9:30 am to midnight. You will have five minutes to complete it.
WRITE and READ	Read all the Discussion topics for Week 4: 1. Post ONE primary post to any of the Discussion topics. 2. Post ONE secondary post to any of the Discussion topics.	Post your primary post by **Wednesday** night, February 1. Post your secondary post by **Friday**, February 3, at 4:00 pm.

← We would have a synchronous workshop to help them with their drafts. I migrated this practice from onsite teaching.

← Diana and I both discuss the workshop draft below.

← Discussion work was again a little lighter this week: To make an analogy with an onsite course, about one class period would be spent onsite in the workshop.

COMPLETE EXERCISE	On the Discussions you will find a citation exercise. Please complete this exercise, which is worth 10 points. *The whole class gets the same grade on this exercise*, so you'll need to work together on it.	Complete this exercise by the end of the week. You should do it before you submit your final draft of Project 1.
WRITE	Complete the final draft of Project 1. Follow the directions carefully. You must submit a copy of the final draft to the **Turnitin** dropbox located in the "Writing Projects" folder. Check to be sure your project • includes the proper sources • accounts for my comments and the peer review comments • has the correct **file name** (see the Syllabus) Also, review the **project instructions** to make sure you have not overlooked something obvious.	The final draft is due **Saturday, February 4 at 5:00 pm**. Please don't submit your final draft late, as there are consequences for your project grade.
READ	You can find instructions for Project 2 in the Writing Projects folder. Please read these instructions carefully. If you have questions, please ask them on "Questions about the course."	You can read the project instructions over the weekend.
MODERATE	This week our moderators will be Ethan and Donald. I will be in touch with them, and then they will moderate some of our Discussions this week. Again, they will be active voices in encouraging conversation, and they will provide a summary of their assigned topics at the end of the week. Thanks to them for moderating here.	The moderators will be working throughout the week to help us keep the conversation on track.

← This citation exercise was a separate assignment. It's easy to focus a Discussion this way to make sure you get the participation you're seeking.

← Final draft instructions! I referred to the assignment instructions and syllabus. The deadline was laid out clearly.

← On to the next project, which was a group project.

It was a busy week. In addition to teaching work on the Discussions, I was finishing up responding to some students' rough drafts while looking ahead to evaluating and commenting on final drafts. I also provided them with the instructions for their Project 2 team project. In Monday's homepage announcement I posted this:

Announcements for Monday, January 30:

- Tomorrow night we will have a **workshop for your Project 1 drafts** starting at 9:15 PM in the live classroom. See the Weekly Plan for this week.
- I emailed the **Project 1 drafts** back to you, using Track Changes to make comments, or I provided a link for those of you who wanted audiovisual response.
- The **Discussions** for this week are now available, as are your latest **grades.**

Every week, I had been updating, quickly and easily, their informal writing and quiz grades in our LMS. That Monday morning I wrote in my planner: "9 AM-12: English 102." I knew I was going to be spending the whole morning getting everything done.

Diana: Preparing for Revision

As I read instructions for the week, my first thought was, "Oh wow. Okay. Project 1 is due this week. I totally forgot." Luckily, I was behind a computer screen so I didn't have to put on a poker face for ProfW. Instead, I mumbled something loud enough for my roommate to ask what I had messed up. One of the upsides to having a live-in companion as a first-year student was being able to commiserate with someone over the fumbles while figuring out how to be a college student.

To be fair, I was following the schedule and had been aware of the Saturday deadline, but this week happened to be my major's "slam" week. It seemed like every course's first project, test, or paper were due at the same time. All things considered, this probably happened to every college student at one point or another. I was just experiencing it for the first time. The good news was my first draft was done. Because ProfW required a draft the week prior, all I needed to do at this point was work through the revision process (unlike the other three papers I had due that didn't require a first draft, which I then put off writing until the last minute).

However, I felt like I was missing something from my peer reviews to move forward confidently with the revision. Don't get me wrong, they were fine. In fact, they probably received A+ grades. They answered the questions provided by ProfW with clear and concise responses, made sure to avoid repeating one another, and addressed areas of my paper that needed work (grammar, spelling, structure, and, most important, my conclusion). I think the problem may have been the lack of a *discussion* over my paper. Up until this point in the course, most of my interactions with my peers had been through dialogue on the Discussion boards. We had productive, intelligent, and, dare I say it, sort of fun interchanges while in our online classroom space. I was beginning to know my classmates and their writing styles, and it felt great! Yet, when it came to an exercise in our course that required some of the most personal interaction of all—peer review—we were writing letters to one another. If we could have moved into an instant messaging space, video chat, or even to the phone, I think I may have received more in-depth suggestions that could have been talked through. But then again, I guess that would have been tough to grade or hold structure to. Nevertheless, I saw on the course schedule that we would have one last workshop on our drafts before the paper was due. Hopefully that would help tie up my revision process.

Scott: Facilitating a Synchronous Online Writing Workshop

Using our live classroom application, I scheduled a synchronous workshop for Tuesday night at 9:15 p.m. I had a meeting for one of my children's sports teams at 7:00 p.m., but I had plenty of time to get home and get set up. Drawing on Peter Elbow and his foundational idea of writing being "a transaction with other people" (76), I believe strongly in the workshop approach when students are revising and working through their drafts. Onsite, I have students work directly on their drafts in a fast-paced workshop, and in line with the migration approach to teaching online, I wanted to migrate that valuable experience into a user-friendly online format.

I created fifteen straightforward slides for the workshop. The first part of each slide provided brief commentary about an aspect of writing, usually based on a collective observation I had made about their drafts. Then, using simple PowerPoint animation, other bullets appeared that gave instructions for them to do some specific writing and thinking about their drafts (see Figure 2).

I verbally included a time limit. When I conduct a workshop like this onsite, I walk around the room, pacing each slide by announcing the time. Online, I am not standing in front of/next to them, but I can still be present. Also, if 9:15 p.m. on Tuesday night didn't work for them, they could self-pace by watching a recording of the workshop. I must point out that what they got out of this experience was strongly dependent on their effort. However, as a way to "close the loop" and create some accountability, I asked them to submit the draft they

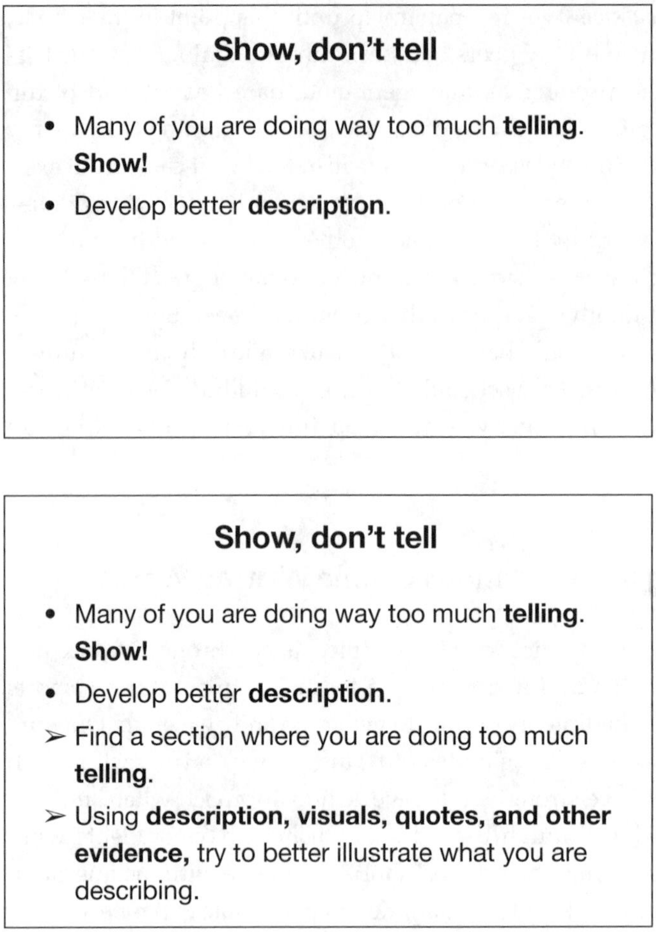

Show, don't tell

- Many of you are doing way too much **telling**. **Show!**
- Develop better **description**.

Show, don't tell

- Many of you are doing way too much **telling**. **Show!**
- Develop better **description**.

➢ Find a section where you are doing too much **telling**.

➢ Using **description, visuals, quotes, and other evidence,** try to better illustrate what you are describing.

Figure 2. Sample PowerPoint slides for our synchronous workshop.

worked on in the workshop as an easy-to-earn informal grade. As stated in the Weekly Plan, that "worked-up" draft "should include all of your notes and any other drafting work you have done; in other words, it doesn't need to look nice. This process is worth 15 points." I emphasized I didn't care how messy that draft was (John emailed me about this during the week, and I responded, "You could hand it in any time during the week—and it can be as sloppy as you like"); I just wanted to see they had engaged in the specific workshop tasks, which included commenting on their peer reviews, reviewing their project purpose, reverse outlining the project by identifying topic sentences and pasting them into a separate document (a pretty cool metawriting activity that is easily facilitated digitally), and looking for places to use evidence to better support their ideas.

Diana: What Revising Actually Looks Like

The workshopping process was surprisingly helpful. Whenever I had workshops in high school, I often felt like they were needless filler activities to stretch out the week's material when teachers had run out of ideas. After looking at my messy, but reworked, paper, I began to get a grasp of what "revising" might actually mean. It's not just a review of my grammar, spelling, and sentence structure, but another closer look to see if there are any stones left unturned: if my ideas are fully realized, my thoughts transition nicely, any claims I've made are supported, and my overall argument is made in an academic matter.

The workshop not only breathed new life into my paper, but also into the online class. While I was doing fine not having an f2f format, the class was beginning to grow a tad bit impersonal and tech-y this week for some reason. Maybe it was just me, but the novelty of it was beginning to wear off, and I was getting very used to the rolling tide of logging in and logging out. I learned when were the opportune times to log on and post to receive the highest number of replies. That way, later in the week when I had to write secondary posts, I had a lot to work with. Basically, when other students (particularly the more vocal ones who were easier to talk with) would log on and off, when ProfW would post replies, and when hard deadlines would be made, I knew it was the best time to post. Though, it occurred to me—was I paying less attention to the rest of my peers? Really, I was only acknowledging the same few individuals—mainly Alan, John, and Karen—who would help my individual grade in the course because they had consistently interesting dialogue and posted around the same time as me during the week. I was aware there were still some classmates I hadn't interacted with, mostly because they posted much later in the week than me, usually too late to add anything new to the Discussion. Was this selfish of me, or even allowed? Sure, if this were an f2f course, I would similarly walk into the classroom only to speak with the professor and a few select peers. I wouldn't walk around the room shaking everyone's hands, asking them their opinions on the topic that week. Maybe I was overthinking my responsibility in these Discussions, or maybe I was beginning to realize the potential online spaces offered for more frequent interactions among a greater variety of peers.

As I mulled over my interactions with my peers, worrying that I was being too selective in who I spoke with, a well-timed assignment helped connect me with the entirety of my class again. Having ProfW appear live on my screen again while other students attended via an online space reminded me that this is a real guy who can give me real advice on my work, along with a real class that I can learn from and interact with. I feel like I'm using this term *real* too much, but it meant a lot in terms of my perception of online learning. *Real* is speaking with other individuals about what I'm learning, how I'm learning it, and what it means. The opposite would be, I don't know, reading Wikipedia on my own. If I wanted to, I could have learned how to write during the summer on my own time using thousands of free Internet sources. But since I was paying for a university class, it was important for it to be real, and that meant engaging in dialogue with an academic and my peers.

The actual content of the workshop was excellent. We worked through a series of strategies to organize our writing and narrow down the content—basically, getting rid of the fluff. None of the strategies was familiar to me, which was exciting and stimulating, and I saw my writing improve in real time as I worked through the process. The only thing that cheapened the experience was the grade awarded alongside the workshop. I would understand if these points were some sort of "attendance" grade, considering professors need to come up with creative ways to assess participation in an online space. However, we were already receiving grades that week for Discussions, quizzes, peer reviews, and an eventual final project submission, so I would assume those would suffice for judging our course presence. Therefore, I wasn't really sure what these points were assessing and rewarding. Our revision process? Our listening skills during the workshop? It was confusing to me because I assumed most of my classmates would want to take advantage of the workshop on their own accord and wouldn't need the motivation of a grade to do so. Sure, there would probably be a few students who would skip the opportunity, but that would be on them, and the quality of their papers would reflect their decisions. It just felt a little odd to be awarded points for something we should want to do anyway.

Scott: A Class "Visitor" and a Group Citation Exercise

I introduced two different types of Discussion threads in Week 4: I set up an argument, but this time with a "visitor," and I asked them to work on a specific aspect of writing, but as a group. Katie had a computer issue toward the end of the week, writing:

> **From:** Katie
> **Sent:** Thursday, February 02 7:50 PM
> **To:** Scott Warnock
> **Subject:** Re: LMS Error
>
> Prof Warnock,
> Since yesterday my LMS account won't let me log on. I can access the sign in page but not any farther than that. A white page just comes up. I can't do my posts be-

> cause I can't access them from any one else's. I'll try logging on on a friend's computer. This is so frustrating. I'm sorry I can't post right now.
> Katie

She ended up trying a different browser and emailing me at 11:00 p.m. that all was well. A little after 9:00 a.m. Friday morning, I emailed back anyway, saying, "It's no problem, Katie. You're always welcome to contact me if you're having problems. I'm here to help."

This week I used one of my favorite OWI threads: the alter ego or provoker (see Warnock, "The Provoker"). I really enjoy taking on the role "The Provoker," a contradictory voice, on Discussion boards. This practice can be pedagogically enjoyable while also, I believe, giving students a focused writing challenge. The Provoker is a rhetorically edgy, devil's advocate–type voice on the class Discussions. I always include a few Provoker threads in an OWC, and in our class, I posted using the alias "Dr. Logoetho" and even logged in to our LMS as "Demo Student" (a function of the LMS that allowed me to see everything from the student perspective), further distancing myself from our "guest." I did make it clear to students that we were playing a rhetorical game (only once was a student confused about this); so it was me—but it wasn't. As you can see, Dr. Logoetho wrote with more than a little cheek:

Author: Demo student **Topic**: Challenge Dr. Logoetho?
Subject: Wikipedia is the worst **Date**: January 30, 4:15 PM

Dear students,

I will be an occasional visitor to your course. My name is Dr. Logoetho.

Perhaps this may shock you, but I have never been defeated in an argument. *Never.* I have decided to give you the honor of trying to beat my undefeated streak this week with this argument, because I have something to say about Wikipedia.

I think that Wikipedia is a completely useless site except as entertainment. No one should ever use it for anything of importance or for real research. Wikis are an unreliable way to build true information. I think the positives of Wikipedia are grossly exaggerated and are only promoted by people who have something to gain from Wikipedia or who don't understand the informational value of the Web.

There. If you want to take me on, at least show a little argument savvy and use some evidence.

I doubt you're up to the task,
Dr. Logoetho

Reply

← I posted this as a "Demo Student" to further distance myself from Dr. Logoetho—although they knew it was me. I bragged about how smart I am, and then I proposed the argument: Wikipedia is "useless."

← Even my normally friendly complimentary close was different! He was more than a bit disdainful.

In these threads, with me, the official professor, out of the center of the frame, I find that students write passionately while also composing interesting, solid arguments. They use evidence, and, in this course, I pushed them to avoid the logical fallacies we had discussed, particularly *ad hominem*, when dealing with a disrespectful interlocutor. They have to think through written, and sometimes emotional, argumentation. When I settled in that Thursday morning in the beginning of February to work on their Discussions, I had some thought-provoking writing to read.

One of this week's moderators volunteered for the Dr. Logoetho thread but did not post much. The students who responded focused mainly on the extreme nature of Dr. Logoetho's language, which is partly what I hoped they would do, while still addressing his argument. The posts were great:

- Diana opened her 660-word post with the tale of a poor Peruvian shoe shiner who was chronicled in the film *Life in a Day*. The boy told the filmmakers that he loved his laptop, and she used that evidence of the openness of knowledge coupled with studies of Wikipedia's reliability to argue that "to say Wikipedia is useless is an exaggeration."
- John, building on (and citing) a class reading about Rogerian argument, focused on Dr. Logoetho's braggadocio: "According to a recent article that we read in this class a couple of weeks ago, there is no 'win or lose' in an argument. Instead, two sides recognizing the others views, accepting them, and having a rebuttal." Significantly, John tied his post back to work we had just done in the course.
- The moderator, Ethan, posted about Wikipedia's credibility and made this provocative point: "I like to think of Wikipedia as an accident with police warning tape all around it. You can see what's going on inside, and you can tell your friends what you think happened via what you saw, but unless you talk to the parties involved or the police officers themselves, I wouldn't go telling the world about how you know what happened because you 'saw the aftermath.'" Dr. Logoetho responded to Ethan, but Ethan didn't reply!
- Rio also said it was extreme to find Wikipedia "completely useless," although she agreed that it "can and should only be used for the purpose of finding out general knowledge."

By midday on Thursday, during my Discussion work, I wrote this post from Dr. Logoetho:

Author: Demo student | **Topic**: Challenge Dr. Logoetho?
Subject: It's not whether you win or lose | **Date**: February 2, 1:48 PM

Dear students in Dr. Warnock's class,

I am glad that you are having such a nice time getting along, and I'm glad that under the tutelage of Dr. Warnock and our textbook that you have all become so (as John describes) Rogerian in your argument approaches, recognizing each other's point of view and whatnot.

← Dripping sarcasm here.

But the fact remains that I, Dr. Logoetho, in fact do not recognize your point of view if you think Wikipedia is worthwhile. So, by my definition, I win.

← As I worked through the posts, I conceded their good points: In this post, I did what I often try to do with the "Provoker": I stubbornly stand by an argument while admitting students steadily chip away at it.

I admit, Diana's anecdotal start about the boy in Peru, with its strong link to all of the rhetorical appeals—*ethos, pathos, logos*—made me waver for a moment. But then I realized, "Dr. Logoetho, stand strong! That boy has a laptop? He can have his stories, but why rely on stories from an unreliable Wiki?"

Indeed, unreliable. Diana was very clever to cite the Nature study, but you know that Britannica issued a rebuttal, summarized here: http://news.cnet.com/Belatedly,-Britannica-lambastes-Wikipedia-findings /2100-1025_3-6053754.html.

Also, let's consider the overall unreliability of any site that the rubes of the world can contribute to. For instance, have you ever checked YouTube's "PronunciationManual"? Look up "Hulk Hogan pronounciation" on YouTube and then go from there. Imagine trying to learn English relying on the darn Internet!

I stand by my original argument so far,
Dr. Logoetho

Reply

I want students to have smart, authentic arguments, and I'd like to provide an interlocutor for them, but teacher-student dynamics can make that difficult. Provoker threads allow students to write and argue without worrying about offending classmates or dealing with the authority-laden quagmire of "debating the teacher." This works especially well online, as some of my comments—like the one above about the PronunciationManual—would be hard to make with a straight face in class. This is enjoyable for me. I'm competitive and debate them head-on. I even get to bust on old "Dr. Warnock." This week, although the posts that were there were great, the thread didn't have quite the activity I had hoped for, but students were set up for a robust conversation when Dr. Logoetho returned in Week 9.

As an interesting aside, in response to John's post about not winning an argument, Diana wrote back, "I think my godfather said it best: a debate should not be about winning or losing, it's primary goal should be to uncover the truth" (she then replied to herself correcting the "it's"). Recall that in Week 3, John and Diana had had a debate on the boards, and John took the opportunity here to reach out to her by responding:

Author: John
Topic: Challenge Dr. Logoetho?: Wikipedia
Subject: Re:Win or Lose
Date: February 1, 9:13 PM

Great saying!

P.S: Nice to agree on something after what happened last week!

Reply

Often, teachers are concerned that students don't return to the boards to see each other's writing, and while that can be true (and Diana mentions it at times in this book), not only were John and Diana following that previous conversation, but Alan added this:

Author: Alan
Topic: Challenge Dr. Logoetho?: Wikipedia
Subject: A change in things
Date: February 2, 1:16 AM

(Insert laughter here). It is nice to see you two reconcile considering last week (sort of since it didn't end in a bitter note). As a culture, we all need to stop having this belligerent perception of an argument. Victory is ultimately meaningless because what have you really won? You can prove a point or two but it does it truly mean that it shall be so forever?

Reply

Thread: Collaboration

We were moving into a complex team project, so while their attention was focused on writing the final draft of Project 1, I also wanted them to start looking ahead and thinking about collaboration:

Author: Scott Warnock
Topic: Collaboration
Subject: Collaboration
Date: January 30, 4:12 PM

Hi all,

Ingalls says you may ask, "Why collaborate?" Well, why, according to her? Why, according to YOU?

What do you like about group work? What do you dislike? (This is a good place to be honest.) What are some common experiences and fears around collaboration? Who are some famous collaborators? What are some critical strategies for creating successful collaborative projects?

Let's work together,
Prof. Warnock

Reply

This metawriting / reflection-type prompt provided them with an opportunity, in *writing*, to describe shortcomings they have had with fellow students in group projects. Our goal in this active thread was to develop expectations so students wouldn't immediately fall into some of the negative behaviors that result in frustrating and educationally unsuccessful group projects.

Thread: What Is an Argument?

As they were finishing Project 1, I wanted to peel back the definition of argument itself: What was an argument?

Author: Scott Warnock　　**Topic**: What is an argument?
Subject: What is an argument?　　**Date**: January 30. 4:10 PM

Dear students,

Throughout the term, we will continue to talk about "arguments." But what is an argument? What is the "rhetorical" goal of argument—and what does "rhetorical" mean again? What does our text say about approaches and components of argument and persuasion in chapter 8?

Choose ONE of the readings in chapter 8 of our text. What's the main idea/argument of the one you chose, and how did the author appeal to ethos, logos, and pathos to make that argument (see p. 231 of our text)? How did the argument fit the way argument is described? Try to be quite specific.

How did you feel about the topic prior to reading the article? Did your view shift at all? Why or why not?

Let's keep going with our good habits. Use in-text citations from our readings, and make sure they are in either MLA or APA style.

Thanks,
Prof. Warnock

Reply

← This thread worked from our course text, but they could choose from several essays to help them revisit key course content / ideas.

← I also asked them, if they wished, to comment on the reading's topic.

← I emphasized evidence again!

I want to reaffirm that since I have asked students to purchase a course text, as part of my teaching ethic, I drew on that text as much as possible. Some teachers don't use a text. That's fine. But if we were going to have a text—and I do think that the "big" texts for FYW courses all have lots of smart, usable material—then you can be sure I'll work from it, regardless of modality. Who knows, maybe they'll mark it up and not sell it back to the bookstore?

That week's chapter contained multiple essays, so students could discuss course concepts through a reading of their choosing:

- Susannah, Aaron, and I had a good exchange based on an essay about a family member donating her liver to another family member.
- A group of students jumped in and created a lively thread about just how inappropriate Halloween costumes for young girls have become.
- Donald started another subthread on Wednesday about the liver transplant piece. He wrote a good, long thoughtful post, to which Susannah responded, but Susannah had written her post late on Tuesday night, so I had to post this:

Author: Scott Warnock	**Topic**: Rogerian, collaboration approaches
Subject: Re:Our Own Warrior Princess	**Date**: February 2, 9:23 AM

Hi Donald

This is a good post, but you would have been better building from Susannah's thread, which already opened a discussion about this reading.

ProfW

Reply

If I wanted to continue encouraging students to *build* conversations, I had to make sure they were talking to each other, connecting conversationally, as often as possible.

- The final subthread stemmed from an essay about the objectification of women. Katie posted a thorough post, John responded, and then Donald commented to both.

Thread: Collaboration and Citation

I wanted to work on citation, as a course and program-wide objective, but teaching citation can, as many teachers know, be stifling and unproductive. So this week I used another type of thread. I asked students to work together as a class-wide team as a way to think about citation. This thread provided them with an opportunity to discuss the mechanics of citation while also working collaboratively in the online environment—which would ostensibly help them as we started on Project 2, a team project:

Author: Scott Warnock **Topic**: Citation exercise
Subject: Working together: Citation exercise **Date**: January 30, 4:09 PM

Dear students,

You will complete this exercise as a class. Everyone will get the same 10-point grade. If we don't hear from you at all on this thread, in fairness to your classmates, you will get no credit.

You will provide correct MLA citations for each of the six sources below. One of the moderators this week will be in charge of indicating to me which are the final, correct "answers" that represent the will of the group!

Good luck,
Prof. Warnock

1. Please create a correct MLA citation for this book: William Mickel's To the Backwoods which was published in 1976 by Windham Press, which is located in Philadelphia.
2. Please create a correct MLA citation for this article in a book: Trisha Walters wrote an article called Nine Degrees that appeared in Joanne Ruth and Cody Andrews' book Changes in Global Climate. The book was published by New York University University Press, which is located in New York City, in 2007. The article appeared on pages 25-51.
3. Please create a correct MLA citation for this scholarly article: The article Refracting the Amblyopic Eye by Michael Shurman, which appeared in Journal of Corrective Lenses in 2005. The volume number was 3 and the number was 2. The article appeared on pages 237-62.
4. Please create a correct MLA citation for this article from a database: Amber Johnson's article A Longitudinal Study of Shut-Ins published in Psychology Behaviors in 2001 on pages 455 to 467. The journal volume was 9 and the number was 2. The database was Academic Search Complete through Drexel at www.epnet.com, and you accessed it on December 2 of last year.
5. Please create a correct MLA citation for this Website: Alan Harmon's piece When It's All Too Much from his Website, Managing Your Daily Budget. The URL is BudgetWhenTooMuch.org. Harmon wrote the piece last April 22, and you accessed it in June 28 of last year.
6. Please create a correct MLA citation for an interview you conducted with Miles Rival on January 3, 2012 at Mr. Rival's home.

Reply

← Emphasis on collaboration.

← There was a grade, but it was low-stakes. That said: They were accountable to themselves and others.

← This was a moderated thread, and I tried to lay out the process clearly to help the students and the moderator. I ended with an encouraging closing. I made up this list of citations for them to "improve." Really, my goal was that the learning would happen in the dialogue that would hopefully ensue.

That thread's moderator, Donald, took the lead and then other students contributed "answers" for these sources. Fifteen of the students contributed thirty posts to the dialogue about what should be done—and why. They confirmed each other's posts—Lisa wrote to Katie, "Great Katie, I got the same thing!"—and Donald pointed everyone to relevant sections in our course text.

This may be a small thing, but I find it remarkable how OWC students can participate in an activity like this. I think, especially because of my belief in social constructivist approaches to learning, that this written environment is an excellent way for students to think through citation.

Diana: Collaborating on the Discussions

While this week's overarching goal was to revise our drafts and send them off for final submission, teamwork emerged strongly in our Discussions. At first, I thought it was a coincidence as I worked through the various threads, but I quickly realized the convenient timing. Having our discussions revolve around collaboration would act as a perfect transition from helping one another revise our individual papers to working together for the group project.

The thread "Challenge Dr. Logoetho?" helped us expand our rhetorical discussions via extensive argumentation from ProfW's stubborn alter ego. Where primary Discussions would usually be followed by questioning or comments from others in the class, they were now followed by extreme, headstrong arguments from Dr. Logoetho. This encouraged more detailed, supported secondary posts from my classmates and, in turn, made for a productive conversation.

Dr. Logoetho's initial argument held that Wikipedia was a groundless website with oodles of false information that was of no help to anyone. I felt it would be tough to comment first, since it seemed like this alter ego was ready to tear any dissenter apart (which would then require more work from me to further defend my point). Sitting at my desk in my dorm room, knowing I had plans later in the evening to visit a friend's birthday party, I replied anyway. I thought, "I might as well post now and have to defend my argument than try to jump in the middle of conversation later in the week." I started the discussion with an anecdotal story about a young, poor Peruvian boy who considered Wikipedia his most valuable treasure. I transitioned into a discussion on the expansive information made freely accessible by those who wouldn't have access to a library otherwise. I then provided statistics on Wikipedia's frequencies of errors being a slight 0.94 percent more than Britannica's, and closed with the following paragraph:

> Wikipedia is a reliable source. It offers information to those all over the world instantaneously, with ease and incredible accessibility. It is an ever-changing source of information, adding stories the moment they break, and releasing that information to individuals everywhere. When even those less fortunate, such as the shoe shining boy, have access to this incredible website, the only source of information they may have, why label it useless?

As described earlier, Dr. Logoetho responded with a stubborn, nitpicky, yet incredibly engaging post. This was quite the Discussion board! The funny thing was, while ProfW was playing this "role" of Dr. Logoetho, this type of professor is very much alive in academia. The professor who, no matter what is argued or supported, stands staunchly beside their argument. Hell, this type of *person* is everywhere! It was a fun exercise for us knowing our professor was playing along, and it was good practice for the stubborn-types we all encounter in life.

A few peers gave a second or even third shot at responding to Dr. Logoetho's obstinate remarks, including John's post (that Scott mentions above) about "how could you 'lose' an argument?" Finally, ProfW, writing as himself, swooped in to settle things down:

Author: Scott Warnock　　**Topic**: Challenge Dr. Logoetho?: Wikipedia
Subject: Just so you know, I'm on your side　　**Date**: February 2, 1:52 PM

Folks,

I'm glad a few of you have challenged not only Dr. Logoetho's argument, as Diana did so well, but also his whole combative premise, as John did.

Just so you know, I'll stay out of it, but I'm on your side, as you can see from this article I once wrote on my blog: http://whenfallsthecoliseum.com/2012/01/27/demystifying-wikipedia/

Good luck. I'm with you!
Prof. Warnock

Reply

To take a break from rhetoric for a brief moment, ProfW had us work on another thread that involved crafting proper citations for six sources. We were to, somehow, work together to produce the proper citation for these sources while fact-checking each other. The logistics of this would be funky, considering everyone needed to post in the thread to get credit, but Donald did a phenomenal job directing everyone to produce a collaborative final product, while also catching a LMS kink we needed to overcome to complete the assignment:

Author: Post naming / Problems with italics, etc. **Topic**: Citation Exercise
Subject: Donald **Date**: January 31, 8:05 PM

Please name your post as follows Source #____ , this way if we have a question about a source we can easily find it. Also if everyone could attach a Word file with the correct italics etc. to your post that would be awesome. Doing this will allow everyone to see exactly how it is done. Thank you Aaron for posting your attachment and letting us see what the citation should look like.

Reply

It was a clunky process as we worked through the task; I thought, "Why is this a Discussion? We're not really discussing anything? We're just fact checking each other and submitting citations?" Then it occurred to me. Remember being in middle school, when a teacher would use the silent birthday order game? Everyone would have to line up based on who's oldest to youngest, but without talking. It required fun but useful collaboration and brought the students together for a moment. This citation exercise was like that, but with the added benefit of learning how to construct proper citation. It was a refreshing exercise and flowed well into the final Discussion: collaboration.

Collaboration is always a fascinating topic for me. A common joke shared among disgruntled group members goes, "When I die, I want the people I did group projects with to lower me into the grave so they can let me down one last time." Of course, the success of this joke comes from everyone feeling like they were the "victim" of group projects one time or another. However, if everyone resonates with carrying the group on their back, do slackers even know when they're slackers?

This theme quickly presented itself as our discussion on collaboration began:

Author: Artan **Topic**: Collaboration
Subject: Collaboration **Date**: February 1, 11:18 AM

I've had a recent problem in collaboration in my engineering 101 class. It was actually last semester. Basically I was the one doing all of the work and my other group members were barely contributing anything. After the first half of the semester, one group member just stopped showing up and would not answer any texts regarding lab reports. He didn't drop the class or anything, he just didn't show up. This made it really difficult for me when it came to basically doing all the work. It basically depends on the people you get for your group that determines these problems.

Reply

Author: Alexa
Subject: Collaboration
Topic: Collaboration
Date: February 1, 12:30 PM

Artan,

I also had bad experiences in collaboration in my labs as well. Last semester for my bio lab, it wasn't that one person didn't want to contribute at all, but this person wanted to be the only contributor in the group and if anyone suggested something she did not like, or if the wording wasn't as intelligent as she would have liked, she shut us down. I absolutely hated group work after that because I was so afraid of contributing ideas because that person was so picky and hard to please!

But I do agree that if done right, it can be extremely beneficial and a learning experience. It can be such a success if everyone listens to one another and tries to understand. I mean, if someone has the right ideas another person can word it correctly. I too worry about collaborative projects, but I'm trying to change my view on it because I know working together can have a much more positive effect than working alone.

Alexa

Reply

So far, I understood where my classmates were coming from. Their situations sounded similar to experiences I've had, but I couldn't help but wonder if they were oversharing. Sure, it's fair to have full disclosure and tell others about concerns you may have regarding a future collaborative project, but was this getting to the point where classmates were coming across as complainers?

Author: John
Subject: Collaboration… I HATE it!
Topic: Collaboration
Date: February 1, 8:24 PM

When it comes to collaboration, you either love it or hate it. In Ingall's case, she seems to be a strong advocate for it. She notes the great collaborators, and shows their great success from it. She puts collaboration as basically bouncing ideas off of one another to enhance ideas. Sure … if it's done right.

Personally, I cringe at the thought of working with another person. I have had MANY bad encounters with group projects or assignments. It always feels like no one else in the group care as much about the project as I do. In one specific scenario, I was assigned a group to put together a very large psychology project presentation in my senior year of high school. This project consisted of an enormous amount of research, and putting together a 10 minute presentation. Well, needless to say, I bore the brunt of the work. But I did have my revenge; when it was time for peer review, they got what they deserved (call me mean, but they deserved it).

I have not had to do one group assignment where there was positive chemistry in the group.

Maybe I have a tainted view of collaboration, and it could possibly be a great tool. However, I am still waiting for someone to prove that to me.

Reply

Some of John's points seemed to push the limits of a classroom conversation. "[Collaboration] could possibly be a great tool"? Where's the debate here? Haven't there been many cases of successful collaboration?

The freeness with which my classmates were sharing their dislike for collaboration was surprising. Weren't they aware future groupmates would be reading their posts, remembering if not referencing them in the Discussion archives, and then, once group projects started, making grounded assumptions on how well they would be able to work together? What about the professor? If groupmates were to complain later that John was hard to work with, the professor had cataloged evidence that John "HATED" collaboration. It was a bold move, one I certainly wouldn't make, but John never really shied away from using a big voice in the class (see our debate in Chapter 3). I felt Discussion boards weren't a confessional for students to share their feelings about a certain topic with no repercussions. This was an academic space. Opposing ideologies were welcomed if they contribute to discussion, but blanket "I hate _____" statements could be perceived the wrong way.

It was interesting to see a sharp contrast in how collaborative we were on the Discussions, only to close the week with some students complaining about how frustrating collaboration can be. I was curious to see how the group projects were going to progress throughout the rest of the semester.

Scott: Final Project Submissions

At the end of the week, the students submitted final drafts of Project 1. I gave them instructions for submitting their project in multiple ways, including in the Friday announcement:

Announcements for Friday, February 3:

- The Week 5 **Weekly Plan** is available.
- Remember the **final draft of Project 1** is due tomorrow.
- Reminder: If you could not attend in person, an archive of Tuesday's **workshop for your Project 1 drafts** is available via the link below. Please submit your **worked-up draft** after the workshop in the link in the Other Assignments folder below. (This is basically an easy 10 points for you.)

I don't know if it seems odd to have students submit a project on a weekend, but in my OWCs, this has never been a source of complaint, as it was not this term: Not one project was late.

Diana: Finally! The Submission

As I cleaned up the revisions made from the workshop, dotted my I's (or, more accurately, placed my commas), I felt confident knowing I had at least worked through what ProfW suggested. Then, I worked through my own revision process, which was a mix of reading out loud and reverse outlining. As I read aloud, I jotted down major notes I had made throughout my piece. At the end of my reading, I reviewed my rough outline, determined how much sense I had made and weighed that against how much time I had left before the submission time (because, if left to my own schedule, I would tweak over and over and over.) My final revision process didn't take long, maybe about forty-five minutes or so, and I was ready to submit.

After I clicked send, I had a brief reflection on my work habits in this new college routine—though, submitting your first big paper in a course will make you do that, as you list the shoulda-coulda-wouldas. I realized that I often work better in an environment full of distractions. For example, I completed the majority of my work this week in a busy café, nestled in a side street of Center City, Philadelphia. I set my coffee on my right, bagel on my left, and zoned out with the buzz of the café around me as I completed Discussions or my paper. I did this in long blocks only a few days out of the week, as opposed to doing it every day. For example, since a large chunk of material was due on Tuesday, and the rest was due on Friday / Saturday, I would sit in the café Monday and Thursday for about three to four hours each day. If I didn't have enough time to finish that work during the day, I would complete the rest in my dorm at Drexel. My roommate and I had relatively opposite schedules, so I rarely had to battle with her tempting me with a party invitation or a game of soccer on the quad. As she was going to bed around 9:00 or 10:00 p.m., I was just starting my work in the living room from about 10:00 p.m. to midnight. This schedule worked for me and would hopefully continue to work as I moved forward in the course—especially since I was addicted to that café's bagels.

In Retrospect: Revising Online

The experience of working through the final draft of a project demonstrates the fundamentally "distant" aspect of much of writing instruction—well before OWI. In different ways, both of us realize that the feedback teachers give has almost always been "virtual" or away from students. For more than a century, courses have been set up and run to help students improve their writing. But were these students in writing-rich environments? In most cases, proba-

Behind the Screen: Revising in Digital Environments

How does modality affect writing and the writing process? This has been a long-standing area of interest in composition, from general thinking about technology and writing by Walter Ong to the specifics of screen-based writing by Christina Haas. This work about revision might inform how you think about and teach revising in an OWC. For instance, in 1987, Lillian Bridwell-Bowles, Parker Johnson, and Steven Brehe found that writers with no prior computer writing experience who went through some prewriting planning were most satisfied with writing on computers, but those who began with drafting were least satisfied. These early researchers—geez, they were pioneers, as were the students—also found that revising surface features was easier on computer while large-scale re-visioning and revising was difficult. A few years later, Carol Klimick Cyganowski examined processes of peer critiquing and collaboration when done on computers, partially in response to negative comments about these processes (which Diana echoes here somewhat). Cyganowski found that combining word processing and collaboration in fact directed writers' attentions to larger composing issues. Interestingly, she found that writers viewed their work in this context as "still writing" instead of revision. Students also felt computers improved their writing. Haas teamed up with Charles Hill and David L. Wallace (Hill, Wallace, and Haas) in an empirical study looking at differences between student and experienced writers using both pen and paper and word processing: How did the computer affect not just writers' products but their processes? How might the computer affect revision not just on the "paper" but in the writer's mind? They determined that task definition plays a greater role in writers' choices than do differences in the revising medium.

Specifically in OWI, Beth Hewett compared oral and computer-mediated communication "peer response group talk" and how it influenced revision ("The Characteristics and Effects"); she found that these conversations "had different qualities when students used different media, suggesting that medium shapes talk." Modality not only offers OWI teachers different ways of teaching revision, but students may also have opportunities to reflect on their own revision process through the lens of technology—and, again, while such practices are not confined to OWI, learning online may lend itself to such metawork.

bly not. An OWC puts students in a peer review–centric, writing-focused environment; that's simply the nature of the experience. Teachers can still engage in many of their *effective* onsite practices but put them into play in online, asynchronous spaces where students' ideas are composed through texts.

In fact, in education we are at a pedagogical moment when almost all revision and peer review happens on computers, regardless of teaching modality.[1] Even if the students were to meet onsite, many times those students will exchange work online to review each other through comments: Think of tools like Google Docs, Microsoft OneDrive, Dropbox, and other cloud applications. While students may be taught revision practices in an onsite format, many have a mindset that it simply is not practical to execute such revision through pen and paper.

During Weeks 3 and 4, students went through the digital revision process. As Diana described, it wasn't perfect. Without face-to-face accountability, do some students engage less in peer review? But the students touched each other's work and interacted with Scott through an intensive reading and writing process—and, again, is that not what we want as teachers of OWCs? Also, the process of working with texts digitally really does not depend on online courses: That process can be reproduced for any modality.

5

Week 5: Forming an Online Writing Team

We wanted the technology to support the complex private and social activities that make up the learning process.

—EDWARD BARRETT, *describing the development of MIT's Networked Educational Online System*

Diana: Feeling Left Out

After completing several midterms the week prior, I received a less-than-average grade in my biology class, a disappointing chemistry lab report final, and my group in my public relations course was dropping the ball on our project. I enjoyed setting aside time every week to dive into this course's Discussion boards and interact with my classmates, but now other classes demanded more of my attention. Even if the amount of writing in ProfW's course was on the heavier side and many of his readings required some serious brain power, it was always enjoyable because I knew I had the chance to talk everything out with my peers. I wasn't just being a nerd about this course either. My classmates also seemed happy to contribute to the Discussion boards. Many of the conversations were positive, energetic, and eager, and rarely did I feel my classmates were only writing to quickly submit a post on time.

And yet, here I was beating myself up because I felt out of the loop on our Discussions. I didn't necessarily fear I was going to commit a disservice to ProfW. I knew I would do my best to submit quality work. Instead, I feared I would simply be left out, worried I wouldn't have the time to read many of my peers' posts or responses to my work. I wouldn't walk away this week getting the gist of what was discussed. Ironically, I felt like I was doing my work "from home."

Yet, good news awaited! I was going to have two opportunities through this week's assignments to directly interact with my peers in other ways: responding to peer reviews and the forming of our new groups. While I wouldn't have time to engage in the Discussions like I normally did, I had the opportunity to connect with several classmates in new ways. After hearing so much from these peers in earlier weeks, it would be refreshing to hear their voices in both a peer review and the casual context of a group forming. These students, Aaron, Susannah, and Artan, would be working closely with me on our second project until the end of the term, so I eagerly dove into our group messaging to kick off our work with a positive start. If I didn't have enough time to interact with all my classmates this week, reaching out to these three would certainly help me retain my connection to the course.

Scott: Groups

We were moving into the next project, as I had let them know with the Weekly Plan:

Week 5: February 5 to February 11

The focus this week is on getting going with your group and developing a topic for Project 2. We'll also think about writing about causes and effects.

What do I do?	What are the specific instructions? Where do I find the work or the assignment?	When is it due? (All times EST)
WORK AS A GROUP	You should have already read the instructions for Project 2 in the "Writing Projects" folder. I will set up a group thread on our LMS for each group. This week, you have three tasks: 1. Propose a team topic. 2. Develop a Group Contract. 3. Provide minutes/progress report to me. All of these matters can be discussed on your group thread. I am thinking of your group work this week as if this were a face-to-face course: You would get together	Your **topics** are due by the **weekend**. Also by the **weekend**, someone on your team will post on your group Discussion thread brief minutes/a progress report of what you have accomplished. At that point, you will also have established the Group Contract. We will work on this project for four weeks, and each week someone different will post

← I was again direct in this week's intro comment: The focus was on launching the teams.

← Time-wise, I conceived a chunk of their work this week as being dedicated to the team project, specifically developing a good topic, *much as if we had in-class meeting time dedicated to this work.* This is following from the idea of *migrating* practices from onsite teaching, especially in terms of how much time the work might take.

	in class one day, discuss topics and create the Group Contract of responsibilities.	the team's minutes/ progress report.
REPLY	You received a peer review from several colleagues last week. In one **memo** on the Discussions for your Project 1 drafts, please write back to the reviewers, addressing the following points: • How helpful was each review? • What was not helpful? • What do you wish they had said more about? • What specific changes were you able to make based on their comments? • Was there anything they wrote that you were unclear about? This is a 10-point assignment.	Respond to them on the Discussions by the **weekend.**
READ and LISTEN	Read the following: • *Course textbook:* Chap. 10, "Writing to Explain Causes and Effects" 47 pages. • *Aux*: Trevino and Youngblood: "Bad Apples in Bad Barrels" 7 pages. • Listen: *This American Life*, "Ruining it for the Rest of Us" 58 minutes.	You'll want to have read by **Tuesday,** February 7 so you can complete the quiz and work on the Discussions.
TAKE a QUIZ	Quiz 5 can be found in the "Quizzes" folder. Please make sure you complete the quiz in the allotted time: five minutes.	As usual, the quiz will be available **Tuesday** from 9:30 am to midnight. You will have five minutes to complete it. Getting used to this?
WRITE and READ	Read **carefully** all the Discussion topics for Week 5, and follow these instructions: • Post ONE primary post to any of the Discussion threads. • Post TWO secondary posts to any of the Discussion threads. One of your posts this week **must** be on "My favorite post."	Post your topics and primary post by **Wednesday** night, February 8. Post your secondary posts by **Friday**, February 10, at 4:00 pm.

← They had weekend deadlines for the team work.

← As I describe below, this brief assignment was designed to create another opportunity for students to dialogue about the student writing in the course—their *own* writing.

← The readings were designed to get them thinking about working and writing collaboratively, with a twist toward what makes teams *not* work. I also assigned a reading about cause-and-effect writing.

← I wrote "Getting used to this?" here as a touch of personality.

← Remember, a "day" of an onsite class would be spent on groups, so Discussion work reflected that. Since the week's theme was about how collaboration worked—and didn't—they would

MODERATE	This week our moderators will be Rio and Deryck. They will have an active voice in encouraging conversation, and they will provide a summary of their threads at the end of the week.	--

have metawriting opportunities to discuss issues and questions about group projects. Note the one required thread this week too.

I reinforced the Weekly Plan with this announcement:

Announcements for Monday, February 6:

- The **Discussions** are up, including an area for **your Group.** Get in there right away so we can get Project 2 going.

They had to get the group project started. I know how students feel about group work; in fact, based on last week's Discussions, I knew how *this class* felt about group work in quite specific ways. I believe in the value of group work, but I have had my frustration with virtual teams, mainly because that one somewhat out-of-it student in an onsite team can more easily slip away and be completely absent online; that *is* a problem of online learning that differs from onsite. Starting this week, we would do our best to create a good, constructive learning environment for a group project. I followed up Monday's announcement on Wednesday:

Announcements for Wednesday, February 8:

- Please get started on the conversation on **your Group thread**.
- Your **grades** are updated.

The group work had clear deadlines. One thing I always try to impress upon groups, regardless of modality, is that they need *concrete actions emanating from their meetings*. The Weekly Plan tried to reinforce that in the "When is it due?" column.

Diana: Getting to Know My Group

Having had thorough group experience in high school, I knew that the best thing to do in this situation was set the stage for my group. I logged onto the Discussion thread and started organizing the work we needed to do (team topic, group contract, minutes) by creating mini Discussion subthreads within the forum. While I wasn't necessarily *doing* the work for everyone, I was creating an easy way for them to start their work. If my group members felt comfortable in contributing (knowing I took the first leap) and had an easy way to do so (because of an organized format), they would contribute. And they did! All my groupmates got a great jump on our assignments and we had an energetic dialogue over the topic for the paper. By the weekend, we had completed everything in good time with good effort.

Though, while I wanted to set the stage for my peers, it was hard making grand plans in the early stages of our group work. Since we were thrown together randomly, it was hard to *really* know what everyone's strengths and weaknesses were. While we had interacted with one another over the Discussions and knew a few things about one another (like how Susannah was really active in her business major and Aaron consistently asked great questions to continue conversations) it would take a few days to assign the larger project roles to everyone.

Scott: Metawriting Work This Week

I had to take my own deep breath that week. I had a good list of things to do that Monday, including for our course. In my planner, I wrote next to "English102" in shorthand: "papers (3 hours), grades, announce, Discuss, quiz." I had a lot to do by the end of the day! (I never did get to the full three hours of evaluating Project 1 final drafts.)

Although it was a busy week, on Thursday I posted their third "Writing puzzle" (I described these puzzles in Week 2).

Author: Scott Warnock — **Topic**: Writing puzzles
Subject: Writing puzzle #3 — **Date**: February 9, 2:04 PM

What do you think?:

"The woman was really honest, so she was able to secure a good price for the very unique painting."

Reply

Alan and Rio both commented about the use of the adverb *very* before a word like *unique*. Our conversation allowed Alan and me to have a brief discussion about words similar to *honest* and whether you can intensify them.

Thread: My Favorite Post

I required one of their posts to be on "My favorite post." I always use a similar metawriting thread in my online and hybrid courses (and I follow up this thread, as you'll see, in Week 10):

Author: Scott Warnock	**Topic**: My favorite post
Subject: My favorite post	**Date**: February 8, 11:57 AM

Hi everyone,

Please look back/think about our Discussions so far and pick one stellar post by one of your colleagues.

This is an evidence-based conversation. Clearly identify the post so the rest of us can find it, and then describe why it was your favorite.

Looking forward to some well-earned compliments,
Prof. Warnock

Reply

A thread like this encourages interaction among students while allowing students to "pay it back/forward." This type of thread also pushes students to return to the Discussion boards to seek their favorite post and evidence to support their choice. OWC instructors can never find too many ways to have students re-touch the written Discussions. Also, the compliments get spread around by students on this type of thread, and I am always fascinated to see who the students think is doing a great job.

Deryck, on his own volition, made an excellent move in the post he wrote introducing himself as the moderator:

Author: Deryck	**Topic**: My favorite post
Subject: Moderator	**Date**: February 8, 4:48 PM

Hey guys,

As a moderator, I feel inclined to present an additional aspect to this post.

Along with describing why whichever post you choose is your favorite, try to incorporate what we've learned from our textbook so far this term:

Chap. 7, "Writing to Analyze"
Chap. 9, "Writing to Evaluate"
Chap. 14, "Using Strategies for Argument"
Chap. 8, "Writing to Convince"
Chap. 10, "Writing to Explain Causes and Effects"

Off the top of your head; are there any techniques you noticed the poster utilized from the chapters above?

Can't wait to hear back,
- Deryck

Reply

This thread, including Deryck's start to it, exemplified the writing work students can compose in an OWC, the imagination and initiative they bring to an online writing environment. In a short response to this intro I told him that this was "very, very clever"—it was the least I could do! Almost all the students posted here, as I asked:

- Multiple students agreed on a few favorite posts. In one case, Aaron agreed about a great post, but he had misremembered who had written it and couldn't find it, which he later acknowledged in a "Woops" message.
- The Week 3 debate between John and Diana reappeared, and this time because Diana complimented John by voting one of his posts as her favorite, titling her post "The John vs. Diana debate." Interestingly, John too said he was pretty happy with his own post ("[sorry if that sounds vain]" he wrote in an aside) but then made this comment: "I found myself checking almost every half hour to see what the next phase in the argument was." John, in a post others clearly thought was provocative, continued to re-touch the boards to see where he stood. Artan too said John's post was a favorite—although Artan kind of violated the "rules" for picking just one post—and he liked the debate. I wrote to Artan, "I too would like to see more debate, so feel free to be a catalyst." Alan, Karen, Alexa, and Deryck also said that the Week 3 debate was good; their conversation went well, but people were violating my rules for this thread! (Though that made me think I should have a "My favorite thread" topic. . . .)
- Four other students, including Alan, who double voted in essence, liked a post by Karen, with Jennifer taking Deryck's invitation and citing the chapters in our book that she felt Karen used effectively in that post.

In his short end-of-week moderator thread summary, Deryck wrote this about being the moderator: "I felt as if I had more authority, or influence than I normally do."

Thread: Discussion about Bad Apples

As I mentioned, there is nothing special about online courses in terms of assigning multimodal "readings" such as videos or podcasts. But as with many aspects of OWI, because teachers and students are fundamentally immersed in digital environments, it may seem easier, more appropriate, or even more natural to have students interact with such "readings"—especially if students are creating projects with multimodal aspects to them.

This week, students listened to a *This American Life* podcast, which was on the core syllabus, about people who don't work effectively in groups. Rio moderated.

Author: Scott Warnock
Topic: Bad apples: This American Life
Subject: Bad apples
Date: February 6, 11:14 AM

Hi everyone,

What did you learn about individuals in public spaces from the stories you heard?

What did Will Felps discover when studying the student groups?

How easy is it to, as Ira Glass, says, "Poison any group"? What happens to teams with the worst people?

How did the measles case illustrate how one's person's decisions affect everyone?

What is your opinion about the vaccination issue, in terms of individual freedoms vs. the good-for-all?

How did comedian Mike Birbiglia ruin a cancer charity event?

Finally, how did Nancy Updike's personality evolve on the Quiet Car? Why did she start to see the value of fascism?

In all of these stories, how do we balance the desires of the individual vs. the good of all?

As we go this week, I may tell you a few stories about my own crazy experiences with those who use cell phones on the train.

Thanks,
Prof. Warnock

Reply

← This video is connected to the course material. The prompt is more complex than I normally like, with too many questions, but the students pounced on it.

← The main point is here at the end.

← I add a personalizing touch at the end: I have my own stories to tell!

This thread was active: There were seventy-five posts. I posted eleven times, including the prompt. The thread also demonstrated how a Discussion thread can evolve. Many students posted long, well-written primary posts by Wednesday, and then classmates built conversations with secondary posts. Rio, who posted twelve times, kept encouraging students after their long primary posts. Diana started a subthread, "Balancing individualist and social needs," with an 815-word well-cited post that spawned conversation among several of us. John provoked conversation with a post "Many > Few." Alan proposed in a subthread "selfishness a luxury," to which several others eagerly posted. I started a subthread "Follow-up: Vaccination," that five students responded to.

When I went to work on the Discussions on Thursday, I realized what an excellent job Rio had done moderating this far-reaching conversation. I felt I did not need a lengthy synthesis post, and instead posted five short response posts to particular students posing questions or asking them to clarify points. Even on Saturday, Rio posted a link about train "quiet cars." In her summary, posted the Monday of Week 6, she wrote:

Author: Rio — **Topic**: Bad apples: This American Life
Subject: Summary — **Date**: February 13, 1:51 PM

Hello again,

Reading everyone's posts/comments about the audio clip from "This American Life" was very interesting. It seemed as if many people had a lot to say about this topic and many exceeded the word count requirement for the primary post! A common trend that I saw people write about was that the people in the scenarios from the audio clip were often selfish and put their needs in front of everyone else's. This was interesting because the audio clip was partially intended to get others to see the cause and effects between the individual and the group as a whole. I didn't think people would analyze this clip on a deeper level than that; nonetheless, everyone brought a different perspective to the discussion and that made this thread all the more appealing to read. One of the most interesting comments about "This American Life" was from John saying that allowing a child to walk around unvacinnated should be considered child abuse. Now, he meant child abuse could go as far as to describe not only inflicting physical or emotional abuse but also putting your child in a dangerous situation. Whether or not you agree with this is up to you, but this was something to think about. Pertaining to the Quiet Car, I was surprised to see that quite a few people in the class have used the quiet car and developed their own opinion concerning behavior in the quiet car. Also, I had asked a question about whether Nancy Updike's behavior in the quiet car was appropriate. Most of you said she was not doing anything wrong in enforcing the rules. In addition, a few people thought, including myself, that her behavior was quite irritating. Karen made a good point on the

← She posted this at the start of Week 6.

← It's not all about quantity, as we've emphasized throughout, but quantity can still matter for writing. Rio notes both in her summary, seeing both the variety of interesting topics while noting that "many exceeded the word count."

quiet car in mentioning that it was going to be difficult in getting everyone to be quiet and balance the needs of all and that how you react to disruptive people should depend on the situation. In conclusion, what was meant to be a topic thread about group dynamics flourished into discussions that brought up many unconventional points that provided deeper insight into "This American Life."

Reply

The conversation trickled into Week 6, when I did offer my own story, for better or worse:

Author: Scott Warnock **Topic**: Bad apples: This American Life
Subject: Re: The Quiet Car **Date**: February 13, 10:01 AM

Yes, we're on to the next week, but I have to say that I have become a kind of quiet car nut. I have gotten into it with several people who were on their cell phones over the years during my train commute to work. Some days, I don't know, I just can't take it to have someone yelling into their cell phone right in my ear. In the days I've had it out with someone, I probably didn't use my rhetorical skills very successfully. I have tried to be a little more clever rhetorically by writing to NJ Transit to institute quiet portions of its light rail train, but so far I've been unsuccessful. For some aspects of public space, I feel incredibly patient, but the cell-phone-in-public deal just makes me livid—and I'm not even sure exactly why. Once I went home and Googled [cell phone jammers], thinking of delicious revenge, but, alas, I learned they are illegal.

ProfW

Reply

A few students did offer their commentary about my hopeless search for cell-phone jammers.

Thread: Organizing a Cause and Effect Project

The team Project 2 assignment was, in terms of its objective, a blend of rhetorical modes: Students analyzed a problem, articulated a solution, and then argued for that solution. In a thread aimed at the rhetorical goals of Project 2, I started with this:

Author: Scott Warnock
Topic: Cause-and-effect project
Subject: Cause-and-effect project
Date: February 6, 10:38 AM

Dear students of English 102:

As I read the textbook this week, I thought that the section on organizing such projects was particularly helpful for what you might do in your teams.

What are the different ways of organizing a cause-and-effect project? Pick one of the readings we read this week and analyze its organizational approach. Also, how does it address causes and effects (for instance, Reich finds a hidden cause behind a well-known effect)?

Interested,
Prof. Warnock

Reply

← Again, if I asked them to read the course text, we would use it.

← The prompt was direct and straightforward, working on content…

←…but there were metawriting opportunities.

I framed this prompt around my own discovery while I read the text, "As I read . . ."—emphasizing for the students that I too was still discovering things specifically designed to help them with their learning, based on their traits and tendencies up until this point.

Participation was light on this thread, although, as usual, some students did excellent work. Lisa composed a 900-word post about one reading and Susannah followed with another long, 630-word, and equally in-depth post. (Again, I can't help but reiterate that these posts, unto themselves, could be high-quality writing projects in many courses.) Four students participated in this thread, conversing about the readings and helping build each other's understanding of how they might organize such a writing project. Remember, if I chose, I could have required that every student participate here, but this was just another way to reinforce the *content* of the course—I was trying to approach the material from many angles.

Thread: Tough Reading of the Week

I assigned a challenging reading this week: an article from the *Journal of Applied Psychology* about ethical decision-making behavior. They didn't bite. The thread had only three posts, two by Jennifer. This kind of low participation can be a critique of OWCs, but teachers in all modalities know that it can be difficult getting students to read. I certainly have observed courses onsite in which it is clear most students have not read the material.

Again, there is a way to address this: I could have required that they post on this thread. However, it is worth noting that although the participation overall was not high, both posters wrote interesting observations about the study results and how, as Jennifer said, "Individuals who have observed the behavior of others and seen that they have been rewarded for unethical conduct or punished for ethical conduct are more likely to make unethical decisions because they come to expect similar outcomes for themselves and therefore, internalize those expectations." In an OWC, you can take a teaching risk with such a tough reading, since the few students who tackle it stand to get a great deal out of the material without having that "pin-drop" onsite class during which you realize the material was over the students' heads—or was barely read at all!

Thread: Peer Review Response

I like to close the loop of the peer review process by having students respond to their reviewers. This is another way for students to write back and forth to each other, and it might help improve future reviews in the class. Diana describes below her experience both giving and receiving response to the Project 1 peer reviews.

Diana: Our First Stab at Reviewing the Peer Reviews

This was my, well, everyone's, chance! After years of receiving peer reviews that ranged from helpful to dreadful, we finally had the opportunity to review the reviews! When the concept of peer reviews was introduced in my early high school years, I thought it was a neat way to receive feedback other than the teacher's while interacting with classmates. As the years went on and the caliber of both my peers and teachers varied, peer review turned into a hazardous endeavor. Would I waste the next few hours putting effort into a review only to receive small changes and a smiley face at the bottom of my paper? Or would I have a helpful discussion about my paper's direction? While I couldn't control the quality of peer reviews I received, nor could my professors, there was one thing I could control: my feedback to them. I always had the opportunity to turn to a classmate and say, "Hey. This is kind of a crappy review. Can you give me more feedback?" Now that this was structured into the review process, I didn't have to worry about offending my peers (and I would receive feedback on my reviews too!).

Both reviews I gave to my peers were positive.

Author: Diana Gasiewski
Subject: Re:Proj1 Peer Review: Diana Gasiewski

Topic: Week 3 - Proj1 Peer Review 5
Date: February 8, 9:49 PM

TO: Susannah
FROM: Diana Gasiewski
SUBJ: Response to Proj 1 Peer Review
DATE: February 8th

Overall, I found your critique very helpful. I genuinely appreciated the compliments and encouragement you provided, which greatly stimulated my writing progress. Also, before you ever gave a critique of what I could improve, you always prefaced it with a praise—always a nice way to go about criticizing someone's work.

From your suggestions, I was able to look at my paper as a whole, and evaluate the sensibility of my developing thought process. I reworked much of what was written previously, and (hopefully) constructed a much more logical piece.

Lastly, I couldn't thank you enough for your conclusion suggestions. In fact, I used your idea to tie my conclusion to the introduction of the couple at White Dog cafe, and I think it concluded my paper fabulously.

The only comment I wish you had elaborated on, or explained more clearly, was your suggestion to delete my original last paragraph. I still don't see how that would have worked, and I wish you would have described your reasoning further.

Other than that, I greatly appreciated the time and thought you put into reading and reviewing my paper. I look forward to working with you on our group project!

-Diana

Reply

Author: Diana Gasiewski
Subject: Re:Proj1 Peer Review: Diana Gasiewski

Topic: Week 3 - Proj1 Peer Review 5
Date: February 8, 9:19 PM

TO: Aaron
FROM: Diana Gasiewski
SUBJ: Response to Proj 1 Peer Review
DATE: February 8th

On a scale of one to ten on how helpful this review was, I found this review to be around an eight. I would have appreciated a bit more direction on improvements I could make to my paper, or suggestions of other creative approaches I could take. Also, other than the grammatical errors you found, I really didn't receive more than three suggestions.

Yet, the encouragement you provided, while I was beating myself up on the progress I had made, was greatly appreciated! You did a fantastic job at pointing out the things I had done well, and you really motivated me to keep plugging away at a project I had almost given up on. Also, I was able to improve my grammar mistakes, which I very well may have missed, because of your findings.

Thanks for the time you took to read and review my paper, and I look forward to working with you with the group project!

-Diana

Reply

Then it was my turn to receive feedback from Susannah and Aaron. Uh oh. I hope I wasn't too harsh! Why did I have to assign a scale to Aaron's post? I wasn't the teacher! Well, if I can dish it out, I better be ready to take it. Susannah's response was positive. She commented on how in depth I went with my critique, saying, "Even just your note about making sure I vary my word choice and sentence structure helped me. I realized I'd be able to add more originality to my paper with just small changes." Reading this felt awesome. I was genuinely happy I could help my classmate improve her paper! Then came Aaron's response:

Author: Aaron
Subject: Re:Proj1 Peer Review: Aaron
Topic: Week 3 - Proj1 Peer Review 5
Date: February 10, 9:39 PM

TO: Diana Gasiewski
FROM: Aaron
SUBJ: Project 1 Peer Review
DATE: February 10th

Pointing out my grammatical errors really helped me out a lot. When I'm writing, I often think too fast and jumble up words, and for some reason when I read them back to myself, I see what I meant it to say.

I've always been bad at writing interesting introductions and conclusions. The part where you said to "paint a scenario, ask questions, propose a radical solution first" in my introduction to spice it up, it really helped. I like to see the path from problem to solution, and you drew that out for me.

I was really doubtful about my essay, thinking that I'd definitely fail it, especially when my topic proposal was off topic. Seeing the reassurance eased my mind.

Honestly, in high school, the only way I learned to write conclusions was in a dull and repetitive way, "just alter your introduction and paste it to the bottom."

Reply

I felt so bad for Aaron. I mean, I'm glad I helped, but I had no idea he was so doubtful of his writing strengths and would be so hard on himself. I saw a tiny aspect of this review turning into more of a therapy session than an analysis of writing, which I could imagine happens quite often. It's easy to admit that learning Spanish, calculus, or physics is difficult, but having difficulties with writing is a different story. Communication is a life skill. It asks us to take all the crazy, jumbled-up thoughts in our brains and repackage them in a cohesive message for others to understand (well, ideally anyway). But what if someone is told they are bad at that? That they're bad at writing? Bad at communicating? If someone doesn't understand astronomy, they don't risk offending a coworker by confusing asteroids with meteorites, but if someone doesn't understand acceptable writing, their ability to properly communicate with others is greatly hindered.

While Aaron may have been struggling with doubt over his paper and fear that he would fail, a really cool thing was happening as we produced these peer reviews. We were practicing writing the whole time! As we mulled over our introductions, conclusions, grammar, and sentence structure, we were practicing perfecting those things. As we discussed how to communicate our topics in a logical manner, we were practicing communicating our ideas to one another. No way could this happen in an f2f writing class. In an f2f environment, the only writing practice students receive may be limited to in-class essays and rough drafts. By the time students sit down with their final papers, they may have only written several thousand words throughout the semester. Yet here we were, practicing effective writing every single day, writing thousands of words a week. Even though Aaron was doubtful, I'm sure his writing wouldn't do anything but improve by the time the course was done. I certainly felt the same way about my writing.

Scott: Groups . . . Forming?

Bruce Tuckman said that groups go through a "development sequence" of *form, storm, norm,* and *perform.*[1] Even if I do not overtly present it in this way to students, I think it's a useful frame for thinking about group work. Where were we with the groups? On Monday morning, I created a thread for each group that was only accessible to members of that team, and I posted welcome posts:

> **Author**: Scott Warnock **Topic**: Discussion thread - Group 1
> **Subject**: Welcome: Let's get started **Date**: February 7, 10:38 PM
>
> Dear Group 1 (Aaron, Diana, Susannah, Artan):
>
> I wanted to introduce you to each other as members of this group. The Project instructions are located in the "Writing Projects" folder. Please read them carefully.

← I greeted each student, which also reinforced who is in the group.

This week you have three goals:
-Topic Proposal
-Group contract
-Minutes (should be covered in the Group Contract who is doing that this week)

First off, you want to create a Group Contract, which I would do in a separate thread. You'll want to address these questions (which are also on the Project instructions): How will you divide responsibilities? How will you monitor the efforts of your peers? How will you make sure that all are abiding by the expectations of deadlines, proper research, and productive communication? This contract will articulate the ethical practices and commitments of your group. Specifically, your contract should address the following elements: Communication, Reliability, Effort, Quality, Adherence to deadlines, and Academic integrity.

Second, you want to have a Topic Proposal posted by the end of the week. You can talk about this here, and I'll help you during the process as well as by reviewing the proposal. Please take some time, because the topic, as you learned from Project 1 (I hope), is key.

Finally, you'll post your minutes/progress report. Again, see the syllabus.

I am here to help you at any stage.

Let's get started!
Good luck, Prof. Warnock

Reply

← I gave them clear goals for the week—which I hope models behavior.

← Step 1 was the Group Contract.

← I reinforced that they must supply minutes and a progress report. I also reinforced that I am there to help.

- **Group 1**. This was Diana's Group, and they had a fast start catalyzed by Diana's Tuesday post that she opened by saying, "I have a couple ideas to start off our brainstorming." She then, by Thursday, had begun the group contract.
- **Group 2**. This foursome also got off to a good start, helped by Karen's initial post. All four members of this group were involved from the beginning as well.

Author: Karen　　**Topic**: Discussion thread - Project 2 Group 2
Subject: Group contract　　**Date**: February 7, 10:17 PM

Hey guys!

I thought that I would already start a thread for the group project. Here are the questions we need to answer:

1. How will we divide responsibilities?
2. How will we monitor each other's efforts?

3. How will we make sure that all are abiding by expectations of deadlines, proper research, and productive communication?

We need to pay close attention to: *Communication *Reliability *Effort *Quality *Adherence to deadlines *Academic integrity

Go ahead and respond to this post with your comments for each aspect of the contract and then we can put it into one coherent document.

Talk to you guys soon!
Karen

Reply

- **Group 3**. John posted on Wednesday to get this group going, and everyone had responded to him by Friday with ideas for the project.
- **Group 4**. Uh oh. By Friday, no one in this group had posted on the group Discussion.

I had made deliberate decisions creating these groups. I tried to put students who were proactive in each group, and, in this class, that was easy to do. Only Group 4 had me concerned.

As the week closed, I posted this announcement. The Discussions and other work were good this week, but I wanted to again remind them to work from my "synthesis" posts, even softening things by saying perhaps "I didn't make this clear enough":

Announcements for Friday, February 10:

- Your Week 6 **Weekly Plan** is available.
- Once again, I want to remind you to get moving with the **group project.**
- We have **750 posts in the course!**
- I perhaps didn't make this clear enough, but while I don't want to dictate your Discussions, I do want you to work from my **"Follow-up" Thursday posts** more than you have been. I'm trying to build a progression of thinking on the threads. Don't get me wrong: You are going a good job. But I want to make sure our conversation evolves each week.

In Retrospect: Going Beyond the LMS?

Technology matters and will influence how a virtual group operates, and unfortunately we both know that a school LMS might not be the best way for students to work. There are certainly advantages to having students collaborate in an institution-supported interface, specifically in regard to privacy concerns, but there are many collaboration tools that even if they aren't necessarily better are more familiar to students. A few years after our OWC, Diana and Scott met again in another course, Writing in Cyberspace. That course had a complex, high-stakes group project. Diana led the charge to successfully migrate the whole project to Google Drive.

In general, teachers should be flexible in how they require students to work in virtual collaborations, and, in fact, choosing a technology could be part of what students learn in a group project. Also, teachers do not need to be that well versed in the technologies students choose; they just need to be able to access the students' work so they are still teaching, and students must be sure their work is transparent so teachers can help them and, when need be, evaluate them.

Speaking of, Group 4 was off to a slow start. Scott needed to know that. Also, the students read about "bad apples," and the teacher, especially in an OWC, had to be on the lookout for such bad apples, who might be causing problems in a group—after all, that's part of the teacher's job.

Behind the Screen: Working in Teams Onlin

I don't pretend to be a world-class expert in collabora tive work, but practices that I have derived from many colleagues through the years and from my own expe ence (mixed in, I suppose, with an interest in facilitating the process well) have helped me conduct team projects in OWCs. Also, I think there is an inherent tea aspect to a well-run asynchronous OWC: Students are always working together. Here are a few resources you might review to help you facilitate team projects and that you might even assign to help students thin more deeply about collaborative work.

The business education literature is full of material on this topic. In *Journal of Education for Business*, Randa Hansen reviews the literature on teams and suggests processes to help business faculty use teams more effectively. Donald R. Bacon, Kim A. Stewart, and Williar S. Silver surveyed more than 100 MBA students in "Lessons from the Best and Worst Student Team Exper ences: How a Teacher Can Make the Difference" to hel provide teachers with empirical data to guide course teamwork. Also, David L. Williams, John D. Beard, and Jone Rymer provided another perspective in "Team Projects: Achieving Their Full Potential."

In an online course, one of the big concerns is that students won't all contribute their fair share. Articles by Daniel Levi and David Cadiz, "Evaluating Team Work on Student Projects: The Use of Behaviorally Anchored Scales to Evaluate Student Performance," and Charles M. Brooks and Janice L. Ammons, "Free Riding in Group Projects and the Effects of Timing, Frequency, and Specificity of Criteria in Peer Assessments," both discus student projects, in particular "social loafing"; Levi and Cadiz provide advice about how to evaluate teamwor while taking such things into consideration.

An accessible writing-focused piece for you and stu dents is Matt Barton and Karl Klint's "A Student's Guide to Collaborative Writing Technologies" in *Writing Space Readings on Writing* (Vol. 2). I discuss OWI team project in Chapter 14 of *Teaching Writing Online*. And Beth Hewett and Charlotte Robidoux edited the collection *Virtual Collaborative Writing in the Workplace: Computer-Mediated Communication Technologies and Processes.*

Week 6: "Homework" in an Online Writing Course

[T]eachers experience the same challenges that their students will face: problems with inadequate computer abilities, learning about the variety of interactive tools, and underestimating the amount of time needed to complete the online readings and homework.

—Dean Caplan and Rodger Graham,
"The Development of Online Courses"

Diana: Classwork ≠ Homework

This week I finally understood how an online class works. Yes, I know how that sounds. It's the sixth week, and I'm just now figuring out how the class works? Well, I had understood the who, what, where, and how of the course. ProfW was my instructor and primary audience, and my peers, while also an audience, mostly provided stimulus to discussion and progression of thought. The class was conducted online, asynchronously, throughout the week, and it was my responsibility to post early and often to ensure successful discussion. I had a high grade in the course, which I had been monitoring via our LMS gradebook throughout the term, and I was moving along just fine. I understood what was expected out of me to succeed in the course from day one. What I didn't understand was the why: Why was this course structured the way it was? Why did I have to do so much damn writing? Why did it seem like I was working so much harder than my friends who had f2f "regular" English courses?

ProfW wrote the following instruction in the course schedule for this week: "You need to allot the appropriate time for this project. With this week's schedule, I'm basically giving you the equivalent of a class period to meet and talk about your project, with the expectation that you'll also do some group-related 'homework.'" Until this point, I felt like everything I contributed to the course *was* homework. The quizzes were homework. The Discussions were homework. The readings, responses, peeps, papers—all of it was homework. Because of that mindset, I thought at times, "God. If I had known how much was expected out of me, maybe I should have transferred to an f2f course a long time ago. The luxury of working from home isn't worth all the effort."

However, because of that grievance, I stumbled upon a critical understanding of the online course's structure. I was *working from home*, which was different from *homework*. Much of my online work was simply a displacement of course meeting time. Instead of meeting in class two days a week, we were meeting online for a total "two days" per week; those days were simply divided into multiple online appearances throughout the week, ranging in duration depending on each participant's schedule and responsibilities. Just like any f2f course, we were expected to do additional assignments on top of classroom participation, and because the online class merged these two activities into one space, everything felt like homework.

With this week's realization, I could now clearly designate aspects of the course that should be perceived as "classwork," while others must be treated as additional assignments. How would this affect productivity throughout the week? Well, I didn't know yet. However, I did know it would greatly affect my attitude toward and motivation for the course and ProfW. Requiring more writing than other courses wasn't ProfW's evil agenda to make us write thousands of words a week. Conversations about course content needed to happen one way or another, so they were performed through Discussion boards. While these posts *were* graded and could therefore be perceived as mini essays, discussions in an f2f class can also be graded as "participation" or "attendance." The purpose behind graded discussion, at least from my perspective, is to promote intelligent conversation about the course material.

If anything, moving classwork discussion to a written, online format created a more structured, inclusive classroom dialogue. Everyone had a chance to speak, everyone received a response, and everyone was responsible for contributing something *new*. Gone was the opportunity for classroom loudmouths to monopolize conversation. No longer did shy students fear speaking out loud, and rarely would a professor's question be answered by awkward silence. Once I no longer perceived classroom discussions as laborious homework assignments, my opinion on the course's workload shifted dramatically.

Scott: Group Norming—and Some Ongoing "Storming"?

The group project, both in our course and the FYW core syllabus, worked synergistically with rhetorical objectives. Students would be developing collaboration skills, collaborative writing specifically, while also achieving rhetorical writing goals, especially problem-solving:

Week 6: February 12 to February 18

The focus this week is on an annotated bibliography for Project 2 and some discussion about writing to solve problems. You'll have time to keep cranking in your groups.

What do I do?	What are the specific instructions? Where do I find the work or the assignment?	When is it due? (All times EST)
GROUP WORK	Your **group goals** for this week: • This week, your group should **create an annotated bibliography** for your project, with a minimum of **eight sources.** The sources should cover the range of evidence requirements, indicating at least some idea of how you will generate *primary research*, the kind of *scholarly evidence* you will use, and a *visual.* • One member of your group should submit your **second minutes/progress report** at the end of the week. You need to allot the appropriate time for this project. With this week's schedule, I'm basically giving you the equivalent of a class period to meet and talk about your project, with the expectation that you'll also do some group-related "homework." If your group contribution has been a five-minute peek at the boards, that ain't gonna cut it. You may need to take out a timer and set it to 80 minutes. Get to work on some aspect of Project 2. When 80 minutes have elapsed, you can stop.	The annotated bibliography and minutes/progress report are due by the **weekend**.
READ	Read the following: • *Course textbook:* Chap. 11, "Writing to Solve Problems" 47 pages. • *Aux*: Atkins, "Collaborating Online" 14 pages. • *33rd*: George, "The Ethics of Medical Involvement" 99-108.	You'll want to have read by **Tuesday,** February 14 so you can complete the quiz and work on the Discussions.

← The introduction this week was again succinct.

← The focus was on group goals. Again, there was redundancy in the instructions, as these goals were mentioned in the course announcements and in the assignment itself.

← I mentioned "homework" here and we discuss this concept throughout this chapter.

← The readings this week focused on collaboration too.

TAKE a QUIZ	Quiz 6 can be found in the "Quizzes" folder.	The quiz will be available **Tuesday** from 9:30 am to midnight.
WRITE and READ	Read all the Discussion topics for Week 6: • Post ONE primary post to any of the Discussion topics. • Post TWO secondary posts. Also note that there is a separate 10-point assignment on the Discussions: the "To be" assignment.	Post your primary post by **Wednesday** night, February 15. Post your secondary posts and the "To be" assignment by **Friday,** February 17, at 4:00 pm.
MODERATE	This week our moderators will be Artan and Karen.	--

← I created posting requirements with the idea that one full "day" of the week would be spent on the group project.

I again pushed the groups to create minutes and clear action items. My philosophy of teaching group work in online settings is inflected by many approaches, including my own onsite pedagogy. I try to think of how time would be spent in my onsite courses, where I don't give students unstructured, "unmediated" team projects; I have compared such work to a lazy gym teacher rolling out the balls and then sitting on a stool for the class period watching kids run around. To further help them, I provided an overt comparison to the time they might spend in an onsite environment. We would have devoted one class to the group project, about eighty minutes. Less than that, "ain't gonna cut it," I said. Much as I do for teachers, I suggested that students use an actual timer to help them dedicate the proper amount of time.

Group Progress and Annotated Bibliography Work

I posted this announcement on Monday:

Announcements for Monday, February 13:

- We need to shift into high gear with the **group project**. Three of the four teams are off to a good start, but I need your week five responsibilities completed so you can get to work on the **annotated bibliography** this week.
- Your **Discussions** and **grades** will be up today.

The primary assignment this week for the team was an eight-source annotated bibliography. Teams were free to break up the work any way they saw fit. The groups were progressing:

- **Group 1.** Diana describes Group 1's progress below.
- **Group 2.** Group 2 was very active on their group Discussion all week. On Sunday going into Week 7, Lisa posted this:

> **Author**: Lisa　　**Topic**: Project 2 Group 2
> **Subject**: Minutes Week 6　　**Date**: February 26, 10:52 PM
>
> What we accomplished this week:
>
> 1. Each member wrote his or her assigned part of the rough draft.
> 2. Our group decided on using a survey as our primary research. Alan gave great questions that we will most likely be using in our survey.
> 3. Our group is in the process of deciding a time to meet with ProfW. It seems like a group vote that our meeting time will be through Wimba on Tuesday night.
>
> To do for next week:
>
> 1. Work on the rough draft. Our group needs to really work on this draft to make it more cohesive, add more sources, add primary research, add a visual, etc.
> 2. When our group meets with ProfW next week, we need to figure-out how we will go about the revision process.
>
> Reply

← She said exactly what each team member had done.

← Their to dos were clear, as was the date of their next meeting.

← They were going to meet me.

My response was simple: "Good work, Group 2," as I made sure to give them a touch of positive feedback.

- **Group 3.** This group was efficient and effective in doing their work this week, including compiling the annotated bibliography. I provided them with a little "boost" post mid-week, and on Sunday Alexa had posted a good summary of the week's work.
- **Group 4.** Group 4 did get materials posted, but not until Tuesday of Week 7. In a troubling issue, one member was not participating at all.

Diana: Divide and Conquer

I had a very light coursework load this week in many of my other classes (a rarity in Week 6 at my university!) so I had plenty of time to dedicate to this class and our group work. I had several friends who were in the same majors as Susannah, Artan, and Aaron, so I knew they probably had a lot on their plates with assignments in other courses. I let everyone in my group know that I had plenty of time this week, so if they didn't mind I could take the reins. I opened ProfW's Weekly Plan to map out not only my duties but help guide my group members' responsibilities as well.

For our project, we agreed to address the flaws in our university's dining plan and propose a solution for different meal "currency." It was a relatable topic for all of us, considering we were all first-year on-campus students, so I knew the material would come easy to everyone. However, I also knew my group members weren't in writing-intensive majors (Aaron said just last week, "I was really doubtful about my essay, thinking that I'd definitely fail it") so I proposed a solution. If they found eight sources between the three of them and gave them to me by Thursday, I would read the sources and write the annotations. I felt this was a fair division of labor because sometimes the hardest and longest part of the research process is finding the actual research. If I gave them that responsibility and then summarized the sources, we would probably be contributing the same amount of time and work toward the process. At this point, we agreed to create a group message on Facebook to quickly discuss things about the project, so I shot everyone a message telling them my plan. Each member got back to me within the hour (a much better turnaround time than our LMS discussions) and said it was fine by them.

While we didn't meet during a "class time" as ProfW suggested in the Weekly Plan to decide all of this, we were on track with a group schedule by Monday night. On Tuesday afternoon, all my group members responded supporting the

Behind the Screen: Researching Online

Digital tools have changed the way we do, well, almost everything, so of course teachers have had opportunities to rethink how they instruct students in the crucial task of conducting research. As Alison Head and Michael Eisenberg wrote in the foreword to *The New Digital Scholar* (McClure and Purdy), "Many instructors are increasingly disheartened by the sense that they are losing pedagogical traction when it comes to teaching NextGen students how to conduct research and how to write" (xii); this collection offers teachers a variety of approaches to address, as Head and Eisenberg continue, "one of the most difficult pedagogical challenges of our time" (xiii). For instance, Mary Lourdes Silva, in her chapter "Can I Google That?," provides concrete suggestions such as giving students help "with generating keywords" and "understanding the limitations of information databases and search engines" (179). Written for students, Randall McClure's "Googlepedia: Turning Information Behaviors into Research Skills" provides similar guidelines and advice.

Digital research tools offer great promise and online modalities place students in environments where such research can be normalized. It is worth remembering that old research habits, what Rolf Norgaard calls "ghosts" of traditional instruction models, may die hard—and not just for teachers. Indeed, Melissa Bowles-Terry, Erin Davis, and Wendy Holliday said students may resist teachers' efforts at information literacy because the "instructional practice was haunted by ghosts of traditional Pedagogy" (228).

idea. By Thursday evening (real evening, not "college student" evening, which falls around 2:00 a.m.) I received all eight sources. I easily wrote the annotations by the weekend.

As we finished this first pass of group work, I realized how risky it was to limit our group work to the online classroom. We were all lucky that everyone actively checked to see if there was new material in our group thread, especially early in the week, but there was no way of receiving notifications when a post was made on the course LMS. We were on to something when we planned to create a little discussion thread on Facebook, but we needed to move the rest of our material to a better shared space. After exchanging sources and annotations over email, Facebook, and our classroom LMS, we decided that working on one specific cloud space would be the best way to communicate for the rest of the project. We settled on having everything—our bibliography, paper, images, conversations—in Google Drive. That way, everyone would be notified of group work instantly (considering we all checked our email on our phones or laptops) as opposed to relying on the sheer will of someone to log in and monitor updates on the classroom LMS. I checked with ProfW to see if this was all right since he wouldn't be able to monitor our discussions, and he gave us the go-ahead, even admitting our classroom LMS wasn't the perfect space for collaboration.

Scott: Homework and [Class]work

This week's reading and informal writing work should have looked familiar to students: We were in the groove. I only used three prompts, and one was a meta-assignment centered on the verb "to be." Two thus-far diligent students, Artan and Karen, had signed up to moderate.

Thread: Discussing Proposals

As a class, the students continued to impress me with their work ethic and writing ability, and it was important to let them know that. This week's first open-ended prompt was not only course text-driven but also asked them to write to learn about content; I asked them to think about proposals we had read in our course text—while gesturing (again) in a positive way overall:

Author: Scott Warnock **Topic**: Proposals we read this
Subject: Proposals we read **Date**: February 13, 4:02 PM

Dear students,

As the course text points out, "Writing to solve problems is prevalent in all areas of your life" (362).

Let's look at some of the proposals/solution approaches you read this week in the course textbook and *The 33rd*. Think about specific aspects of how these proposals work. For instance, what organizational approach do they take (see p. 386)? What kind of rhetorical approach do they take (in particular, is Ellsworth "invitational")? How do they address audience? How do they establish audience? How viable is the solution that is advanced?

Perhaps we could again start a separate thread for the different readings.

One thing that I like that you've done this term is to critique our readings. As you've probably noticed, they are not all prime examples of great essays; they have their flaws. I like your confidence in noting the good but also pointing out the flaws in our readings.

Looking forward to your responses,
Prof. Warnock

Reply

← We worked directly from the course text.

← . . . and, again, the texts provide numerous good examples that also gave students some posting choices.

← I complimented them specifically about the work they have been doing.

It was interesting to see how dialogue-based writing was taking place in a thread where I overtly encouraged students to create subthreads. In Figure 3 you can see a representation of how this dialogue evolved, particularly the subthread "Failing Our Ancient Rhetoricians." Again, the student's name is followed by a postword count:

Thread: Further Thinking about Collaboration

The pacing of the class had become familiar: I would often ask students to read a more complex article than perhaps they were used to and discuss it on the boards. This week, they read Atkins's piece on collaboration, and Karen moderated that thread, which I started like this:

Author: Scott Warnock **Topic**: Atkins on collaboration
Subject: Atkins on collaboration **Date**: February 13, 4:05 PM

Hi everyone,

So we've got ourselves off and running (or stumbling) on the group projects. Was there anything in Atkins' article that you could find directly applicable to what you are going to do? What are some technologies you might use to help you have success with your group? Are there any specific tools to help you

← Again, a prompt can get students into a reading and then connect them with their actual work in the course.

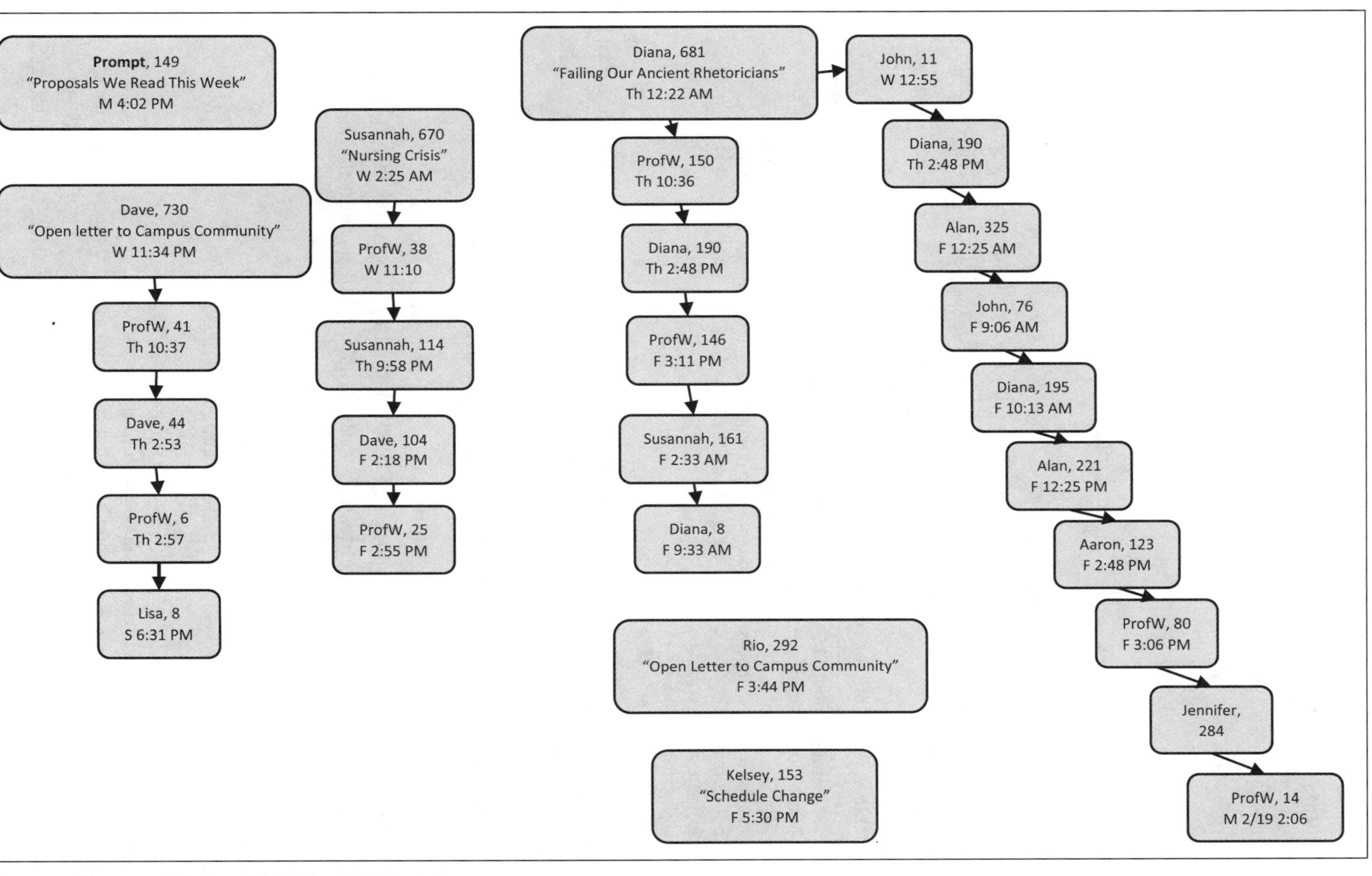

Figure 3. "Proposal We Read This Week" in Week 6.

with drafting/editing your project? How does Atkins say technologies might help you keep other group members accountable? I will ask you to present your final products to the class in some way: Did this article give you some ideas in that area?

Let's talk it over,
ProfW

Reply

As I said in the other reading-based thread this week, this thread had a lot of dialogue, spurred on by good moderation by Karen. To provide yet another perspective about the kind of work students were doing, Table 1 provides a numerical representation of the posting work in this thread.

Table 1. Post Totals for Collaboration Thread

Total student posts: 35	**Total # of moderator posts: 9**	**Total # of instructor posts: 8**
Total student participants: 14 Average number of posts per student: 2.6 Average word count: 284 Highest word count: 445 Lowest word count: 21 Total words: 5,773	Average word count: 137 Highest word count: 225 Lowest word count: 2 Total words: 697	Average word count: 57 Highest word count: 104 Lowest word count: 13 Total words: 489
Total posts: 52		

Thread: Metawork with That Troublesome Little Verb

Again, metawriting opportunities are a major part of why I believe OWI and writing studies coalesce so nicely: The students have a vast corpus of their own informal writing to mine and work with. This week, I wanted them to explore their use of verbs:

Author: Scott Warnock **Topic**: Not "to be"
Subject: Not "to be" **Date**: February 13, 4:53 PM

Hi all,

This is a separate, 10-point exercise from the other Discussions this week (although if you comment on someone else's submission, that can count as a secondary post). Please submit your "assignment" here, preferably as an attachment that you worked up using Track Changes.

← It was easy to have students participate: I required it and gave a low-stakes grade.

The verb "to be" is the most commonly used verb in English. You know the verb forms: am, is, are, was, were, be, being, been. Now, there's nothing wrong with the verb "to be" in small doses, but since verbs are the engines of your sentences, you can often make your writing stronger and clearer by choosing stronger verbs.

The assignment: Choose a few paragraphs (about 250 words) of something you have written in this course—a piece of Project 1, a post, anything—and, using Track Changes if possible, go through that document, removing the verb "to be" wherever you find it and replacing it or removing it (which sometimes might involve some rewording).

This could be an eye-opening experience, as this little verb lurks everywhere (including five times in this post!).

Take care,
Prof. Warnock

Reply

← "How do you *teach* grammar and mechanics?", writing teachers are often asked: I believe in having students work (really, play) with their own texts.

← Assignment instructions were clear and short—with a little playfulness myself at the end.

Artan took on the challenge of moderating this thread, and the students generally posted attachments (in message boards with very good WYSIWYG editors, these posts could simply be directly in the threads—our LMS was not great in that way).

As often happens, students struggled mightily to even identify these verbs—they do hide in plain sight—and they ended up engaging in some unsure hypercorrecting, while often reintroducing other forms of the verb *to be*. Their posts provided many interesting teaching moments that allowed us to discuss conventions of grammar. Some of their comments:

- Aaron asked, "Surprisingly, I looked through about a dozen of my responses and didn't see to be all that much. Is that a good thing or a bad thing?" As it turned out, he missed many of them, but I wanted to reinforce that "It's not a bad thing, as I said, but you can often use stronger verbs."
- Deryck: "A lot harder than expected."
- Katie: "This assignment proved to be very difficult. At times, I realized I had to completely rearrange an entire sentence just because the verb form was holding the sentence together."
- Nate: "I found that my first paragraph had many more uses of these verbs. I also thought it funny because I can speak a bit of German and the language rarely uses these verbs."

- Rio: "This exercise was harder than I thought it was going to be."
- Alexa: "Definitely eye-opening."

Artan contributed this moderating post on Wednesday, obviously feeling some confidence:

> **Author**: Artan   **Topic**: Not "to be"
> **Subject**: Ways to change "to be"   **Date**: February 16, 10:52 AM
>
> Hey guys,
>
> So the most effective ways of removing the "to be" verbs are:
>
> 1. Substituting the verb with another verb.
> 2. Rearranging the sentence differently.
> 3. Changing another word in your sentence into a verb.
> 4. Combining sentences.
>
> These being said, I would like to see you guys to start using these methods at least once to replace the "to be" verbs. This is optional, but I think by following these steps at least once each time can make it really effective.
>
> Thanks,
> Artan
>
> Reply

I replied, in the spirit of language play: "Nice job, Artan. I am enjoying your moderation of this thread, or should I say, 'I find your moderation of this thread enjoyable.'"

Diana: Thrown Together Randomly

My group members and I were working alongside one another perfectly, having been paired without a choice. In high school, having control in your group was a life-or-death scenario. Regardless of how large the high school was, chances are most students were aware of one another's strengths and weakness after attending multiple classes with their peers and being able to observe them over a period of months or years. Therefore, if a teacher gave students the chance to pick their partners, they better jump on that opportunity to avoid working with the prima donna who always turns the project into her latest theatrical production or the burnout who forgets what class he's in every other hour. In college, however, it's unlikely that classmates have met before, nor is it likely they will have class with one another again. Everyone is entering the classroom unaware of each other's true talents and faults, so partner selection becomes less critical to group achievement. With that being said, picking up on "good student behavior" is still easy, even if students only see each other three times a week for half of a semester. The know-it-all who talks over everyone else or the bum who always shows up late naturally stand out in the classroom, so it's likely most students would want to avoid working with a select few peers if they have the choice.

Even if I were to pick my partners based on their Discussion performance, how was I supposed to know if they were a cooperative team player, or even a normal human being? In an f2f class, ideal group member traits can be observed in how a student listens to others, interacts with the professor, or contributes to class conversation. Online, all I could go by were the Discussions (and the only thing I knew for sure about potential teammates is that John hated collaboration, so that might have been rough if I was paired with him). Nevertheless, even if I had a choice, it would be easier to simply let the professor pick the groups randomly (or on purpose, for all I knew).

So here we were, grouped without a choice, and we were working together wonderfully. Maybe it was because there were only four of us, so it was easy for everyone to be held accountable. Maybe it was because we all communicated well and stayed in touch easily. Or maybe it was pure luck! Needless to say, it was pretty cool realizing I had never met my group members f2f, nor did I have a significant online relationship with them, and we were collaborating perfectly. Moving forward, I knew I could rely on my group members and trust that we would complete the project successfully.

Scott: Some Grade Questions

Toward the end of the week, Jennifer sent me a pair of emails about grades. First, she said, "I was just looking at my grades and wondering why in Week 4 I got 28/40 points." Not long after, she wrote the email below as well, to which I responded:

From: Jennifer
Sent: Friday, February 17 11:14 AM
To: Scott Warnock
Subject: Engl 102

In addition to my last email, I was wondering if there's anyway that I could possibly re-do my project 1 paper in any way to gain more points back. I know that it may be unorthodox, but I know in some of my other classes if we redo our papers or do some sort of extra credit we can gain points back on them. I really want to do well in the class and I was just wondering if there's anyway that I could do anything because I lost a lot of points on that assignment. I could meet with you to go over it or redo it someway and go over it with you or anything. If anything at all possible let me know, thanks.

> **From**: Warnock, Scott
> **Date:** Friday, February 17 1:24 PM
> **To:** Jennifer
> **Subject**: RE: Engl 102
>
> Hi Jennifer,
>
> Good to hear from you; I put both of your emails together below.
>
> In week 4, I do not have you as having completed a secondary post. If you did, please tell me where it is, and I'll update your grade. That week you also received, as did the whole class, 8/10 for the citation exercise thread; 8/10 for your primary post; and 12/15 for your draft work based on our workshop.
>
> Unfortunately, you cannot re-do Project 1. I'm more than happy to go over it with you, but at some point in the course we need a final grade so we can move on. Note that there are 1,000 points in the course, so you have many opportunities to improve your grade, and I'm available to discuss this with you as well.
>
> I hope this helps, even if it's not exactly the news you were looking for,
> ProfW

I no doubt disappointed her in response to the Project 1 question. Others may grade differently and be surprised by my approach, but you can see I couched my response in the context of the overall FLS grading in the course.

In Retrospect: Homework and Group Projects

For students and teachers, the issue of time in an OWC is in some way a question of what is the nature of homework in online learning. You could probably start addressing that question by acknowledging there is no standard of homework in higher education. Students will be the first to say that expectations of homework vary wildly from course to course. Online, teachers might get a sense of homework if they reverse engineer their teaching in line with the "migration" approach that Scott discussed in *Teaching Writing Online*. Such an approach allows a teacher who has taught a course that is moving online to rely on experience in determining how much time students should be spending on work, avoiding making courses too time-consuming or far below the mark in terms of rigor.

A group project puts the issue of homework under increased focus. Group projects place students in various learning situations, some constructively frustrating, others just frustrating. Onsite, teachers can create structure by providing students in-class time to work as groups, particularly in courses where learning the dynamics/process of teamwork is part of course learning objectives, as it was in ours. (In capstone and other advanced courses, teachers may assume students have "learned" how to work in teams and so evaluate work based on content/product.)

All these things considered, it was evident in Week 6 that the groups were not operating at the same pace. It is difficult to know exactly why, but in a limited, short-term project such as the one in our class, perhaps it is enough to have one hard-charging, dedicated student on your team. But for teachers, certainly creating a clear-cut set of criteria and expectations can help students stay on track. However, the downside is that the more scaffolding you put in place, the more frustrating it is when one or two teams stumble along when other teams, randomly assembled, are making the project work. But that is a key teaching challenge: figuring out how to help students at different levels succeed. Making it clear and overt that they need to conceive of some of the time they devote to a class as *homework* may be a big factor in helping them.

7

Week 7: Reading and the Literacy Load

At the college level where the traditional classroom approach to learning is disrupted by digital tools, we need to pay more—not less—attention to basics like reading.

—Beth Hewett, *Reading to Learn and Writing to Teach: Literacy Strategies for Online Writing Instruction*

Scott: Group Drafts on Their Way

We were creeping out of winter in the Northeast. I was handling the dynamic of group writing in much the same way that I handled individual writing projects, focusing on process and revision. Interestingly, the group "norming" seemed to mirror the way the class as a whole had come together in a conversational community. The Weekly Plan elaborated on group requirements:

Week 7: February 19 to February 25

This week I'd like to see a draft of Project 2 and set up a meeting with some or all of your group.

What do I do?	**What are the specific instructions? Where do I find the work or the assignment?**	**When is it due? (All times EST)**
GROUP WORK	Your **group tasks** for this week: • This week, your group should **create the first draft** for Project 2. The draft need not be perfect or complete, but it should be developed enough to get feedback and contain a minimum of **eight sources;** the sources should cover the range of evidence requirements, indicating at least some idea of how you will generate *primary research*,	The rough draft should be together and posted on your group thread by **Thursday,** February 23. The minutes/progress report are due by the **weekend**.

← Again, I used the space at the top to help reinforce that week's focus.

← The group instructions were explicit, including what a draft should include.

	the kind of *scholarly evidence* you will incorporate, and a *visual.* • One member of your group should submit your **third minutes/progress report** at the end of the week. • Set up a **half-hour meeting** with me to discuss the rough draft; I'd like to meet your entire group face-to-face, but that may not be logistically possible, so I'll meet representatives if that's the best we can do, and we could use the class online meeting space. Probably the best way to set this meeting up is for you to figure out schedules on the group Discussions. I am flexible, but here are some times I will be available to get you started: • Friday, February 24 from 9 to 11. • Friday, February 24 from 1:30 to 4:30. • Tuesday, February 28 from 9 to 12. • Tuesday, February 28 from 1 to 4:30. • Wednesday, February 29 from 9 to 3. If nothing works, let me know, and we'll see about facilitating a meeting at a different time.	
READ and WATCH	Read the following: • *Aux*: Trimbur, "Consensus and Difference" 14 pages. • Watch: "Howard Rheingold: The New Power of Collaboration" TED Talk. 19 minutes.	You'll want to have read and watched by **Tuesday,** February 21 so you can complete the quiz and work on the Discussions.
TAKE a QUIZ	Quiz 7 can be found you know where.	The quiz will be available **Tuesday** from 9:30 am to midnight. You will have five minutes to complete it.
WRITE and EVALUATE	As a 10-point assignment, please **email** me a brief, informal evaluation of the contributions of your teammates. *These evaluations will be between you and me only*, although, as appropriate, if a number of people in the	Please email me at sjwarnock@drexel.edu by the end of the **weekend**.

← I wanted to meet with them in whatever way was most convenient. I gave them some suggestions on how to organize a meeting . . .

← . . . and I tried to be flexible. All the meetings ended up taking place in Week 8.

← Writing about Writing–style, they read an article by John Trimbur about consensus in collaborative learning. They also watched a TED Talk about collaboration.

← I hoped the *pacing* (see Guideline 35 of *Teaching Writing Online*) of the course would be well established at this point.

← I provided them with an opportunity to evaluate each other's contributions to the team this week as another way

	group have an issue with one person, I will follow up. First, I want you to allot a total of 100 points to the four members of the group including yourself, based on contributions. Does everyone get 25? Does one person get more or less? Then, please address the following questions for each person: What does this person contribute to the team? Has the person done his/her fair share? Is the person prompt in responding to posts? Does the person go above and beyond in any way? Would you like to be on a team with this person again?		to help me understand how well each group was functioning.
WRITE and READ	Read all the Discussion topics for Week 7: • Post ONE primary post. • Post TWO secondary posts.	Post your primary post by **Wednesday** night, February 22. Post your secondary posts by **Friday,** February 24, at 4:00 pm.	← The amount of Discussion work was again determined based on the understanding that one full day of *class time* would have been spent on group work.
MODERATE	This week our moderators will be Susannah and Aaron.	--	

Thursday was the group draft deadline, and I asked that the next minutes/progress reports be posted by the weekend. In the draft, I pushed them to use evidence and sources. I also wanted to set up meetings with the groups (and reminded them of this in a homepage announcement). I knew it might be challenging to get them all together, and maybe impossible onsite, so I took the pressure off by simply indicating I knew it might not be "logistically possible." This may seem like a small thing, and perhaps it is, but I have found that many students—as I've mentioned throughout—can be anxious about forgetting something. I feel bad when students write a lengthy apology about missing a post when the problem is *that I have failed to post the prompt*. Effective Practice 3.1 in the OWI *Position Statement* says teachers "should use written language that is readable and comprehensible" (Conference 12), and I think teachers should use a clear writing voice to encourage students and reassure them that, well, everything is going be okay. Students must *read* most of our instructions in an OWC, so we have to be especially mindful of the language that represents our teaching—and our very selves.

Diana: How to Write One Essay with Four Writers?

Distributing the responsibilities as I did in the previous weeks for our project, I created a way for my groupmates to provide helpful content while not feeling overloaded with writing, since that happened to be their weakness and my strength. I asked everyone if they would be okay reading through each of the sources on their own, then providing thorough summaries of the most important points from each source in relation to our topic. After they did so, they would organize the information they found in the outline we discussed, designed, and agreed upon. This way, my group members didn't have to worry about perfect writing, but they were still contributing greatly to the content and ideas behind the paper (each member wrote approximately four thousand words of content). Plus, everyone would have read the sources and have a good understanding of the direction of a paper. After my group members completed their summaries and organization of material, I would synthesize the material into a cohesive first draft.

Even though I would be doing significant work writing the clean first draft, I was shar-

Behind the Screen: Reading in OWCs

The titles will likely look familiar: in the *ChronicleVitae*, David Gooblar's "They Haven't Done the Reading. Again"; John Warner wrote in *Inside Higher Ed*, "When Students Won't Do the Reading"; Keith Parsons said in the *Huffington Post*, "When Students Won't Read." Faculty are perplexed as to how to encourage their *college students* to read the material for their courses. Think about OWI in this context. In an asynchronous, text-driven OWC, the students are faced with an enormous amount of reading, a huge literacy load. This is a good thing and, in fact, an advantage to teaching writing in this way: To function in the class in any way they must read.

You might make this increased literacy expectation explicit to students. If you are seeking some quantifiable evidence, June Griffin and Deb Minter showed there is a measurably higher reading load for OWI teachers, especially in asynchronous-type courses, and the overall literacy load is heavier for both teachers and students compared to onsite teaching. Of course, this makes sense when you consider that the fundamental conversations of the course happen in writing. A superb book (from which the epigraph of this chapter is taken) about this topic is Beth Hewett's *Reading to Learn and Writing to Teach: Literacy Strategies for Online Writing Instruction*. It contains strategies for teachers but also general perspectives to help students think about these literate, electronic environments. Hewett's work complements what the OWI Position Statement makes explicit: "Furthermore, given that OWI typically is a text-intensive medium where reading is a necessary skill, addressing the accessibility needs of the least confident readers increases the potential to reach all types of learners" (Conference 7).

ing half of the writing process with my peers. While I didn't doubt that they were contributing their fair share, I wondered—could I write a proper essay if *I* haven't thoroughly read our sources? I was reading my members' summaries of the sources and briefly skimmed our references to make sure everyone was on track, but I was relying on my group members to pull out the most relevant and interesting information. Even though each of my group members was providing summaries for all sources so accuracy could be accounted for, would I still have a thorough understanding of what the sources offered our topic? My group members would be able to provide insight on this, but I'd have to wait until I finished the first draft. I also wondered if I'd get in trouble if ProfW found out this was how we constructed the paper. I figured I'd run it by him at our meeting the following week.

Scott: New Reading Challenges on the Discussions

The students were *studying/studenting* collaboration, reading and thinking about how to collaborate while engaging in that very activity. This week I did introduce students to several different variations of Discussion threads, so I'll go into some detail in describing the action on the threads.

Thread: Summarizing a Challenging Reading

Getting students to read course texts is a widespread teaching challenge that some believe may even be worsening with the distractions of the digital world (see this week's "Behind the Screen"). As mentioned, I have used quizzing as a constructive way to encourage students to read assigned texts, but if they are participating in an OWC at all, they are also reading thousands of words each week, building their reading "muscles." I take on the reading challenge straightforwardly with many WaW readings, but I keep in mind that I am still also teaching them how to read well too. The group summary is a specific Discussion thread that combines several prompt types to help students work on reading and summarizing: conversations about a text, work on an aspect of writing, write-to-learn, and develop community:

Author: Scott Warnock **Topic**: Summarizing Trimbur
Subject: Summarizing Trimbur **Date**: February 20, 3:37 PM

Dear students,

Everyone must post to this thread. There are 15 pages, so, with a moderator, it works out perfectly (one person will finish here with the Works Cited page).

← A lot was happening in this prompt.

Last term you should have developed and honed your ability to summarize. Let's use those skills to collectively summarize the Trimbur piece. Our goal as a class is to summarize the entire article, so everyone will have to contribute here. Each person will summarize ONE page; you will want to pick up from the previous page/summarizer, especially if your page starts in the middle of a paragraph.

The first person who posts here should tackle the first page, perhaps using the "does-says" approach to summarizing (what does your page DO in the article—helps build the writer's ethos, etc.—and then, what does it SAY).

Each subsequent poster will then tackle the next page. Make it crystal clear which page you are summarizing; you may want to post and declare your page so people don't end up working on the same pages. Also, you should BUILD from previous posts when appropriate.

Don't forget to quote (and cite) Trimbur when appropriate,
Prof. Warnock

Reply

← Trimbur was logistically perfect: His fifteen-page article + works cited lined up with the sixteen active students in the course.

← This was a required thread.

← I gave them a summarizing strategy, "does-says," and connected that to approaches they should have learned last term.

In a thread like this, I have them work on the literacy load by building a chain of summaries. For those who scoff at the writing of mere summaries, note that in my work in the Drexel Writing Center, a recurring issue we have even with graduate students who visit us is that they have difficulty composing a good summary. Summarizing is not as easy as it sounds. Of course, this thread also helped them work together—the thread served a variety of course objectives. Could they just read their part/page and the parts/pages around it? Yes, they could, but they had some responsibility to each other and themselves as well. This thread was an opportunity for me to *encourage* students to interact closely with their texts. There was no guarantee of "eyes on page" (is there ever?!), but these students took on this prompt with considerable vigor; the logistics of this thread were different from others this term, so I myself will summarize here in some detail:

- Diana jumped in, posting Monday only two hours after my prompt with a 420-word summary of page one. She described Trimbur's overall purpose and even used some rhetorical basis for her summary, discussing the *logos* of his argument. This post was fortunate, because, as in any thread, having a few good students get the ball rolling prevents mishaps down the line; if I had a weak summary Monday night, the possibility increased that other students would have followed suit before I could right things Tuesday morning.

- Four hours later, Lisa took on page two. The top of that page introduced some tough terms and concepts, and I responded to her summary by asking, "You're clear on all of the terms and concepts?"
- Just after midnight on Tuesday, Aaron stepped in as moderator. He wrote:

Author: Aaron | **Topic**: Summarizing Trimbur
Subject: Moderator | **Date**: February 21, 12:11 AM

Hi guys, just wanted to let you know that I'll be moderating this topic. Diana posted page 1 as a response to ProfW's post, to solve your possible confusion.

When you're about to begin writing your summary, it may help to make the new topic first, saying that you'll be doing a specific page. This way, people who log on to do a page aren't writing a page you're currently working on.

I'm looking forward to working with everyone this week.
~Aaron

Reply

← Aaron did what I kept hoping moderators would do: take over a thread.

I complimented him, saying, "Great job jumping in here as organizer." Although what Diana did was fine, Aaron had suggested an alternative organizing strategy, so Diana, being a good team player, responded with "Shoot, sorry. I'll repost it to the main thread," which she did. In the middle of the week, Aaron also emailed me for advice about moderating this somewhat unusual thread:

From: Aaron
Sent: Wednesday, February 22 10:47 PM
To: Scott Warnock
Subject: RE: English 102: Moderators for week 7

Hey Prof. Warnock,
I was wondering if you could give me some tips on how to get discussion going in the Trimbur post. It's basically just summaries so the first thing I thought was organization, but I want to get an actual discussion going and I'm not sure how.
Thanks,
Aaron

From: Scott Warnock
Sent: Thursday, February 23 9:24 AM

To: Aaron
Subject: RE: English 102: Moderators for week 7

Hi Aaron,
Thanks for writing to me about this.

You've already done a good job interacting with your classmates, such as your dialogue with Alexa. By the way, you've gone above and beyond, as the moderator did not have to summarize a page, but you already did that!

This is a tough article, of course, so you could do a couple other things. One is to make sure that the summary each student submits is accurate. You can do this without being overly critical, perhaps making sure that terms and concepts are clear (see, for instance, Rio's question about the article in "Questions about the course"). You can also check to make sure about the quality of the summaries, even things like the proper citation, are in line. Also, since we're only up to page six, you can also nudge people to get moving with commitments.

Basically, you're doing a great job here,
ProfW

- Alexa "claimed" page eleven in a short post at 11:00 p.m. Tuesday night, prompting a conversation between her and Aaron about how to "claim" a page on the boards and where the threads should go. They were basically self-organizing the thread.
- Tuesday night around 7:00 p.m., Aaron himself summarized page three.
- Over the next few days, students posted short posts "claiming" pages, and then they followed up with 200- to 400-word summaries of those pages. In those summaries were many moments of writerly and readerly excellence, and they were citing and quoting the article liberally and appropriately.
- Susannah, in "Page Eight of Trimbur Summarization," described in some detail how Trimbur was referring to theorist Kenneth Bruffee's ideas of "struggle." Her post spurred a brief exchange among her, Donald, and me.
- John and Aaron, working from Susannah's post, carried a conversation through Saturday about "struggle" in school group projects.

- With Aaron's prompting, the summaries continued throughout the week, and all but one page ended up being summarized. Aaron used a pleasant bit of encouragement on Saturday afternoon to call out that one student:

> **Author**: Aaron — **Topic**: Summarizing Trimbur
> **Subject**: Page Fourteen — **Date**: February 25, 2:47 PM
>
> Hey guys,
>
> Everyone's doing a really good job with your summaries, but we still need page 14 (I can't check from here, but I'm pretty sure 15 is just the work cited). Anyone who hasn't done a page yet needs to get on top of it.
>
> Thanks for your cooperation everyone :)
>
> Reply

As I mentioned, the summaries were often great, as students made a strong effort to interpret a reading that was not easy for them. The following Monday, I posted this:

> **Author**: Scott Warnock — **Topic**: Summarizing Trimbur
> **Subject**: Summaries — **Date**: February 27, 10:00 AM
>
> Folks,
>
> There are numerous impressive aspects to what you did here.
>
> Your summaries are good, sometimes great. Interestingly, you operated in a collaborative way to summarize a tough (some might argue overly tough) reading. You came together in a virtual space, imposed order through your posts and the strong work of our moderator, and systematically handled the task.
>
> Really well done,
> ProfW
>
> Reply

This is something I have said multiple times: In OWI when the students do well, you can't just let it sit; you should write your thoughts to them directly. I also wanted to encourage them in terms of the specific reading; they might have found it challenging, but collectively they did a good job understanding it—and sharing their understanding.

As we moved into Week 8, the only person who didn't post sent me an email, which I responded to in the hope that he would finish up Trimbur for us:

From: Ethan
Sent: Sunday, February 26 10:32 PM
To: Scott Warnock
Subject: Trimbur Article? (Discussion post)

For the Trimbur article this week. My computer was glitching for some reason because when i looked at the discussion the class had only gotten up to page 5. So i did page six, then when i went to go upload it, it refreshed and then i saw that everyone had done them all. And page 15 is just the works cited. What should I do here?
-Ethan

> **From**: Scott Warnock
> **Sent**: Monday, February 27 9:57 AM
> **To**: Ethan
> **Subject**: RE: Trimbur Article? (Discussion post)
>
> Hi Ethan,
> As I said in the directions, I was hoping someone would summarize the Works Cited as part of these summaries: What's on there? Why? How does it help build the article?
> Thanks,
> ProfW

Alas, while a placeholder post appeared from Ethan, we never did get that final post up.

Thread: Modeling: Putting My Writing, Myself, Out There

The writing play that an OWC offers can be one of the most enjoyable and educationally stimulating parts of the course. This week, I went all-in with a modeling-type approach. For several years, I had been writing a biweekly (or so) blog/column for the website When Falls the Coliseum called "Virtual Children." These 500- to 1,000-word pieces keep me writing, and about 20 percent of them get reblogged or republished elsewhere. As a writing teacher, it's a good story to have: In addition to my scholarly work, I'm actively writing throughout the year.

I also use these short pieces for teaching. (By the way, modeling approaches are reinforced in the OWI Principles, which suggest that one way to help students is "Modeling by writing at the level that is being required of the student" [Conference 13].) I write about topics relevant to my courses, but they are also convenient to use to demonstrate my writing *process*. While writing a piece about

Wikipedia (a post I also referenced in Week 4), I deliberately compiled drafts. I separated my efforts into six discrete, time-stamped drafts and then pasted them all into one file, simply making each draft a different text color so the students could more easily differentiate versions. The prompt asked students this:

Author: Scott Warnock **Topic**: Warnock draft process
Subject: Warnock draft process **Date**: February 20, 3:44 PM

Hi everyone,

Please look over the Warnock article process file in our Course Materials folder. I know, I know, it's not pretty.

I have been insistent all term that you revise more effectively, as I think of revision as the absolute cornerstone of good writing. What do you think of the process I went through in this article? How significantly does the article change from version to version? How much did I have to cut and change things as I wrote? Did I give up anything that you think I should have kept? Does any of this connect with the way that you write and revise?

I hope these drafts are helpful to you. As I look back on it, much of this is raw and some of it is almost embarrassing to show in public. But I'm pretty happy with the final product, and, more importantly, I'm happy to have shared this with you if it's helpful.

Please feel free to comment or ask questions—that's why I used this as an example,
Prof. Warnock

Reply

← I used a humble tone here (contrast this with Dr. Logoetho!).

← In the prompt "instructions," I emphasized how I'd like them to *read* about my revision process.

← Again, I'm self-deprecating—but I'm also modeling how teaching should be open.

I urged them along by noting that "it is almost embarrassing" for me to show these to others. This thread had only four posts—their attention was focused elsewhere this week—but those posts were good, demonstrating what students can gain when you reveal your process to them:

- Lisa said, "I have to say that the first draft and the sixth draft almost seem like two completely different papers. . . . In the sixth draft, it is very clear how you took those initial ideas from the first draft and revised them, expanded on them, and made them flow better in order to create the final product. . . . After reading these drafts, I can definitely see how I need to improve my revising process and it gives me one more example of why revising is so important because it can completely change a paper."

- Katie wrote that early on I had "become more comfortable with your writing through each draft, but almost too comfortable," and "In your final draft, you have much more solid information. You also use a more solid vocabulary."
- Alan, who was turning out to be quite the thought-provoking writer, said "It feels a little strange reading your drafts" and then compared our processes. He then wrote this, in one of those delicious diversions that I think are another strength of OWI:

Author: Alan **Topic**: Warnock draft process
Subject: Draft process **Date**: February 24, 12:14 AM

Just out of curiousity, what would you do when your children head for a higher education. As a professor with a PhD. in English, would you provide guidance for them in how to write better along the way or would you let them learn the hard way on their own and then come along and help. My teachers in my high school were parents themselves (or had experiences that would match a parent's) with a fairly high proficiency in their art. I'm not sure if it's true or not or where I heard this but I hear that how a teacher or professor teaches would reflect (eventually) how they'll approach their parenting. My teachers were fairly lenient but had some high expectations from us students. I always felt that if they were my parents, I would probably be treated the same way even if I wasn't a student at the school. I don't know, I felt that I'd throw that out there.

Reply

- In response to Alan's post, Jennifer said, "Looking at the amount of revisions, and additions that you put onto your work was eye opening to me and made me realize that I should probably plan more in my writing."
- In that subthread between Alan and Jennifer, I wrote "I'm glad you got something out of this, folks," and then directly to Alan I said, "Alan, you ask a provocative question. I have to say that I am not overly intrusive about my own children's writing education." The students, through Alan's question, were able to see another side of me.

The students who did participate on this thread were able, through some close reading—and it appeared many of them did read these dense, chaotic drafts closely—to gain some insight into how someone who fancies himself a writer works.

Thread: Collaboration, TED Talks, and the (Further) Appeal of Video-Based Threads

OWC threads that emanate from audio- and video-based course materials seem to be more active, which may reinforce ideas about student literacy habits. Indeed, it does seem, as we mentioned in Week 2, that *if you give them videos, they will come*. I assigned a nineteen-minute TED Talk, and they pounced on the thread associated with it. In my prompt, I just asked them a series of questions based directly on what they watched:

Author: Scott Warnock　**Topic**: Rheingold and collaboration
Subject: Rheingold and collaboration　**Date**: February 20, 3:43 PM

Hi everyone,

Rheingold touches on a number of topics in his brief talk. What is the prisoner's game, and why do some propose that we fundamentally don't trust each other? Why do proposers in the ultimatum game end up near 50/50? What would you do if someone offered you $4 in such a game? Why do some think that altruistic punishment might be the glue that holds society together? What does Rheingold want to see with his idea of a transdisciplinary "cooperation project"?

Think it over,
Prof. Warnock

Reply

← There is nothing fancy about this content-driven prompt. I asked them a series of questions and wanted to see where they took the conversation: Some drilled closely into the video; others were open-ended.

That simple prompt turned out to be all they needed to get going:

- Susannah moderated, introducing herself confidently: "I'll be checking all of your posts, adding my own ideas and comments as well as encouraging the conversation by posing different questions for each of you!" In general, moderating in this course, I thought, was going well.
- Almost every student in the class posted on this thread, which had seventy-one posts encompassing over fourteen thousand words.
- There were several typically long, well-thought-out posts.
- There were also numerous well-developed, dialogic subthreads, about fourteen in all.
- Interestingly, though, I still had to push a few of them to build on the thread dialogue and not just respond repeatedly to my initial prompt.

Diana: To Read or Not to Read

For one of the threads, everyone needed to summarize at least one page of a difficult reading, which would accumulate to a full summarization of the article after everyone submitted their work. It really wasn't a hard decision to decide which page to summarize. After doing a lot of work directing the work on my group project, writing the first draft, and studying for a test in another class, the last thing I wanted to do this week was read and summarize a difficult article—so, I made sure I was the first person to claim a page, and I claimed page one. That way, I only had to read one page of the article. If I selected page four, eight, or ten, I would need to read all the pages prior to my page in order to summarize what was being said correctly.

Sure enough, I was the first person to jump in. I claimed page one, quickly wrote a nice summary, and clicked "submit." The next day, I logged onto the Discussions to contribute my secondary posts and peeps, and I decided to check out the Trimbur thread to see how everyone was doing summarizing the article. After seeing the hard work all of my peers had done, I felt guilty about my choice. Was I using a loophole to get out of work ProfW purposefully designed for us? I had also forced my classmates to do more work than me.

Part of me thought, why should I feel guilty? Work smarter not harder. If there was an opportunity to contribute work and receive credit for it while, in fact, spending very little time on that work, why should I feel bad? But I knew this was a pattern for me. I *always* tried to get out of reading. I did it in my group project. I just did it for the Trimbur thread. I've done it many times before, and I'll probably do it again. I knew technical reading was an important skill required for academia and, well, life, but I couldn't stand it. Could I survive throughout the rest of my college career if I kept avoiding reading? After all, I was doing well so far despite focusing my attention on writing over reading. Maybe I could just be the amazing, magic journalist who writes perfectly and never reads (kidding). I decided to make a goal for myself: I would opt for the more difficult, lengthy article for the week, and focus on directing my attention toward reading more in my classwork.

Scott: Team Evaluations

As another way to help the groups function more effectively, I asked each team this week to evaluate the contributions of the other team members, as I wrote on the Weekly Plan. This is a common team teaching practice, providing some opportunity for students to report to me about their progress working with one another. The 100-point system allowed students structure to do this. While I attempted to be hands-on in the groups, I wanted yet another method of finding out if students felt their group members were pulling their weight.

This type of evaluation system was no different from something I might do in an onsite group project. Their evaluations, which I received via email, were not surprising for the most part, but in two cases I was able to sniff out a potential problem with a student whose group members had provided consistently low ratings for his/her performance. This was the kind of useful comment I received: "_____ really has not gone above and beyond at all, but he has not managed to not do what he is supposed to do. There is not a huge significant thing that I can think of [him] contributing. I do not think I would want to work with him again, but I hope that we can learn to work together for this project." In Group 4, one student was apparently not doing much of anything. Several students indicated they were relieved that they had the chance to provide feedback before the high stakes of the grade.

I pushed the two groups that were lagging, including in a midweek announcement:

Announcements for Wednesday, February 22:

- I posted your **Group grades** for the annotated bib and topic proposal. You will note that I still don't have a topic proposal for two groups.
- Again, check out your **group tasks.** Make sure you get your **first draft** together and talk over a **meeting time with me.** Know also that I am just an email or phone call away if you want to discuss anything about Project 2.

Group 4 was finally starting to get on track, though. While I had replied to the other groups in Week 6 about their bibliographies, I wrote on Group 4's thread a post that I hoped was encouraging while still letting them know there was work to be done:

Author: Scott Warnock **Topic**: Project 2 Group 4
Subject: Comments about your Final Annotated Bibliography **Date**: February 22, 10:38 AM

Hi Group 4,

Thanks for getting this together. You have continued to gel after your initial bumpy start. You have some very interesting sources here about school spirit, I must say.

I did wonder where your primary and visual evidence pieces are, though.

As I look at these sources, I'm wondering how exactly they are going to come together for your project; there is an interesting theme around sports and school spirit, and perhaps that could be a primary focus?

The bib doesn't really explain how the sources will be used in the context of your project. I'm looking forward to meeting with all of you, and I'm certainly available before you start creating your final draft.

Best,
Prof. Warnock

Reply

I was also getting ready to review rough drafts on Friday in anticipation of meeting the teams.

Diana: Making the Final Connection

Boy, did I beat myself up this week. I was so worried that I was going to get in trouble with my groupmates or ProfW for creating this system of summarization for our paper. The last thing I wanted was an accusation that I "wrote" the whole thing while my groupmates did much of the grunt work. I was also concerned that posting early in the Discussions for the week was some loophole to get out of reading the whole assignment. I thought I skipped out of too much work, avoided too many responsibilities, and took advantage of ProfW's classroom system. By the end of the week, however, I realized I was wrong. I hadn't manipulated myself out of work at all. In fact, I was doing exactly what ProfW wanted us to learn that week.

How could I have missed this connection? The Discussions prompt, "Summarizing Trimbur," was designed *exactly* like the plan we decided on for our group project. While I divided summarization work among my group members to expedite our research stage, ProfW was modeling the same exact plan in our online space! In fact, (I kind of gave myself a pat on the back after realizing this) I beat ProfW to the punch! My groupmates and I thought up this process of dividing work among us and having everyone summarize the material *before* ProfW even showed us how to do that in class! Proud of my group and the straight direction we were heading with our project, I had a wave of relief come over me.

Then came the second realization. Even though I posted early for the "Summarizing Trimbur" prompt, I really wasn't getting out of much reading. In fact, the majority of my reading didn't always come from the reading assignments. Most of my reading was done online—reading my peers' thoughts and questions. While it may take me twenty to thirty minutes to complete the week's readings, I'd spend thirty to forty-five minutes reading my classmates' posts each time I logged on. Before I wrote a post, whether it was a primary submission or a small peep in a subthread, I wanted to make sure I wasn't repeating something that had already been said, heading off topic, or neglecting to address someone's specific question. Therefore, I needed to spend significant time reading through each thread and getting a firm grasp of the conversation. I had no idea until this point that participating in classroom Discussions required a significant amount of the classroom reading load! Because I was in an online space, I read significantly more than I would in an f2f class. It was great news. Now, I didn't have to worry that I was skirting around responsibility, but was, in fact, right on track with what ProfW wanted from me for the course. Plus, there was also a quiz question about Trimbur!

In Retrospect: A Vast Corpus of Texts

The archive files that we drew from in this course are eye-opening: Each Discussion, from the group forums to the Dr. Logoetho threads, contained thousands of student words. Writing teachers want their students to be better readers, and that training involves practice and immersion in texts. Aside from the raw number of words that students must digest and contemplate in an asynchronous, text-driven OWC, teachers can approach literacy and reading from a variety of creative angles and assignments.

The summary Discussion thread / assignment provides one way, and modeling writing for students provides another. Interestingly, a study in the *Turkish Online Journal of Educational Technology* compared how multilingual students' summary writing improved through collaboration in online (wiki-based) vs. onsite groups (Wichadee). This study, which is mentioned in some detail here because of its interesting convergence with both this week's general theme and the specifics of the summary thread, found that both groups improved their summary writing skills, and the online, wiki-based students did slightly better. The wiki-based student groups identified more advantages than drawbacks to that method and felt that by using a digital method the teacher was more likely to be able to identify their individual efforts, which they found motivating. Of particular interest is that students could work on the skill of reading and a demonstration of that skill—summary—in a collaborative way through the use of digital tools. There are lots of assignments and prompts that teachers can use in a similar spirit.

Week 8: Writing Collaboratively in Online Learning Spaces

8

The first steps to learning to think better, therefore, are learning to converse better and establish and maintain the sorts of social context, the sorts of community life, that foster the sorts of conversation members of the community value.

—Kenneth Bruffee

Diana: What Does Collaborative Writing Look Like Anyway?

By Sunday night, I had already received all my group members' summaries—detailed with excellent observations, citations, and succinct analyses. I was more than prepared to write the final paper, and I was thrilled that we had devised such a functioning work plan. In fact, I'll admit it: I was pretty proud of what we came up with.

Collaboration requires one key, crucial skill from every member in a group: communication. From day one, all my group members spoke clearly about their talents and flaws. Some were eager to take on the task of finding resources and searching through databases, while others expressed interest in organizing information and laying out our argument. If we hadn't been so open with our skill sets, we may have wasted days trying to figure out who should do what, or worse, given someone an assignment that was totally wrong for them.

After communicating, everyone was then responsible for the tasks they claimed. Because of this accountability, jobs were completed quickly and efficiently. After the researchers finished their assignments and the summary writers completed theirs, I wrote the first draft; after everyone gave everything a final review, it was my job to jump into the role of editor.

That's where we lucked out again. In prior group projects, there has been the occasional Queen Bee battle. Who's going to make the calls? Who's going to direct the project? Who's going to be in charge? When this isn't agreed upon on the first day, one of two things happen: Everyone falls into the role of follower, or people butt heads over who should take the lead. In both situations, little gets done. In this group, however, everyone was fine with me taking the lead. Why that was the case, I really had no idea. Maybe it was because I posted so quickly and extensively in the beginning of our group work (after all, I wrote approximately 400 words for our first group thread post and suggested two well-researched ideas). Or maybe it was because I already demonstrated my strong voice on the Discussion Boards, and they felt comfortable knowing I would speak up for myself and for them throughout the project. Either way, there was no contention over who would direct the project, and everyone was comfortable with their roles.

With all of this considered, I happily opened a new document and also opened my peers' summaries and research, and I was proud to synthesize all of my group members' hard work into, what I knew would be, a successful essay.

Scott: Wrapping Up the Group Project

The Weekly Plan again had them zero in on the group project:

Week 8: February 26 to March 4

This week you'll get into final gear with the group project. The readings and other work are light here.

Note that I moved up the deadline for the primary post to **Tuesday.**

What do I do?	What are the specific instructions? Where do I find the work or the assignment?	When is it due? (All times EST)
READ	• *Course textbook:* "Making Effective Oral Presentations" 7 pages. • *33rd*: Falcone, "I Will *Not* Be a Murderer" 55-58.	You'll want to have read by **Tuesday,** February 29 so you can complete the quiz and work on the Discussions.
TAKE a QUIZ	Quiz 8 can be found in the "Quizzes" folder.	The quiz will be available **Tuesday** from 9:30 am to midnight.

← Saying "light," I meant it. Only one primary and one secondary post were due, and I moved the date of the primary post to Tuesday to help them focus further on the team project. I tried to move their other work closer to the beginning of the week as well. Everything this week was designed around having them prepare the final group projects and getting ready to present those projects. The work that they were doing in the groups was

WRITE and READ	Read all the Discussion topics for Week 8: • Post ONE primary post to any of the Discussion topics. • Post ONE secondary post.	Post your primary post by **Tuesday** night, February 28. Post your secondary post by **Friday,** March 2, at 4:00 pm.
TEAM WORK	Your **group tasks** for this week: • Your group should **create the final draft** for Project 2. This project is challenging enough; please avoid simple problems by reading the instructions carefully before you submit on your group Discussion thread. • One member of your group should submit your **fourth minutes/ progress report** at the end of the week. *Remember, minutes are not a recording of how much time you put into a project: See the project instructions.* • You should have set up a **half-hour meeting** with me to discuss the rough draft; some of those meetings will happen this week. I'm looking forward to meeting you. • Prepare to **present** your project via a PowerPoint in our online meeting space to me and any other members of the class who are available next week.	Post your final draft by **Sunday** night, March 4, clearly marked on your group thread. Your meeting minutes or progress report is due by the **weekend**.
PEER REVIEW	I have created a Discussion topic and placed all of the group projects there. I am asking each of you to choose some other group's project and give a thorough review of it based on the guidelines I provided on that thread.	The peer review is due by **Friday** at 6:00 pm. It is worth 15 points.
MODERATE	This week our moderators will be Jennifer and Nate.	--

rigorous enough, I felt. I also assigned only a short reading in our textbook about oral presentations and one brief—although argument-rich—reading in *The 33rd*. As always, there would be a quiz.

← I asked each student to review another team's project, using criteria described below. This was worth 15 points.

Their presentations were scheduled through a simple Discussion thread.

Author: Scott Warnock | **Topic**: Schedule a Presentation Time
Subject: Schedule a Presentation Time | **Date**: February 27, 11:24 AM

Hi all,

Next week I am going to ask each group to make a five- to ten-minute presentation about Project 2. You should create a streamlined PowerPoint that captures the main ideas of your Project 2 argument, and then we'll all meet in our online meeting space to make these presentations. This will probably be a different kind of presentation for many of you, but it will be a good experience to practice presenting electronically.

You probably want to work a time out on your group threads and then have one person report back here. Here are a wide range of times I could be available to log in to our online meeting space to see your presentation:

-Monday, 3/5: 9 am to 12 pm, 2 pm to 5 pm, 9 pm to 11 pm
-Tuesday, 3/6: 9 am to 11 am, 3 pm to 5 pm, 9 pm to 11 pm
-Wednesday, 3/7: 9 am to 5 pm, 9 pm to 11 pm
-Thursday, 3/8: 9 am to 2 pm, 3:30 to 5 pm, 9 pm to 11 pm
-Friday, 3/9: 9 am to 5 pm

Let me know if you have questions or need more options,
Prof. Warnock

Reply

← There are many other ways to schedule appointments, of course, such as using an app like Doodle or a tool like Google Calendar, but I like to keep it all in the LMS when possible. Also, there were only four groups (as opposed to, say, scheduling a whole class full of one-to-one conferences), so it wasn't much of an issue to find slots.

The students were working hard this week, and that made me reflect again on the reputed time crunch associated with *teaching* online. Simply put, my workload was not that heavy in Week 8. The work was being done by the students. I was there, as always, as a "guide on the side," but this week I was very much on the side, serving to help and answer questions. While I did need to reserve time to meet the four groups, I was, to put it bluntly, not buried with work. In addition, because I was teaching online, my teaching schedule was flexible.

Of course, teaching was only a part of my job, and I had a lot going on in the other aspects of my job—I had thirteen meetings that week—and personal/family life, including that my kids had their annual school "variety show" at the end of the week.

Diana: After Eight Weeks, We Finally Meet Face-to-Face

Not only was I about to meet my group members f2f for the first time, but I would soon meet the famous ProfW nearly two months into the course! It was a

Behind the Screen: Collaborative Online Writing Projects

Although he was cautious, John Barber said in 2000 that OWCs could offer new opportunities for learning focused around collaboration. While a pedagogy of student written collaboration drove the entire OWC that Diana and I are writing about, the group project concentrated that approach even further. Managing any group project can be challenging, of course, and doing so online creates additional challenges, but there are many resources to help. In their *Pedagogy* article "Transforming the Group Paper with Collaborative Online Writing," Peter Kittle and Troy Hicks provide suggestions for using specific Web-based tools for collaborative writing projects. You might find interesting a study by Nans Sri Handayani that investigated specific strategies for helping students complete collaborative written assignments; Handayani observes that due to varying participation among the students, teachers need to get involved, sometimes "more strictly" (378). Both you and students might read Anthony Atkins's piece from *Writing Spaces*, "Collaborating Online: Digital Strategies for Group Work," which includes practical advice.

If you are looking for specific support for group projects in your OWC, David Passig and Gali Schwartz found that when comparing collaboratively written academic assignments by graduate students in both online and onsite environments, the online group wrote papers the authors described as of a "higher quality" (395). For further historical perspective, see a piece Marion Fey and Michael Sisson wrote twenty years ago for *Computers and Composition*; Sisson was a student in Fey's teaching practicum, and they describe how the class used "Internet collaboration" to expose students to classroom technologies and help students "experience the liberatory effects of collaborative pedagogy in long-distance, computer-mediated writing classes" (37). Sisson provides a valuable student's view of the collaborative process—the "studenting" we are trying to illustrate in this book.

By the way, APA's style guide has a statement about collaborative writing: http://www.apa.org/research/responsible/publication/index.aspx (American Psychological Association); and NCTE/CCCC has a useful position on collaborative scholarship; see bullet #6: http://www.ncte.org/cccc/resources/positions/scholarshipincomp.

strange experience to prepare for. It's always a little nerve-racking meeting with a professor one-on-one. Will he be overly critical of my work? Will he be "grading" me based on the meeting? Will I ask any stupid questions? Then add to those fears having to meet someone in person for the first time. Is he just as nice in person? Will other people be there too? Will he allot enough time to meet with us? I realized all this overthinking wasn't going to help make a good impression, so I sucked it up, gathered my materials for the project, and walked to the other end of campus.

ProfW's office was in the Drexel Writing Center, which was in the basement of the College of Arts & Sciences building. After climbing down stairs, walking behind the kitchen for our cafeteria, and passing the center for drug and alcohol addiction, I finally reached the Writing Center. I felt bad that ProfW's office was tucked into this weird spot and that any students who needed help with their writing had to walk all the way down here too. Once I was inside, though, the space was bright and airy. The receptionist was a young student, probably only a few years older than me, and the common space had a few students who seemed to be working on their papers with tutors. The receptionist directed me to a table, where one of my group members, Aaron (who actually appeared a lot less nerdy then he described himself), already sat.

Aaron told me Artan wasn't going to make it because he had class, so it'd only be three of us representing our group. We had an awkward exchange since he was a bit shy, but to break the ice, I decided to say, "Working online is just the weirdest thing, isn't it? Good thing Professor Warnock is great." He replied, "I'd prefer this online course over a face-to-face class any day." I was shocked, expecting the usual round of complaining most students exchange when given the opportunity to talk about a course. I asked him why that was the case, and he explained, "I really don't participate in class. I get awkward. I don't know. This just makes it easier." Before, when I had criticized the course for having a unique schedule to get used to, I never considered the social benefit it could have for others. I'm outgoing in class, both f2f and online, but it didn't occur to me that students who were quiet in class could have the opportunity to be more vocal online. In hindsight, I don't know how I couldn't have seen that, but it was interesting hearing it from my group member, a real member of the class. A few minutes later, Susannah arrived, quickly said hello, and immediately started pulling out materials needed for our meeting, jumping right into work mode. I was happy she was on the ball and really wanted to start talking about the project.

Then, out came ProfW. He was much more smiley than I imagined he would be. Also, he was definitely "youngish," not "oldish" like he described in the first week of the course (but I guess that's all relative). He greeted us warmly, complimented our performance so far, and got to work. To my surprise, we did a lot more talking than he did. I figured this would be more of a top-down meeting where he told us everything we should be working on, but he spent most of the time listening to us explain our project. At first, it made me nervous just having him sit there and nod occasionally, but eventually it felt cathartic being able to talk with my group members about our work process, knowing we were all on the same page. In the last five minutes of the meeting, ProfW gave suggestions on small changes we should make and goals we should set for ourselves, but he again gave us a big smile, shook our hands, and wished us luck on what he was sure would be "a really interesting project." I wrapped things up with my group members, made a few plans to get in touch with one another next week, and we all went our separate ways.

Scott: Meeting with the Groups

This week, I would meet all the groups to discuss their projects, and from there, the teams would continue on in their uneven paths toward project completion.

- **Group 1** continued working well. On Sunday night, Diana posted a lengthy "list of things we still need." She said, "I'd appreciate if each of you claim a task or two, and let me know what you'll take care of." The "categories" were finding a scholarly source (per assignment instructions), pictures, conducting a key source interview, creating the PowerPoint, and reviewing and editing. The group had a dialogue over the next day and a half, and Diana circled back with a summary of that conversation. Artan started a thread to schedule their presentation and Aaron added, "What ProfW said about our paper is that it flows very well (uncommon for a group project) and we need to make sure we have that in our power point too." They quickly had a meeting set up with me on Tuesday afternoon, face-to-face in my office—as you just read above.
- **Group 2** met with me Tuesday evening via our online class space; they had "voted" on their Group Discussion to meet then. That group wanted to focus on "how to go about the revision process." This was after I nudged them: "Your group has not set up a meeting with me. You need to get moving on this pronto." We had to squeeze in between schedules: One student had a class until 9:00 p.m., and one had an exam at 8:00 a.m. the next morning. And, oh, I had a Board of Education meeting that night until 9:30 p.m.! So we scheduled for 9:30 p.m. Lisa did post their minutes with clear "to dos."
- **Group 3** had hashed out the group meeting the week before, with Katie pushing everyone to meet onsite. Only two of the group members were able to meet with me Wednesday afternoon. Their forum was mainly quiet, and it seemed there was some confusion, as in a thread about their rough draft this exchange took place:

Author: Katie **Subject**: Re:Topic Proposal draft (open for edit from all members)	**Topic**: Project 2 Group 3 **Date**: February 26, 11:13 AM

Is this our final then? Should we repost it as "final"?

Reply

Author: Alexa
Topic: Project 2 Group 3
Subject: Re:Topic Proposal draft (open for edit from all members)
Date: February 26, 11:14 AM

I guess so, if no one has anything to change, I guess we should! Haha, I'll just re-post that now.

Reply

Group 3 also sorted out their presentation time on the boards, posted minutes (by Alexa), and posted their, as Alexa put it, "long overdue topic proposal." As I've said, as a teacher I prefer to receive something late as opposed to never.

- **Group 4** was another group I sent a "you haven't met with me" message. Ethan did say that they had agreed on a date but hadn't communicated to me, and they eventually gathered all together for a meeting Tuesday afternoon. Ethan posted the minutes from the previous week that Sunday. The rogue group member continued not to participate.

In these meetings, I served in many ways as a group tutor, working from the skills of one-to-one response/conferencing. Of course, working in this way was different because I was often talking with multiple students, but I have this idea that writing instruction is a fractal endeavor: At all levels the interaction/instruction is fundamentally self-similar, focused around deep reading, listening, and conversation. These meetings were an embodiment of that idea.[1]

As a teacher, I do try to do a good job, and I want my students to succeed. I normally can counter any complaint about OWCs with an analogous problematic dynamic in onsite courses: issues online with retention, identity, plagiarism, and inactivity all have analogs in onsite courses; I'm ready to make those arguments. For a long time, I could endorse online group projects by saying—to students and colleagues—that I had never thrown a student off a team. Well, this term, that changed. I won't get into the details, but that student in Group 4 was doing nothing. I finally felt that I had no choice, as he wasn't even responding to me: I "exiled" him to completing the entire team project on his own. To his credit, when we finally got in touch on the phone, he admitted that he hadn't been doing the work. This was a final decision I had to make after weeks of inactivity and frustration by his teammates that manifested itself on the Week 7 group evaluations. Of course, that's why I conduct those evaluations.

Each group also received AV feedback from me. I discussed AV feedback earlier, and it's especially useful for group projects. I sent a version of this email to each group:

From: Scott Warnock
Sent: Monday, February 27 2:20 PM
To: Jennifer
Subject: Comments about group Project 2 drafts

Hi everyone,

I have recorded comments about your Project 2 drafts, and you can access those comments here: [URL] Just click on your group's name, and you will hear a brief recording in which I discuss your draft.

I initially just created the comments in RealMedia format; you can download Real Player in about one minute here: http://www.real.com/. However, I also created a couple of the comments in Windows Media (so some groups have two links, but the info is exactly the same in each link). At any rate, if you can't access the comments, let me know and I'll help you.

Looking forward to meeting with your group,
Prof. Warnock

(This method relied on Drexel's Streaming Media server. Since then, I have begun using even more streamlined methods, such as Jing.) Two students had technological difficulties accessing the comments, but we were able to solve those problems quickly.

Diana: Writing the Group Project

When it came to writing the essay, I knew I had to tie up a few loose ends before diving into the composition. After reading through the summaries one more time, I realized a bit more organization needed to take place. While my groupmates had done an excellent job finding relative sources, summarizing them appropriately, and coding them based on topics we wanted to discuss in our piece, they were varied. For example, while one group member thought a particular point would fit under, say, our introduction, another group member categorized a similar point under our third argument. That was another issue: There were a few repeat points in the summaries. Not many, but a few. While we made sure earlier in the work process that sources were varied and covered different information, that wouldn't stop two group members from summarizing a similar point. As I scanned through their summaries, I realized about 10 percent of each member's summary repeated information in another summary.

No worries. I tweaked the outline here and there, planning to add more research if any section seemed thin. In this outline, I would rephrase a point my peer made in my own words, add the appropriate in-text citation, and repeat. This way, all the arguments would present themselves in a logical order, there was no risk of my groupmates claiming I plagiarized their writing, and I would have my citations ready to go with each point.

Because summaries and arguments are typically the easiest to write, I started on the body paragraphs first. Working from my outline, I would again rephrase each point; therefore, the wording was now, hopefully, three times removed from the original source to avoid any unintentional plagiarism. Proceeding from point to point and argument to argument, the body paragraphs came together quickly and nicely after about three hours of work.

My next task was to tighten up these body paragraphs. While the content was now down on "paper," I needed to double-check my transitions and wording. Were my arguments clear? Was the progression of discussion logical and easy to follow? Did one group member's perspective on an issue coincide with another's? Were there contradictory arguments? This process took a bit longer than anticipated—another two hours that night and one more hour in the morning. While my group members were on the same wavelength with shared perspective on our issues, some of the language was wonky. I was surprised by this, considering I had rephrased their points twice now. The problem, however, may have been my group members' unique tones and styles of writing. Even though my writing would produce consistent work throughout our piece, one group member's tone was more casual than another group member's blunt style. Interestingly, these styles were coming out in my own writing. So, to remove any inconsistencies in tone, I read my work aloud and rewrote any phrases that didn't sound like "me." Even though this was a collaborative paper, and each member should be represented equally in the final product, that didn't mean each member needed to be "heard" in the final product. Our readers didn't need to hear four different voices providing commentary in our piece—one voice was enough.

After cleaning up the body paragraphs, I began working on the introduction and conclusion. For others, this order of production may not work, but since I hated producing content that would only be deleted later if it didn't apply to everything else, I saved the "cap" sections for last. The introduction and conclusion came together quickly and easily, to be frank. We'd been talking about this project for weeks now with our group members, ProfW, and other classmates. If I didn't know how to introduce and conclude my topic by now, there would be a problem. This portion of writing only took about an hour.

I gave the whole paper one more read-through. Using a practice from the workshop ProfW led for our first project, I reverse-outlined the piece. I caught just a few changes here and there during this editing process, but overall I felt it was pretty clean. After approximately two-and-a-half sessions of writing, I was ready to pass the final draft off to my group members for one final review. Everyone quickly replied with a small "Looks great!" email, and we were a few days ahead of schedule for submission, just in time to receive feedback from my other classmates. The funny thing was, this was the first project in the course that felt exactly like an f2f classroom assignment. It didn't matter what classroom environment this project could have occurred in; my group members and I would have gone about it with the same plan.

Scott: A Tough Topic

Again, this was not an overwhelming Discussion week, with three threads (you could argue there was barely enough to go around for the moderators), plus a quick presentation scheduling thread.

Thread: A Divisive Topic

Usually in a class on persuasion or argumentation, I want the students at some point to tackle at least one of the "classic," contentious argument topics (I once taught an FYW argument course using the book *Current Issues and Enduring Questions*). Through a short *33rd* reading, I introduced them to a Discussion about abortion:

Author: Scott Warnock	**Topic**: Falone: Tone and approach
Subject: Falone: Tone and approach	**Date**: March 1, 1:23 PM

Hi everyone,

Abortion certainly makes the short list of the most divisive topics in America. What do you think of the argument that Charles Falone makes in "I Will Not Be a Murderer?" What do you think of his solution? Using some of the tools of argument we have learned this term, can you analyze how does Falone construct his argument? What do you think of the tone and point of view of the essay? Who is the audience?

Interested in your thoughts,
Prof. Warnock

Reply

← I focused the questions about the way Falone constructed the argument, although by asking about his solution, I provided students with an opportunity to weigh in with their opinions.

This prompt fell into several of the categories I mentioned in Week 2. It worked from a text. It asked them to explore a specific aspect of writing. And while I didn't encourage them to argue about the topic, I did ask them *to argue about the author's approach.*

What did students do when faced with a thread about a challenging topic like this so late in the term? I'll summarize briefly and include some metrics:

- First off, they didn't shy away from the topic.
- There were sixty-one posts totaling about 10,500 words, and I only posted three times.
- I think you will find it interesting to see a brief summary of some of the subthreads that emerged in response to the prompt:
  - Jennifer on Tuesday afternoon wrote the 750-word "I Will Not Be a Murderer": Six posts followed over the next two days, commenting on her idea that "I believe that viewing yourself as a murderer in a way that people probably hadn't thought of before is extremely effective and would make a lot of people who voted for this amendment, change their stance." She and Aaron had a good dialogue.
  - Alexa on Tuesday evening wrote a 410-word post "I Will Not Be a Murderer": Four students responded.
  - Lisa, Ethan, and Donald all posted Tuesday evening: Multiple students responded to each.
  - John on Tuesday night posted "Falone's Tactics": Three students responded.
  - Alan late Tuesday night posted "To murder or not to murder? A misleading title (this post I mean)": One student responded.
  - Deryck on Wednesday night posted about "tone and approach": Three students responded.
  - Diana on Wednesday night wrote the 780-word "A Schizophrenic Rhetorical Appeal": Twelve posts followed in a dialogue that extended through Saturday.

In my Thursday synthesis post, I recognized Jennifer for doing an excellent job moderating (she posted twenty-two times on the thread!), and I focused that synthesis post on some of the instruction about argument, specifically tone and point of view and warrants:

Author: Scott Warnock
Subject: Murder and warrants

Topic: Falone: Tone and approach
Date: March 1, 2:30 PM

There are so many good posts here, and Jennifer has done such a thorough job of moderating, that you scarcely need me. I just wanted to (further) raise one point.

Ethan is one of the first below to question the use of the word "murder." Susannah and Diana agree with his critique. It is a loaded word, yes, especially in terms of legislation. If there is a funding bill for fixing potholes and people vote against it, does that make them murderers if someone gets into an accident and dies because of the pothole? You could probably name a lot of legislation that if you follow it all the way to every possible end could result in someone's death (this rhetoric found its way into the health care debates about Obama's plans). Donald raises a point that illustrates this dynamic.

However, the word "murder" hangs around the abortion debate, and that's precisely why Falone uses it, I'm sure. Diana, in her clever post below, brings up Toulmin in analyzing the argument. So, now to my question: In terms of warrants, how does the word "murder" here work? If you accept it, you're probably on Falone's side. If you don't, you probably don't see this his way.

Thanks,
ProfW

Reply

In addition, the conversation about this tough topic was conducted respectfully, even though several students did identify their position. Jennifer summed it up well:

Author: Jennifer
Subject: Quick wrap up

Topic: Falone: Tone and approach
Date: March 5, 12:05 AM

Just to summarize a bit of this thread, I would like to say that I really appreciated everyone's excitement and involvement, and it was interesting to get the chance to read and respond to everyone's very opinionated posts. Overall, it seemed like everyone either felt very strongly that they agreed with Falone, or were extremely offended with what he said, and did not agree with him at all. Falone made interesting arguments that were clearly made to get a rise out of people. Although everyone wasn't excited about what he said, he definitely got a response out of everyone and got people thinking about the amendment that he so adamantly opposed. As abortion is a very heated topic, it was great that no one offended anyone else, besides Falone, and everyone respected everyone's thoughts and generally I thought it was interesting that there seemed to be more people that disagreed with him. Great thoughts everyone.

Reply

What I hoped would happen did: Students had a conversation about the text and the approach, studying, if you will, the *writing*, even though the topic inspired polarizing opinions.

Thread: Presenting the Group Projects

I provided them with another meta-opportunity prompt to discuss learning in the group project:

Author: Scott Warnock　　**Topic**: Presenting Group Projects
Subject: Presenting the Projects　　**Date**: February 27, 11:51 AM

Hi everyone,

Do realize that your group project is not a competition. I hope you all get an A.

← I started out with what I hoped was a friendly comment.

I am going to ask you to present Project 2 next week in our online space. You'll create a simple PowerPoint based on your project, and I'll load that PowerPoint. You should each present one part of your project.

← The context also served as a reminder.

In a separate thread, I have set up a schedule. I will be in the audience, of course, and anyone from the class is welcome to listen in too.

Can we talk about this a bit? As you are thinking about this, are there any presentation questions or ideas that you might share, whether they are ideas about site design or whether they are technology tricks? What rhetorical strategies are key to an effective oral presentation? Looking back, maybe you could even think about what tips might Cicero offer to someone who is about to present to a live audience?

← The way into the prompt is easy: "Can we talk…."

← I connected with other texts.

Perhaps this thread can help all of you be better prepared for the presentations.

← The goal of the prompt was reinforced.

Thanks,
Prof. Warnock

Reply

In contrast to the dialogic thread about the abortion essay, students only posted nine times. Disappointing? No. As long as the class was having robust conversations on the Falone thread, it was fine that their writing accomplished different objectives here. Three students, including moderator Nate, discussed this topic, and on Wednesday afternoon Karen dropped in a 1,100-word post, reflecting on numerous aspects of presenting and working collaboratively. Two students and I responded to yet another example of what students can do when they write in a structured, audience-friendly environment. Really, in onsite courses how often do students articulate such in-depth thoughts about topics like group presentations?

Thread: Team Project Peer Review

I asked each student to review another team's group project. Peer review, as I mentioned earlier, is to me primarily of benefit to the writer/reviewer. Many students do an excellent job providing reviews for their colleagues—this class had a high number of strong reviews—but the process of thinking through and providing detailed written commentary is the goal: As I mentioned during the Project 1 reviews, I often believe peer reviews are the most "real" writing students do in my courses, even if the students do not always see it that way. The OWC once again provided a strong venue for review, as students who hadn't met each other often face a complex rhetorical task: They must balance how to provide constructive criticism, in writing, on a multimedia project.

Diana describes specifics of her experience with the review below, including the peer review prompt I wrote (I created threads for the four groups). Several other students provided lengthy, thoughtful reviews. Karen posted nearly 700 words reviewing Group 1's project; she said, "I think that one of the most impressive aspects of your paper was that you were able to sound very unified. It seems as though you all sat down and wrote it together. Yay!" Susannah wrote an 800-word review of Group 4's project, going paragraph by paragraph, and while she was positive, she ended with this honest comment about a less-than-complete final draft: "Right now the outline is good, but it's hard to critique when I'm not seeing sentences, evidences and your exact train of thought, the way you would present it in your final draft."

Diana: Oh, No . . . Abortion?

Okay, is ProfW trying to kill us? We're trying to finish our papers, produce peer reviews, work on all our other classes, and now he wants us to tackle a discussion on abortion?! Not only that, the reading wasn't the best! Well, okay. Maybe I'm right, or maybe the author is pulling "A Modest Proposal" on us. Either way, since this was one hell of a Discussion thread he wanted us to jump into, I figured I might as well get it over early and get writing. As I began to stew over my Discussion post, I actually got a burst of energy and considered posting a fun argument:

Author: Diana Gasiewski | **Topic**: Falone: Tone and approach
Subject: A Schizophrenic Rhetorical Appeal | **Date**: February 29, 1:21 PM

Charles Falone is a murderer of rhetoric skills. You may be confused, at this point, as to how writing an argumentative paper accounts to murder of the English language. However, Falone's writing is far from a proper rhetorical argument. His paper is simply an instructional on how to use logical fallacies. Imagine, attempting to construct an argument while littering the piece with inappropriate attacks. That, in my eyes, is poor rhetoric. That, in my eyes, is laziness. If you have any literary intellect, whatsoever, Falone's writing should disgust you. Every individual in this class who has the audacity (or is it cognitive dissonance?) to label him or herself a "college-student" while advocating for this purely emotionally charged paper is responsible for the degradation of higher-level writing skills (Falone).

I hope my introductory paragraph sounds familiar to you. Essentially, it is simply a brief derivative work from several lines in Charles Falone's essay, "I Will Not Be a Murderer." I also hope you realize how ridiculous it sounds. Name-calling, ad hominems, and guilt by association—all of these are recognized as logical fallacies, but Falone heedlessly litters his piece with them regardless. The majority of his essay exhibits aspects of a fine rhetorical approach. However, his consistent use of inappropriate arguments ultimately eclipses the good.

To reiterate my former comment, I sincerely believe the majority of Falone's essay was well written. He clearly understands the meaning of attention grabbing. In order to single himself out from the crowd of abortion debaters, he twists an idea commonly used by pro-lifers—the murdering of innocent lives—and uses it to support his thesis. All the while, he is introducing his claim, indicative of Toulmin argumentation. Falone then proceeds to introduce data supporting his claim. He highlights, "... only 3% of all services provided by Planned Parenthood nationally in 2008 were abortions. In contrast, 34% of services involved testing and treatment of sexually transmitted diseases, while 17% involved cancer screenings. These services are overwhelmingly provided to low-income women, for whom Planned Parenthood is their only option" (para. 2). Falone effectively appeals to logos, providing sufficient evidence that heightens the benefits of Planned Parenthood. Logically, to follow his use of data, Falone introduces his warrant. He states, "Taking away funding from Planned Parenthood means taking away life-saving medical care from these women" (para. 3). Falone connects his data to the claim of the paper, and appeals to logos and pathos. Lastly, by addressing an argument posed by low-tax supporters, Falone states his appeal, claiming, " ... in 2008, Planned Parenthood prevented approximately 621,000 unintended pregnancies, thereby preventing abortions ... your tax dollars are being used to provide sexual education and low-cost birth control; preventing unwanted pregnancies prevents abortion" (para. 4).

I wish Mr. Falone had stopped here. He may not have fulfilled the length requirement listed by his professor, but at least his argument would have been sound. Unfortunately, Falone followed with an array of logical fallacies. Considering his audience was primarily those of voting age, judging by Falone's final plea to entice his readers to out vote the "murderers," one would think he would be conscientious of possibly offending any major demographic (para. 9). Instead, he offends nearly every "pro-life" individual by saying, "Every American who has the audacity (or is it cognitive dissonance?) to label themselves 'pro-life' while advocating for an amendment that would kill women is responsible for this amendment" (para. 8). His aggressive, intolerant, and smug tone deters readers from listening to his agreement. Falone also claims, "There is not moral or logical ground from which you can defend the Pence amendment. If you have any compassion whatsoever, the prospect of killing women should disgust you" (para. 7). He unfairly dismisses any further arguments an advisory may have, silencing a potential audience member, and, once again, turns him or her away from his favor.

Last (but certainly not least, only so for length's sake) in the logical fallacy line-up, is Falone's constant use of the word "murderer," which is used to define those who support the cutting of funds for Planned Parenthood. It is nearly laughable how inappropriate this word choice is. Not only does it neglect to make logical sense in association to the amendment supporters, it is a textbook ad hominem argument. Falone is attacking his opponent's character rather than the issue at hand. For instance, I would never claim Mr. Falone disrespects the rules of the English language because of his profuse use of logical fallacies. Instead, I would indicate that I am sure Mr. Falone is a wonderful man, rich in intellect, and I would not want to give any impression that I think poorly of his character; however, his writing does not exhibit proper rhetoric skills.

What this all comes down to is the importance of acknowledging one's audience. Falone failed to appeal to all audience members with his schizophrenic tone—jumping from concrete rhetorical arguments to logical fallacies throughout the piece. It seems I have written an essay of my own this time, so I thank you for taking time to read my lengthy response. I know how busy we all are, and how time is cut short as finals approach. In that case, perhaps I have misjudged my readers as well!

Take care, Diana

Reply

Honestly, if the discussion hadn't been so controversial, I doubt myself or any other classmates would have had the energy to produce quality work on the Discussion boards, and boy did we have a lot of energy. Others responded to my post:

Author: Alan **Topic**: Falone: Tone and approach
Subject: Re: A Schizophrenic Rhetorical Appeal **Date**: February 29, 11:09 PM

Wow, Diana. I did not think that Falone had used logical fallacies. I felt that he was a little too passionate and insulting throughout the paper and Falone's argument felt incomplete. I knew something was wrong, but I couldn't put my tongue at it. Now I realize that it was mostly logical fallacies that were in mind. The emotions that readers get aroused by from his words really made most of them overlook this, I think.

Reply

Author: Karen **Topic**: Falone: Tone and approach
Subject: Re:A Schizophrenic Rhetorical Appeal **Date**: March 2, 12:22 PM

I am just catching up with the whole Falone debate, but I couldn't help but crack up when I read the posts about the schizophrenic aspect of his essay. I guess I was laughing mostly because that is exactly what I thought when reading his paper, but I did not know how to put it into words. I guess "schizophrenic" is a pretty appropriate way to describe his approach. Most of what I would have wanted to say about the essay has already been mentioned (and I do not want to sound repetitive) but I found myself getting sort of upset by his jumpiness when reading. It was one of those moments where I wanted to talk to my book as I read because the paper really made me want to voice my opinion. I do not know if that is a good thing or a bad thing, but I definitely think that his paper was compelling enough to spark such a large debate within the class. There has to be something that he did right if so much can be said about what he wrote . . . I am just not exactly sure if I can pinpoint what that "something" was.

Reply

Author: John **Topic**: Falone: Tone and approach
Subject: Re:A Schizophrenic Rhetorical Appeal **Date**: March 2, 11:31 PM

And isn't that the point—getting the attention of the people and provoking a reaction. Even though I'm going to give Diana props on this post, I still particularly liked Falone's piece; not so much for the information he used, the way he presented it, or the ideals he so brazenly put out there, but for the way he KNEW how to catch ones attention. I mean, Diana, didn't it work? Despite your strong feelings towards this topic, he did get you to write a fairly lengthy response to it. Turning "sheeple" into people who think for themselves (sheeple are those that see one person doing something, and follow right along; like a sheep does when it's with other sheep, hence the word sheeple) was the goal. As true as your argument may be Diana, I must admit, Falone still won.

Reply

Author: Diana Gasiewski **Topic**: Falone: Tone and approach
Subject: Re:A Schizophrenic Rhetorical Appeal **Date**: March 3, 2:57 PM

Thank you for the "props," but I cannot see how Falone won. There are loads of horrible writings that people pay attention to, but recognizing a unique piece doesn't correlate to following through with his request. Remember that Falone's goal was clearly to convince his readers to protest the amendment. Yet, through the usage of logical fallacies, he turned away a majority of readers (including those who were initially against his argument, and those who may had followed through, but chose not to after his catty attack.)

Reply

Despite having to do loads of other work this week, I once again found myself getting into a fun debate with my peers on the discussion board. Either my class happened to be an energetic group of writers that day, or ProfW expertly placed an exciting discussion in the middle of a week he *knew* we would be reluctant to participate in.

Scott: Evaluating Posts against Our Rubric

In the pre-chapter, I shared with you my overall grading approach as well as a custom rubric to help evaluate Discussion posts. At this point, you have seen a lot of student posts and informal writing. I had been evaluating each post, primary or secondary, based on that rubric. I want to make it clear that I did not go through the rubric checklist-style for each post, but, instead, as I mentioned, the rubric was a clear representation of the course grading to help the students—and me—understand the evaluation. The rubric is easy to use. Looking at Diana's lengthy post above, "A Schizophrenic Rhetorical Appeal," against the rubric, you can see how to evaluate posts. In terms of the "General," binary categories, her post had no "Gross mistakes" nor "Ethics" issues, and it was timely and of the appropriate length. Looking at the writing categories, I found it was in the first/best column for all eight categories, including in:

- "Evidence": She built her post from a variety of evidence sources.
- "Audience and context": She connected to her audience, her classmates, especially at the end of the post.
- "Style" and "Originality/creativity": I felt she took "productive risks" in an "original," "creative" post.

Maybe this was an easy one, but you can see how it doesn't take long to map students' posts onto the rubric and then use a number, usually 9/10 or 8/10, to communicate with students how they are performing on those posts. If they have questions, they can ask.

Diana: Frustrations in Peer Review

By the end of the week, ProfW asked us to review other groups' work based on similar guidelines provided in the previous peer review activity.

Author: Scott Warnock **Topic**: Peer Review of Project 2
Subject: Peer Review of Project 2 **Date**: February 27, 11:24 AM

Dear class:

I've started four different threads with rough drafts of each of the four group projects attached. Please choose one of the projects and provide a peer review of it on that thread, using the questions below **as a guide**. Make sure that if you are not the first reviewer that **you take into account what the other reviewers said before you write your review; in other words, I don't want the authors to get obviously redundant comments.**

You can choose any of the group projects to review, but let's spread around our commentary evenly.

Your review will be a **150-word memo to the authors;** please review the project, framing your comments around these areas (do NOT simply answer these questions—and don't feel obligated to address every question):

- Does the project fulfill the assignment (look at the assignment directions again)? Why or why not?
- What's the purpose? Is this a good, interesting topic?
- Do the writers account for audience effectively?
- Is the problem clear? Do the writers successfully use techniques of persuasion and argument in proposing a solution to this problem?
- Can you suggest sources that would make the project stronger?
- This was written by several people. Does it sound unified and logical?
- Comment on the grammar and mechanics. Do recurring, glaring errors interfere with the project's message?
- You are doing a similar group project, of course. How do you feel about your project after reading this one? Did you get any ideas to help make your project better?
- Do you have any ideas to help the group think about the final presentations?

Remember, reviews must be wrapped up by Friday. And while I don't want you to be mean, remember that a common flaw with peer reviews is that they are too *nice*.

Please let me know if you have questions,
Prof. Warnock

Reply

I thought the timing of this is peculiar, considering we'd only have a few days to make appropriate edits based on peer feedback. If this occurred earlier in the week alongside our other review from ProfW, the revision process would be more cohesive. Nevertheless, it was annoying to have another peer review placed so late in the writing process. I understood that this may have been due to the condensed term lengths we had at our university, but I wondered if there was a better way to schedule the assignment.

What also made this peer review difficult was disrespectful tardiness from some classmates. Many groups submitted their projects late or incomplete. From my perspective (and I can't be alone on this as an undergraduate), peer review is both a helpful step in the writing process and an altruistic endeavor to some degree. While peer review helps sharpen analytical skills and transfers over to one's own writing process, it also relies on the motivation of all parties to succeed. In this case, my peers contributed an iota of the effort I was trying to give them. It was Week 8. I was studying for three exams in other courses, working on two other papers, wrapping up homework, *and* trying to finish a group paper in this very course, and those who reviewed our group project basically handed me an outline for a paper. While I cared about the quality and improvement of another group's work, it became less of a priority when that group demonstrated a lack of appreciation for the review. If they didn't respect my time enough to submit their own work by the due date, why did they deserve a quality review from me? In the real world, people *pay* for peer review and feedback on work, but now my schoolwork (that I'm paying thousands of dollars for) is delayed because some group couldn't get their work together in time for a review. I tried my best to compose a professional review of Group 3's draft:

Author: Diana Gasiewski — **Topic**: Re: Group 3
Subject: Re: Group 3 — **Date**: March 1, 2:54 PM

To: Group 3
From: Diana Gasiewski
Date: March 1
Subject: Project 2 Peer Review

It's always nice to start with the good news first, right? With that said, I feel as though your usage of sources is great. Luckily, you have a chosen a project that offers loads of information. I feel well informed, and trust the information that you have provided. Looking over your paper, however, it seems as though you still need a works cited. Definitely do not forget that. Because of your lack of a works cited, I do not know if you have included a primary source yet. Even if you have, I know of a wonderful Drexel faculty member that would have plenty of information for you guys. His name is [instructor], and you can reach him at [instructor]@drexel.edu. He has studied the education system in the Philadelphia area, and would source as a wonderful contact for you.

As for the bad (well, we'll look at it as constructive) news. Obviously, just from glancing at your paper, I notice that you still need a title, works cited page, as well as MLA format. Do not forget that. Also, make sure you compose this writing into the proper medium for which you would like to present it. In addition, as I read through your piece, I kept stumbling upon grammar and mechanical errors. I suggest you read it aloud to yourselves, or have a professional edit the piece, so you can eliminate those errors.

However, that is just the little stuff, and is easily fixable. Your content, however, needs work. For example, I found your introduction quite boring. It reads like a textbook, and exhibits no character. You do a fine job introducing your topic, informing the reader of what you will be discussing, but I can assure you the reader is not excited or eager to do so. Get something interesting in there—an anecdote, controversial statement—anything that will grab the reader's attention. As you continue into the meat of your argument, I feel as though it is simply a mundane cycle of presenting the problem, following with evidence to support it, and presenting another problem, and, yet again, providing data to support it. Try to rework the format of your argument in an interesting manner.

Speaking of the presentation of your information, it is critical that you guys add transitional sentences between paragraphs. Many times, I felt lost as you jumped from one topic to the next, without explaining why you were doing so. I saw this specifically between paragraphs one and two, three and four, and six and seven. Please, make sure you do this. It would improve the cohesiveness of your paper tenfold. My last suggestion would be to look over your argument and make sure you didn't make any blanket statements without supporting them. I noticed specifically in your fifth paragraph, when you said " ... there are no bad students, only bad teachers" and "This is a growing epidemic ... and is only getting worse," that those two statements really needed evidence behind them.

You guys have quite a bit of work to do, but the content and information is there. Just remember to consider your audience. This class, as well as Professor Warnock, reads textbooks every day, so we look forward to writing filled with excitement! You guys have the ability to make this interesting; all you need is to put the effort into it.

Good luck and keep up the hard work,
Diana

Reply

I wasn't the only one frustrated by delayed submissions. Those who also reviewed Group 3's work had similar sentiments:

Author: Alan **Topic**: Re: Group 3
Subject: Re: Group 3 **Date**: March 2, 6:55 PM

Like Diana has said, I believe that a better introduction is needed. It sounds so much like a textbook and it lacks personality (like Diana said). I like how you presented the problem, which is quite a concern for me personally as I'm one of the few in my family that graduated high school. It's a problem I can relate to somewhat. Good job on using your sources but I think you could have better elaborated in your survey. Give a solid statistic for example.

On the fourth paragraph, you slipped a personal pronoun, here "I", nearing the end. The sentence I refer to is "This would lead to a chain of events, consisting of, as I stated earlier, teachers teaching in areas in which they were not trained." There is no need to use "as I stated earlier" and it should be omitted. As one of those basic things on writing, don't use personal pronouns. It is a little detail, so I'm fussing too much about but it would be a bad idea to leave that as is.

Diana already addressed this but the flow of the paper feels a little too sudden. You did a good job in keeping on subject in explaining the roots of excessive dropouts, but a transition from one reason to the next would make it easier on the readers. Another thing I would want to bring up is a little hard for me to articulate. I feel a slight dissonance of tone if that makes sense. It's slight but every paragraph gives a subtly different feel than the last. Well, if you edit well, this won't be a concern at all but try to read the paper out loud and you might get what I'm trying to say.

Your solution seems solid but how does that persuade us to improve the schools in Philly? As I read through the paper, I can see what can be done but I feel that there isn't a way for me to get involved in bettering schools for its students. I don't know how others in the community can also pitch in. I think readers feel excluded from the solution and when they feel like that, they might have a little more apathy to the problem. The tone is very professional and it is a bit of a wedge for me between myself and your cause.

I tried to avoid redundancy as much as I could but I think Diana gave you better guidance on how to improve on your paper. The emotional side of the paper is something I think is what you should better refine at. Physical edits and more logic and facts help well but it won't help if it alienates the readers who could support your cause. Eh, make it feel like it's another person, not a robot, that's talking.

Reply

Group 3 never posted another draft, even though I and other classmates advised them to do so.

A positive aspect to this peer review process was being able to complete the reviews in an online format. It really did make the feedback process easier, regardless of the quality of effort from my peers. When doing peer review in f2f classes, sometimes the process can be cut short if someone is a slow reader (like me) or the feedback can be compromised if people can't articulate their ideas quickly out loud (also like me). By doing it online, I had the luxury of taking my time, reviewing my wording, and double-checking everything to make sure all suggestions were clear and appropriate.

Scott: The Occasional Student Disaster

Unfortunately, students are going to have a few disasters during the term. On Thursday I received this message from Alexa:

> **From**: Alexa
> **Sent**: Thursday, March 01 3:16 PM
> **To**: Scott Warnock
> **Subject**: Issue

Hi Professor,
It's Alexa from your online english class. I know I am supposed to moderate for next week but my laptop just broke and I need to get the screen fixed and my mom isn't too happy about that and wants me to wait a while, so I feel like I won't be able to update on the posts that I am assigned to moderate as often since I will have to use the computers in the library, so I just wanted to let you know that I will do my best with that, but I apologize if it won't be as engaging or up to date.

Alexa
Sent from my Verizon Wireless BlackBerry

Alexa had been doing a good job in the class, and in fact was anticipating a problem for the following week. As I have mentioned throughout, I felt I had to move quickly into calming mode. There was obviously a lot going on in her email; I could sense the stress. I replied the following morning:

From: Scott Warnock
Sent: Friday, March 02 8:55 AM
To: Alexa
Subject: RE: Issue

Hi Alexa,
I think this will work out. You don't have to pop in every hour to be a good moderator; a few thoughtful dips into your thread may even be better than many short visits. If you schedule some time at the library, or, really, on anyone's computer you should be fine: A little time on Wed., Thurs., and then again on Fri. should do the trick.

Thanks for keeping me in the loop,
ProfW

It didn't take much. She replied to my message less than a half hour later, saying, "Oh okay! That's perfect then. I just thought I would have to reply to each post constantly so I got worried as to how that would work out. But since not, I should be perfectly fine! Thanks, Prof!"

In Retrospect: Writing—and Reviewing—Collaboratively

As we have wound toward describing the last few weeks of the course, we are aware that readers of this book will have an acutely different perspective from that of the teacher or students of this class. Discussion dialogues may not be action- or plot-driven; they may not always make great theater. But each week, the participants had new readings to challenge them and were writing "in front" of a group of other people who had become increasingly familiar. Teachers can choose to use strategies like structuring the course so their students become comfortable in the beginning, and then once the students are warmed up teachers can add provocative readings like Falone's.

Students were running on parallel tracks this week, as they engaged in the group project while also composing individual assignments on the Discussions. Even within those two broad categories, they had different tasks. This parallelism feels natural in an asynchronous OWC, where keeping people on the same topic *at the same time in the same place* is unnecessary and, perhaps, undesirable.

Students were working together on a high-stakes (read: worth a lot of their final grade) project. That writing had its own challenges, but many of those challenges are the same as in an onsite section of composition. However, in an OWC there are organizational challenges students may find as obstacles; they will certainly need to find their way around them, because while there is indeed art and talent in writing, in a group project, you also need someone who can put the words on the page. But some questions about collaborative writing in student projects remain unanswered, as Diana reveals here: How much must each student contribute to be a "writer" on the project? Can/should technological tools help teachers discern that? Can better technologies be developed for online writing projects? What is the ultimate learning that is achieved?

Thinking about the writing work that was done this week, Diana's frustration with the reviews stand out too. Reviews must be structured well, as Scott discussed in Week 3, so the student being reviewed gets useful feedback, but perhaps teachers simply have to make more explicit that the reviewee learns a lot: Help students understand their rhetorical role and what they have to gain in the "studenting" experience of review. The authority issues inherent in providing a "useful" review between students, especially with the added rhetorical load represented by a project like the one described here, may be a high barrier to good writing/reviewing. Scott, after thinking this over, admits the difficulty of getting into a student's shoes: Like many teachers, he has done so much reading and reviewing of writing over his career that he wondered if at times that experience might obstruct his understanding of the complex rhetorical situation reviewing students are in, particularly with something similar to the group project in this course. However, the back-to-back reviews of Diana and Alan demonstrate both great reviewing—and great writing.

9

Week 9: Portfolios and Compiling Student Work

Digital portfolios, then, precisely because they are digital, privilege perspective and multiplicity and a representation of palimpsest. Or: that is the hope.

—Kathleen Blake Yancey, *"Postmodernism, Palimpsest, and Portfolios: Theoretical Issues in the Representation of Student Work."*

Scott: Final Goals for the Groups

We were finishing Project 2 with group presentations this week:

Week 9: March 4 to March 10

This week you will present your group project. You should have already set up a time. I welcome any of you to "attend" the other teams' virtual presentations by logging into our online class space at the time of their presentations.

You will begin thinking about a revised version of the writing portfolio you started in 101 (if you didn't start a portfolio in 101, don't panic; see below).

What do I do?	What are the specific instructions? Where do I find the work or the assignment?	When is it due? (All times EST)
GROUP WORK	Your **group goals** for this week: • This week, you will **present Project 2 via our online class space** to me and any other members of the class who are interested in logging in during your presentation time. I will load your PowerPoint slides for you, so please send them to me prior to the presentation (even a few minutes before is fine).	The presentations will all be completed this week. The post-mortem is due on **Saturday**, March 10.

← In a brief comment at the end of the intro, I wanted to calm them a bit if they hadn't already created a portfolio.

← I provided their final weekly goals for the team project.

	• You will each write a **postmortem**, which you will post to your group thread. See the Project 2 instructions and the Ingalls article we read in Week 4 for guidance about the postmortem.	
READ	• *Course textbook:* Review Appendix A, "Constructing a Writing Portfolio" 7 pages. • *Aux:* Sen, "Reflective Writing: A Management Skill" 14 pages.	You'll want to have read by **Tuesday,** March 6 so you can complete the quiz and work on the Discussions.
TAKE a QUIZ	Quiz 9 can be found in the "Quizzes" folder.	The quiz will be available **Tuesday** from 9:30 am to midnight.
WRITE and READ	Read all the Discussion topics for Week 9: • Post ONE primary post. • Post TWO secondary posts. One post must be on the Sen thread. Everyone must also post on the "Analyzing your own argument" thread. That is a separate, 15-point assignment.	Post your primary by **Tuesday,** March 6. Post your secondary posts and the "Analyzing your own argument" post by **Friday,** March 9 at 4:00 pm.
THINK ABOUT REVISING YOUR PORTFOLIO	You should have created a writing portfolio in English 101 in the fall, preferably using Drexel's ePortfolio system. Directions for the portfolio are in the "Composition Projects" folder. I wrote the portfolio assignment instructions to help you with this process. Use them. *If you already have an ePortfolio account and portfolio,* this week simply begin thinking about what you will include from English 102 in that portfolio and how you will revise your cover document. You could also take a look again at the format of the portfolio. *Also, make sure you follow the instructions to make me a reviewer.* *If you didn't set up an ePortfolio portfolio in the fall, don't panic:* We will get you up	If you don't have an ePortfolio portfolio, you should set it up this week. Make sure you make me a **reviewer.**

← I assigned a short piece from our text about portfolios—I had asked them to read the portfolio assignment instructions at the end of Week 8. In line with the core syllabus, I also assigned a longer piece about reflective writing by Sen. This reading was challenging, and I didn't want them avoiding it, so I required one post on that thread. They also had another metawriting thread.

← I provided detail here about setting up and revising their writing portfolios. A conversation about this end-of-term project had been also occurring in our Discussions.

	to speed quickly. Start off by emailing me that you need an ePortfolio account. Then, based on the readings above, you should begin deciding what should be in the portfolio and writing your cover document (as a letter, memo, essay, or report).	
MODERATE	This week our moderators will be Alexa and Lisa.	--

Students were completing their group work in the course and beginning the intensive, reflective, and often personal work of a writing portfolio. In our program, many of the students would have already set up electronic portfolios in their previous FYW course, English 101.

As I mentioned, I wanted to maintain the learning opportunity of an oral presentation in this course. While presenting online was different than standing in front of a live audience, I thought presenting remotely from different sites was a good skill for them to practice; Jacqueline Cason and Patricia Jenkins discussed how in online courses instructors might think about how "presentational" aspects of f2f courses might translate, and I think it is worth it for students to have an opportunity to have the same experience, considering how much of this type of presenting they may do in other aspects of their lives. However, because the presentations would be a synchronous activity, I couldn't guarantee an audience. After posting all the week's work, I posted this announcement (which also mentioned that the course themes for their English 103 spring FYW courses were now posted):

Announcements for Monday, March 5:

- Looking forward to your **Project 2 presentations**. Make sure you post your group's time on the Week 8 Discussion thread so everyone knows when these presentations are taking place.
- Your **materials** for this week are available.
- The themes for English 103 in the spring are available on the FWP website.

Diana: The Final Presentation

The final stage of our group project (as is the case in many group projects) was to present our work. To delegate responsibilities fairly, we decided to use the same steps of production we created when constructing the paper: The other group members organized the content and the sources, and I put together the final PowerPoint. Everything went without a hitch, and we all "arrived" in the online classroom on time. As we logged in, however, we were met with a disappointing atmosphere. None of our classmates was online to view our presentation. ProfW was the only attendee. Everyone's presentation time was posted on the course site, so others were aware that we were presenting. As the first group to volunteer, I'm guessing the process wasn't set in stone. Also, ProfW hadn't made it a graded requirement to attend, hence the lack of effort on my peers' part. The funny thing was, I had lamented over ProfW's small graded, required tasks many times earlier in the course, and here I was, wishing he was giving a quick, graded assignment to my peers.

Our presentation now felt overdone and misdirected for our audience. If we had known our audience was so specific and small, we would have constructed the PowerPoint differently. Rather than spending time explaining the ideas and goals behind our project (which ProfW was already well aware of, since he helped us throughout the whole process) we could have talked more about our findings and results—a more worthwhile conversation for both ProfW and our group. At the very least, we could have created a recorded presentation. That way the presentation would have been a lot cleaner, and classmates could log in at their preferred times to view our work and provide feedback.

The presentation experience did bring an f2f vibe to the course. Who would have thought I would eventually present work with three classmates—who were in remote places across the city (or beyond)—live to our professor in an online space? It was a refreshing change in the cycle of write-submit-receive feedback that many courses, both f2f and online, fall into.

Scott: Groups Wrapping It Up

The teams were presenting this week; mid-week, I encouraged them with this announcement:

Announcements for Wednesday, March 7:

- The **Project 2 presentations** are going well. Thanks for making this environment work.
- The themes for English 103 in the spring are available on the FWP website.

The online presentations introduced worthwhile challenges for the students, and I think to maximize those challenges they had to present synchronously.

The way our software worked, I could load slides into the live classroom and then any course member could log on and watch. I asked each team to present in a short time frame and be prepared for a brief Q&A.

In most cases, I was the only audience member and the only one asking questions. There are ways I probably could have addressed this audience issue. I could require each student to attend one other team's presentation; barring significant scheduling snafus, this should work. I could take a page from a strategy I use in onsite tech and business writing course presentations: invite guest audience members. This practice works well for those types of courses, as I have had students presenting pitches and proposals and audience members playing roles as clients. Online, of course, such audience "visits" would be easier to facilitate, as long as the LMS allows guest access: No one has to travel. (True story that shows another possible benefit of online learning: In an onsite business writing course I taught one term, one audience member got a flat tire on his way to the presentations and was unable to attend!)

The presentations were a mixed bag:

- **Group 1** finished their strong work throughout the project with a unified presentation, as Diana described.
- **Group 2** struggled. Despite having operated well during the course of the project, the presentation was, as I candidly said in my written, end-of-project evaluation, "a mess." The slides were fine, but I said, "You were unprepared in terms of technology and organization." One group member said he had a bad connection—whose source I never discovered—and another didn't have a mic. Background noise was an issue, although I reminded students several times to turn off their mics if they weren't speaking, and they talked over each other and seemed to disagree about the presentation content. I wrote, "Well, this was a low-stakes lesson about presenting as a group in a virtual environment, which is certainly a challenge; I hope that you take from this the understanding that you need to be prepared, especially when the stakes are much higher."
- **Group 3** also had several problems in the presentation. In the evaluation, I wrote, "Plain and simple, you were not prepared: My hope is that you take a lesson with you from this experience." Two of them logged in right at the presentation start time. Their slides weren't ready nor were they proofread. As with Group 2, I noted, "You were talking over each other and didn't seem to know who was doing what." I added that the

presentation issues "seemed to be representative of the issues with the project itself in terms of how you worked as a group."

- **Group 4**, on the other hand, while having issues in the project overall, did a good job presenting. I wrote, "You had a great design for your slides, and you provided some good information from the report/ project. As with the project, the solution could have been more clearly presented rhetorically, but you are all accomplished speakers, and you handled the brief Q&A well." Because they did a good job, I provided some nuanced feedback, such as "When presenting, especially electronically, make sure you identify who is speaking."
- The student who had been exiled into his own project space? Well, he was confronted with challenges you might imagine someone would encounter when trying to complete an entire group project on their own. He survived the project—but barely.

After the presentations, I posted evaluations on the Discussion forums for each group. Here is the full evaluation for Group 1:

Author: Scott Warnock | **Topic**: Project 2 Group 1
Subject: Comments on Group Project | **Date**: March 9, 1:55 PM

Dear Group 1 (Aaron, Diana, Susannah, and Artan):

← I addressed them not just as a group but as individuals.

You did an excellent job throughout the process, getting a group project together under challenging circumstances. Your final article looks excellent and contains a lot of thoughtful argument. In terms of a solution, as they say, the devil is in the details, so in order for City Dollars to work, a lot of the "all we need" stuff about implementing it would have to be thought over quite a bit more. Still, this is an excellent project.

← I opened with an overview that emphasized that working in a virtual team isn't easy.

Main idea and rhetorical focus of project: Good. As I mentioned, I have seen lots of projects about Drexel's meal plan, but I think you offer an interesting twist to this with your proposal of City Dollars. The problem is well established, and your ability to include information from other institutions only strengthens it.

← I chose to organize my response by category, providing an overall assessment for each category, like we were using a loose rubric.

Audience/rhetorical role. Good. The idea of writing this as a newspaper article is just excellent. At the end of the article, you shift into writing to an audience of, I guess faculty?:"your classrooms"? This is a strange shift in POV, but overall, you're fine.

Writing: Excellent. Watch your hyphens, but, especially for a group project that has to incorporate many voices, the writing here is strong and clear.

Organization: Good. The newspaper layout is effective not just for appearance but for organization.

Evidence/sources: Excellent. You found some great evidence to provide a different approach to the meal plan project. You have a good survey and many other strong resources. I was struck by this aspect of your project when I looked at the annotated bibliography, and you've done well to incorporate this material into the project.

Document/site design: Excellent. What can I say here? This is really well done design- and presentation-wise.

Presentation: Good. You did a good job presenting in the online environment and making it all work. You provided a good outline slide to let the audience know what was coming, and your slides were good and clear with minimal text. The presentation felt unified; you all knew what was coming. You had a good sense of visuals, and you are all accomplished speakers. You handled the brief Q&A well.

Teamwork: Excellent. You worked together as successfully as any team I have had in a long time. You stayed on track, helped each other, and had open and frequent communications. It seems different people stepped up at times to make sure the team weekly benchmarks were met. Congratulations. You worked together virtually to complete a team project.

Grade: 237/250, A.

Good work,
Prof. Warnock

Reply

← The "categories" of our rubric contained some specific details for this type of project, such as "Presentation" and " Teamwork."

← The evaluation ended with the grade and a complimentary close.

The overall grades for Project 2 ranged from this A to a C+. I want to note that in general I am always concerned about providing a crusher grade to a whole team. Group 4, the C+ team, despite concentrated efforts by me to help them get going and the fact that they gave a good final presentation, was unable to get the project together. In the evaluation overview, I wrote:

> You struggled in the beginning of the process, but I do think you were able to find a way to come together as a group and hit your benchmarks. Your final project is not very persuasive. It's oversimplified and you use a lot of unsubstantiated claims. Where is your visual? Where is a scholarly source used? It appears to be written by four people, as there is a lot of redundancy and some inconsistency. This is all, of course, a product of not handing in a real rough draft.

I wanted to emphasize their issues with teamwork:

> **Teamwork**: Fair. This was a team in need of a leader. You did bring it around, and while you were late with some benchmarks, you eventually made the project work. While I think the final project could have been stronger, I do want to congratulate you for working together virtually to complete a team project.

Interestingly, this weak project from Group 4 arguing that Drexel should have a football team (an oft-discussed campus topic) still was accompanied by a "Good" presentation. This group struggled, and how much of that was connected to the online environment is an open question. Certainly, as with online learning in general, the fact that students didn't have to look one another in the eye in the same physical space could have been a factor in their success (they had the one nonparticipating group member, as I mentioned, whom I removed from their team). Such physical proximity for this group might have alleviated problems ranging from the poor evidence in the final project to the lack of a clear leader. However, because the project, like the class, is virtual, students may be able to "perform" more effectively because they don't have just to allot the time that they are together in class to work on the project. The project can lurk in their consciousness throughout the week, part of that blurry homework/classwork OWC line. Considering the teamwork issues and final project problems, perhaps a C+ was generous, but I think regardless of modality or subject matter, teachers must be careful about grading team projects too harshly.

Diana: The Course Is Finally Done! Right?

The winter weather was finally starting to break. I was eager to start exploring Philadelphia, eat at outdoor cafés, plan my spring break, and attend backyard parties on frat row—all the typical distractions for a first-year college student. Not to mention, our group project was finished, our presentation was delivered, my work was reviewed, and it was Week 9—this term should be wrapping up by now. In my high school English classes, if we finished papers and final assessments ahead of schedule, the last few weeks were usually filled with movies. Of course, I wouldn't complain, and the semester would fizzle out with a slow, lazy cinematic experience. With everything being said, now that I was paying hundreds of dollars per class at a university, I didn't want to feel like the last few weeks were a rip-off, but I also didn't want to jump into another extensive project right before the end of the term. I opened the week's announcements.

Announcements for Friday, March 9:

- The final **Weekly Plan** is available. How about that?
- You all need to make me a **reviewer in your ePortfolio account**. So far, no one has done that.
- Your **group evaluations** are on your group Discussion threads.

It looked like we would be crafting our portfolios. While I constructed a writing portfolio in my last college English course, my grasp of the concept was still loose. Was this just a folder with all my best papers thrown in it? Would I have to write more? Would this portfolio be reviewed as a whole rather than each individual paper receiving a review? Would I include Discussions I wrote as well? While I knew *how* to construct a portfolio, I hadn't yet grasped the *why*. If I was really lost, I could always email ProfW for further clarification or even walk down to his office (now that I knew where it was).

This assignment, whatever it would turn out to be, did seem like a logical and appropriate final task for the course. I decided to focus on my other tasks for the week—Discussions, group evaluations, and other coursework—before jumping into this portfolio, since ProfW suggested in the Weekly Plan that "based on the readings above, you should begin deciding what should be in the portfolio and writing your cover document. . . ." Also, my other obligations could be completed quickly and easily without much hesitation since I had been doing them all term. Then I could focus on this final project during the remainder of the week—and term!

Scott: Preparations for Reflection

On the Discussions, I had them reflect in structured ways about their writing in the course.

Thread: Analyzing Your Own Argument

I again used the low-stake Discussions environment to help them dig into their own writing.

Author: Scott Warnock **Topic**: Analyzing your own argument
Subject: Analyzing your own argument **Date**: March 5, 9:43 AM

Okay folks,

I'd like you to choose a post YOU wrote from earlier in the term in which you

← I used an informal greeting.

make an argument. Please cut-and-paste that post here and then provide an analysis of the argument you made using any of the tools and terminology we have discussed this term. How do you appeal to *ethos, pathos, logos*? Is your argument Rogerian or does it better follow another model? How do you connect with your audience?

This is a 15-point assignment that is separate from your other Discussion work this week. I'm looking forward to seeing your analysis of your own argument methods,

Prof. Warnock

Reply

← They were to work directly from their own texts.

← I graded the assignment in an FLS way.

I wanted them to work with a manageable amount of *text that they composed*, but without the high-pressure constraints of looking back at a major project. I wanted them to use the composition skills they had learned over the term to analyze that material: As you can see from this prompt, I was asking them to connect with course concepts, such as if the post had elements of Rogerian argument to it. The assignment scaffolding was simple and straightforward.

Thread: A Final Go-Round with Dr. Logoetho

Dr. Logoetho resurfaced for one final round of debate with the students. This week, I had the good doctor go after a vulnerable area, college costs:

Author: Demo student **Topic**: Dr. Logoetho & college
Subject: Dr. Logoetho on college costs **Date**: March 5, 10:21 AM

Dear students,

I'm tired of hearing everyone complain about the cost of college. Considering how much people benefit earnings-wise over the course of their lifetime based upon the degree they have earned (see http://www.acinet.org/acinet/finaidadvisor/earnings.asp?nodeid=21), I argue that college should cost MORE money than it does now. I would ask if you agree, but how could you not?: I make a very reasonable and logical argument.

Yep, that's what I think,
Dr. Logoetho

Reply

← I again posted from the role of "Demo Student."

← Dr. Logoetho launches right into it, even using some "evidence."

← Tone-wise, Dr. Logoetho is again aggressive.

This was an active thread with fifty posts and all but two students participating.

The moderator, Alexa, did a good job on this thread in which students expressed a variety of opinions about Dr. Logoetho's stance.

As I worked on Discussions Wednesday and Thursday, I again had to synthesize the various comments students were making. Throughout the term, my mid-week "synthesis posts" were written based on the collective development of the conversations. For this thread, as we were near the term's end, I responded individually to many students, pushing them to develop their arguments. Some highlights of the way the students addressed Dr. Logoetho:

- Alan: "Also, if you put it bluntly, a college is a business that sells knowledge or education. No one is required to go to college. And yet it is a beacon for those who want to learn or improve upon skills."
- Lisa: "While the graph does make a point about higher education level equaling a higher median weekly earning, I still think that your idea that college should cost more is completely insane." Dr. Logoetho responded: "Lisa says my idea is 'completely insane'? If I weren't a person of great internal confidence—which is what you get when you NEVER lose an argument—my feelings would be hurt."
- Alexa: "With that being said, Dr. Logoetho is right, in a sense. Education is advancing and it is true that it does have a higher value than before."
- Donald: "I'll give you the example of what I did to pay absolutely $0.00 for going to Drexel. Even though it did cost me 5 years of active military service, it is well worth it. I even moved across the country so I had to pay nothing. I shopped around and I suggest you do as well."
- Rio: "Therefore, can we assume that a college's cost should cost more only if the education there is worth more?"

Students conversed with one another on this thread, and that is captured in Figure 4. This thread provides fascinating comparisons with the conversations captured similarly in Week 2 and Week 6, as this conversation was far more involved and dialogic.

Thread: Some (Light) Conversation about Writing Portfolios

If a teacher dedicates part of an onsite class to discussing portfolios, that could be time well spent, but if students don't talk, the class could be a bust. This week, I opened a conversational thread about portfolios:

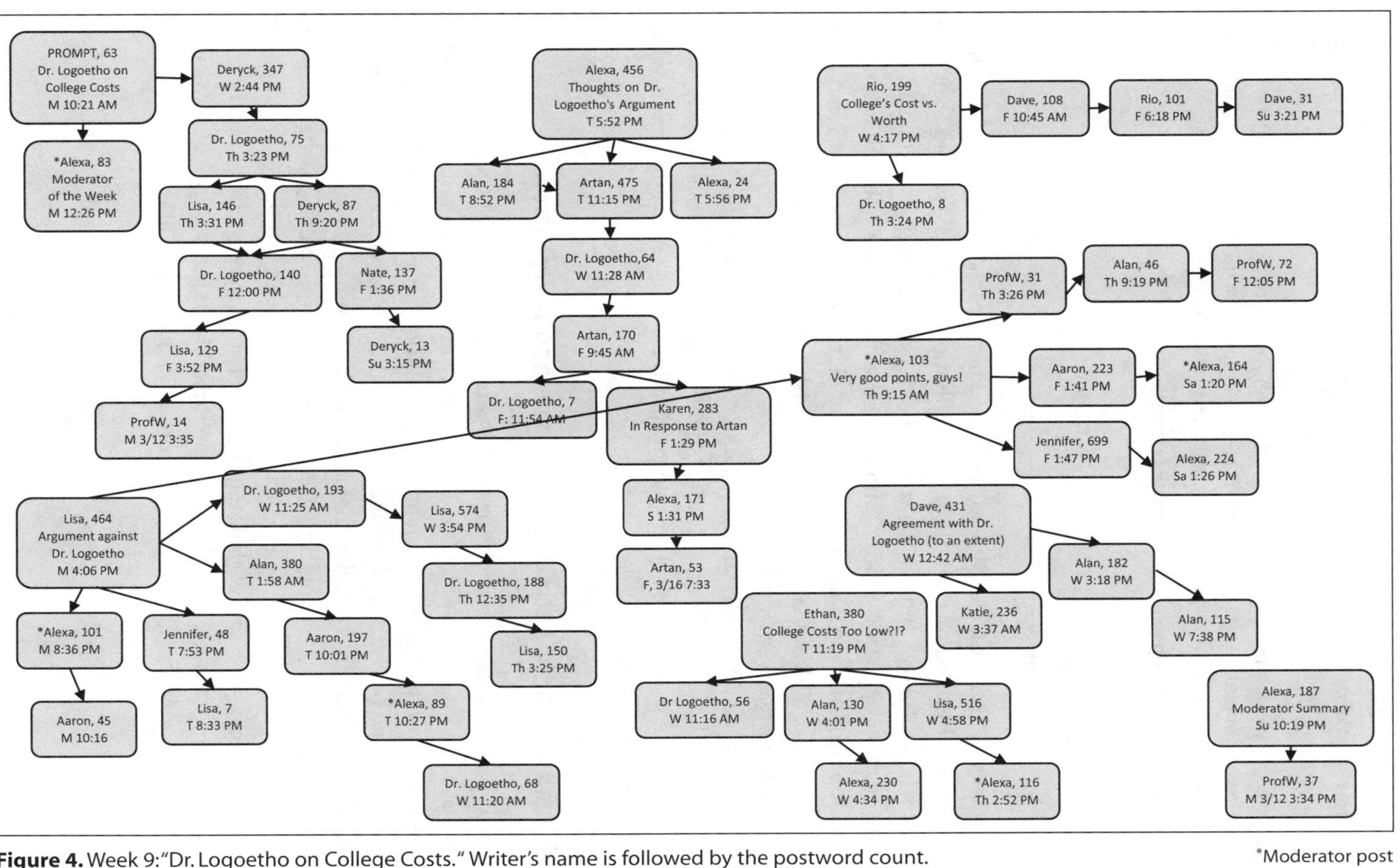

Figure 4. Week 9:"Dr. Logoetho on College Costs." Writer's name is followed by the postword count.

*Moderator post

Author: Scott Warnock
Subject: Portfolios

Topic: Portfolios
Date: March 5, 10:22 AM

Dear students,

I am asking you to update (or, in some cases, create) your writing portfolio. What might you include from this term (and it doesn't have to be just from this class)? Why would you include those artifacts? How might they help you professionally down the line?

Use this thread to help you think about your portfolio,

Prof. Warnock

Reply

This was a lightly traveled thread, as the moderator Lisa lamented at the end of the week: "I was somewhat disappointed that only 2 people shared their ideas for their portfolios." But for the students who contributed, including Lisa, the conversation appeared focused and helpful in answering questions about the development of their portfolios: Rio received advice about what to include in her portfolio, and Diana had a dialogue with Lisa and me about what theme/topic her portfolio should follow.

This thread demonstrates again the simple benefit of parallel learning afforded by asynchronicity: For the students who participated here, there was value, but all students didn't have to squirm through a class conversation in which they were not interested.

Thread: Trying to Encourage Dialogue about Reflection

I also posted another straightforward, reading-based prompt about the more complex reading about reflection. The particular way the Sen article approached reflection won't appeal to all teachers of writing, but based on simple starter questions, the conversation unfolded during the week, with various subthreads emerging. Students can tackle threads about complex readings as long as there is some structure (clear posting guidelines), encouragement (teacher and perhaps student moderation with colleague support), and a touch of requirement (as I mention above, one of their required posts had to be on that thread).

There were nineteen posts on the Sen thread from the majority of students—it was a *required* thread—building a core of conversation about the content of this piece.

Behind the Screen: Portfolios in an OWC

Portfolios are a long-trusted way of having students gather, reflect on, and present their work in a writing course; as Richard Larson said, portfolios could be compared to capturing a student's work as a motion picture, not a snapshot (274). With the emergence of digital tools, eportfolios have seen increasing use. You can find lots of information about portfolios and eportfolios, as teachers and writing scholars have discussed approaches to portfolios for decades. In fact, the use of portfolios is often a best/effective/recommended practice for writing instruction; for example the Conference on College Composition and Communication said in "Principles and Practices in Electronic Portfolios" that "portfolio assessment has become an important part of the learning-to-write process." For some suggestions on differentiating between the broad classification of portfolios as product- or process-based, see Marc Zaldivar, Teggin Summers, and C. Edward Watson's "Balancing Learning and Assessment: A Study of Virginia Tech's Use of ePortfolios." "Postmodernism, Palimpsest, and Portfolios" by portfolio expert Kathleen Blake Yancey is an excellent piece to help frame your use of portfolios. The collection of essays edited by Barbara Cambridge, Susan Kahn, Daniel P. Tompkins, and Yancey, *Electronic Portfolios: Emerging Practices in Student, Faculty, and Institutional Learning,* offers numerous ways of thinking about and using portfolios in courses. Another good overall resource is Katherine V. Wills and Rich Rice's *ePortfolio Performance Support Systems: Constructing, Presenting, and Assessing Portfolios.*

If you are looking for advice about using eportfolios specifically in your OWC, there are many resources as well. First, eportfolios should be accessible, and Sushil Oswal's "Accessible ePortfolios for Visually-Impaired Users: Interfaces, Design, & Infrastructures" focuses on such issues. Christine Tulley, in "Migration Patterns: A Status Report on the Transition from Paper to Eportfolios and the Effect on Multimodal Composition Initiatives within First-Year Composition," provides a perspective on the growing use of eportfolios, particularly in the context of multimodality in composition courses. The *OWI Position Statement* says of the text-heavy OWC, "These opportunities make OWI ideal for multiple drafting opportunities and portfolio-based assessment" (Conference 14).

If you are looking for some thoughts about how to evaluate portfolios, Yancey, Stephen J. McElroy, and Elizabeth Powers provide perspectives, including many examples, of how to think about assessing portfolios, in their digital publication, "Composing, Networks, and Electronic Portfolios: Notes toward a Theory of Assessing ePortfolios."

Diana: Discussion SOS

I'm glad I worked through the Discussions before diving into my portfolio. As a matter of fact, there was a discussion thread created *specifically* for talking about the portfolios. I quickly submitted a post early in the week.

Author: Diana Gasiewski | **Topic**: Portfolios
Subject: Obtaining Direction through Organization | **Date**: March 7, 3:36 PM

As soon as I read the prompt for this discussion thread, I knew I had to make my primary post here—not because it seemed like a fun topic, but because I terribly need help constructing my portfolio. I am awful at synthesizing collections of work. Therefore, taking a moment to evaluate the process will do me well.

Indecisiveness is my main obstacle. I will look at one essay of mine, think that it's the next "Ulysses," and then come across another piece that seems to put my first essay to shame.

My options eventually blur together, and I lose direction. The fear of embarrassing myself in front of potential readers also hinders my decision making process. I have no idea what will impress one reader from the next, so I try to cover all bases and include as much work as possible. Therefore, my portfolios usually turn into an overcrowded, undirected mess.

I believe, however, that Appendix A helped to strengthen my selection process. This chapter details what questions I should ask myself prior to making a selection, how I should reflect upon what I have written, and, most importantly, offers two ways in which I can organize my collection. These outlines may save my portfolio. I would have never thought to organize my work according to learning goals or purpose (618-620). Before, I simply included what I thought was best; however, our text's methods will clarify my portfolio's direction.

With that said, I expect to organize my portfolio according to purpose. Throughout this past term, I have written on an array of topics—all of which vary from evaluative to persuasive to creative approaches. Therefore, constructing my portfolio to reflect my diversity in writing abilities will showcase my range as a writer. For example, I will surely include my piece for English 102's second project, for it exhibits my ability to write journalistically and persuade an audience. Also, by including my piece analyzing society's addiction to the media, written for my Com 150 class, my evaluative abilities will be displayed wonderfully.

Realizing that organization was the key to constructing my portfolio has helped me greatly. Having a clear and concise direction will be wonderfully beneficial as I work to formulate my collection. In addition, it will appeal to future employers as they either look for specific skills in my prose, or for a wide range in writing ability. A strong direction in my portfolio will improve decision making, both for future employers and myself.

Reply

ProfW replied to my post:

Author: Scott Warnock **Topic**: Portfolios
Subject: Re:Obtaining Direction through Organization **Date**: March 8, 12:23 PM

Hi Diana,

This is a good prompt to get us thinking here. I'm sorry, but after working with you all term, I find it hard to believe that you are "awful at synthesizing collections of work." However, this indecisiveness could be an asset and certainly a topic for you, because what it reflects is the way that your own view of your writing shifts significantly. There is a great question here: Why is that?

Regardless, learning goals and/or purpose are great ways to structure your portfolio, and they are also a way for you to have a portfolio that might appeal to different audiences.

Let me know if you have questions,
ProfW

Reply

I guess I was being too hard on myself. ProfW's words of encouragement were extremely helpful, particularly the bit about my concerns being an asset rather than a hindrance. I moved forward feeling much more confident about the direction I was heading with my portfolio, and already had a few pieces in mind I was going to use for the portfolio.

While I was making progress, I was still nervous about crafting the cover document. I had just reached an understanding of what my portfolio needed to include, but I still needed to reflect on everything in my own words. Luckily, ProfW created somewhat of a "practice round" in our Discussions. A prompt titled "Evaluating your own argument" challenged us to find a primary post we made earlier in the course and reflect on our rhetoric. I chose to reflect on one of my favorite threads in the course: arguing with the infamous Dr. Logoetho:

Author: Diana Gasiewski
Topic: Analyzing your own argument
Subject: A Rhetorical Evaluation of "Wikipedia and The Shoe Shiner"
Date: March 7, 7:43 PM

For my reflective analysis, I chose to evaluate my rebuttal to a favorite prompt this term—Dr. Logos' problem with Wikipedia. In this argument, I feel as though my greatest achievement was appealing to a wide range of opinions and personalities. While I was only writing for one audience member—Dr. Logos—I had a feeling this was a sophisticated individual, who looked for an argument that would cover all the bases.

Keeping that in mind, I began with a pathos appeal, relaying the story of a poor Peruvian boy who greatly appreciated his access to Wikipedia. While it may not have been the strongest of my arguments, it certainly caught one's attention the most. I feared boring my audience with an introduction filled with statistics, so I chose to take an anecdotal path. In addition, I was able to grab a hold of emotion first, a strong aspect of one's decision making processes.

Making sure I didn't elaborate extensively on the pathos appeal, I promptly transitioned to a discussion of experimental evidence regarding the efficiency of Wikipedia. Here, I provided statistical proof equalizing Wikipedia's quality of information to that of the renowned encyclopedia, Britannica. Through comparative reasoning, I appealed to the logos of the audience.

After outlining a couple of my own arguments, I proceeded to offer a rebuttal to Dr. Logos' original argument. Responding to the original claim that "Wikipedia is useless," I brought to attention an ethos-focused argument. Wikipedia provides free knowledge to those who have very little access to information otherwise. Therefore, Wikipedia is acting as a public servant, enlightening community members in a virtual and direct manner. In addition, to contribute one additional logos based argument (since my audience was "Dr. Logos" after all) I made a point to recognize that "Wikipedia offers information in over 273 languages."

All the while, with each argument proposed, I was building up to my main thesis. Through this process, I utilized inductive reasoning—transitioning from specific examples to a general claim. Therefore, as I stated my thesis I concluded my essay with a final summary of arguments made. Then, to completely wrap up my piece, I brought attention back to the boy discussed in the introduction, bringing my argument full circle.

Reply

Just as I would analyze the work of a peer, colleague, or author, I had to do the same with my own writing. Of course, it would be more awkward because I had the tendency to both self-loathe and be overconfident in myself (I'm from Philadelphia, after all) so an unbiased reflection on my work would be difficult. In this post, however, I felt confident in my analysis and ended up receiving an A from ProfW. This grade, along with this week's other Discussions, bolstered my confidence significantly. I reached the end of the week and began working on my portfolio.

In Retrospect: Analytical and Reflective Work

The type of course we describe provided a strong platform for the fundamental thinking that underlies portfolios: Edward White, William Lutz, and Sandra Kamusikiri used portfolio assessment as an example of a promising way for teachers "to gain power over assessment and hence over the definition of what is to be valued in education" (9). Although our course was not portfolio-centric, the well-run OWC presents opportunities for a rich textual recursiveness. Students need not conceptualize it like that, but the opportunities for writing about their own writing are extraordinary.

As Diana pointed out, though, students need to be "okay with writing—a lot." They will compose thousands of words in a "quality, thoughtful, productive dialogue," not just "I agree" posts. This body of work created in the dynamic Discussion environment then combined with the major project work students engage in seems to provide an intriguing opportunity for a deep, multigenre, reflective portfolio—not one in which they are thinking only about high-stakes work that they have discussed with the professor, but a range of posts and conversational writings that may allow them to get a much broader view of who they are as writers.

As we moved into the final week of the course, the students would have several final opportunities to further strengthen their reflective skills . . . and write!

Week 10 (and 11): Reflecting, Evaluating, Moving On

Sharing texts over a computer network enables students to observe, and hence reflect upon, each other and themselves in ways not possible in a traditional classroom.

—L. Lennie Irvin

Scott: Reflecting on a Term-Long Writing Experience

At the top of the last Weekly Plan, I emphasized that students needed to focus on their portfolios. I myself was not only finishing up the term but was heading to a national conference—and I could accommodate both due to the wonders of online learning.

Weeks 10 and 11: March 11 to March 19

As we close the term, you will focus on updating your portfolio. We'll also read about some things that might lie ahead for you writing-wise.

Please make sure to complete the course evaluation, which is on our course site. It's worth 10 points.

What do I do?	What are the specific instructions? Where do I find the work or the assignment?	When is it due? (All times EST)
READ	• *Aux*: Singh-Corcoran, "Composition as a Write of Passage" 12 pages. • *Aux:* McCarthy, "A Stranger in Strange Lands..." 32 pages. (I know, this seems like a long reading. But there are three pages of references and a couple pages of tables; it'll be okay.)	Read by **Tuesday,** March 13 so you'll be prepared for our final quiz.

← I'll discuss course evaluations below and in the next chapter.

← In our curriculum, we had been thinking about transfer and not only how writing transfer was happening at Drexel but how we might, Writing about Writing–style, teach students about it. The

TAKE a QUIZ	Quiz 10, your final quiz, can be found in the "Quizzes" folder.	The quiz will be available **Tuesday** from 9:30 am to midnight.
WRITE for GROUP	This week, you will write your postmortem of the group project. From the Project 2 instructions: **Postmortem Reflection:** At the completion of the project, members of your group will each compose a **reflective analysis**, in which you look back on the project, think about its many facets, and evaluate how it has impacted you, your learning, and your perspective on collaboration. You will post these brief reflections on your group Discussion thread.	The postmortem is due Wednesday evening**, March 14.** Again, post them on your group Discussion thread.
WRITE and READ	Read all the Discussion topics for Week 10: • Post ONE primary post. • Post TWO secondary posts. Make sure one post is on the "My favorite poster" thread.	Posts are all due by **Friday,** March 16, at 4:00 pm. You have more than shown that you can sustain a conversation in here without multiple deadlines.
COMPLETE PORTFOLIO and MAKE IT ACCESSIBLE	You will complete work on your writing portfolio and make sure it is accessible to me.	Portfolios should be completed by **Friday**, March 16. I will begin evaluating them on Monday.
COMPLETE COURSE EVALUATION	The **final anonymous course evaluation** will be available on our homepage. Please spend some time on the evaluation, which, again, is anonymous. I take my evaluations seriously, and I read them closely to see what I can do to improve as a teacher.	The course evaluation will be available until **Monday**, March 19. You will receive 10 points for completing the evaluation. The evaluations are anonymous, but at the end I will

readings this week, both available on our LMS, reflected that: McCarthy was long, so I gave them a heartening parenthetical.

← I'll describe the "postmortem" assignment below. It was a way for them to reflect on their work in the team environment.

← Final discussion work. I thought of them as spending "class" time working on portfolios and time on course evaluations.

← I provided more information about the course evaluation here. This term I tried tying the evaluation to a small informal grade.

		see a list of who in the class has completed an evaluation and who hasn't. This is an easy 10 points.
MODERATE	This week our final moderator will be Katie.	
If you have reached this line, folks, you have completed English 102 online. Almost all of you made the most of the opportunities presented by the online learning environment. I very much enjoyed working with you, and you worked hard not only to develop your own writing and techniques of persuasion but to help each other. It's been a pleasure to work with all of you.		

← This was a final note of goodwill and respect for the work they had done.

On Monday, I posted an announcement urging them to set up their portfolios. Not all would . . . :

Announcements for Monday, March 12:

- Your **Discussions and other work** for Week 10 will be available today.
- Let me know if you have questions about the **portfolio.** I just checked my ePortfolio account, and I only see *five* of you listed. See the Weekly Plan and the portfolio instructions; I provided further instructions on the Questions about the Course thread in a response to Rio.
- Please be sure to complete the **course evaluation**.
- Your **group evaluations** are on your group Discussion threads.

Diana: Pushing through the Last Stretch

This was it! My portfolio and postmortem were due after working on them over the weekend. These were the last assignments in the course, and while I knew I had performed well throughout the term, I didn't want to screw up my grade last-minute with a shoddy essay. Plus, this week wasn't occupied by any other coursework. Most of my classes held their finals during "finals week," which would be Week 11 in the term calendar. Since ProfW decided to have everything due Week 10, I had plenty of time to complete his assignments and still study for my other classes. This scheduling was very much appreciated, and I wondered if ProfW did this purposefully. In my past classes, I felt like most professors decided due dates by throwing a dart at a calendar. Papers would overlap tests, tests would happen after a holiday, and major presentations would be due during finals week despite having many weeks prior to present them. Yet, in ProfW's class, I had a small feeling he was looking out for his students with this scheduling (or at least wanted to get his grading over with earlier rather than later).

My only gripe was the inclusion of a quiz and Discussion board posts. I mean, come on. Technically this is the last week in the course and we're still doing these little assignments that we've been doing *all* semester? I've already written nine weeks' worth of Discussions. I counted, and I wrote sixteen primary posts and sixty-two secondary posts, a total of 12,510 words. That's a lot of writing! It'd be cool if ProfW had an exemption for students who were consistent "posters," so we didn't have to submit posts for the final week. But then again, that would be similar to a professor letting the more vocal students skip the last classes of the course because they've consistently participated. One last week of Discussions wouldn't kill me, so I opened the prompts for the week and got to work.

Scott: Looking Forward, Saying Our Goodbyes, and Recognizing Great Work

This week's Discussions were woven in with the portfolio: They were designed to help students reflect on their work and write about that reflection in a specific way for our portfolios. Peppered throughout the week were also student goodbyes to the class, to each other, and to me.

Thread: Final Reflections on English 102 (and 101)

I gave them a reflective prompt, asking one last time about their overall FYW experience:

Author: Scott Warnock	**Topic**: Final reflections on English 101/102
Subject: Final reflections	**Date**: March 12, 11:20 AM

Dear students,

You are reflecting in your portfolios, and I wondered if you might have a few overall comments about your experience in English 101/102 over the past two terms that you want to share with us, perhaps in the context of Singh-Corcoran's article.

What have you learned since September? Do you think this knowledge will transfer, as she says? What would have helped you more in your writing classes? What has changed since high school? How well prepared were you for college writing? What are your writing expectations as you pursue your major and your career? Were your experiences similar to any of the students in Singh-Corcoran's article?

Let us know,
Prof. Warnock

Reply

This thread was very strong, perhaps, fittingly, one of the best in the course. There were twenty-eight posts comprising 5,500 words, and thirteen students participated. To describe this thread, I'll categorize the comments in a range of categories relevant to the OWC experience.

Accountability

"English 102 also taught me that online classes are not the place for me. I am not good with deadlines online, as I am very forgetful. It is also too much extra work for me, considering I am an engineering student. Overall, it was a positive experience in the fact that i learned a little more about myself and my way of getting things done." —Katie

"A lot of my friends thought that it was crazy when I said I was going to do my English course completely online. I thought that it was crazy too at first and I was skeptical of how it would work. I think that everyone should have the chance to experience an online English course. The online course does not allow leeway for slackers. The teacher can see exactly who is talking and doing their work instead of begging people to raise their hands during class. Throughout my entire life, I have always relied on a participation grade to be that extra push at the end of the quarter if I had a borderline grade. If you were the kid that didn't talk and raise your hand in class at all, you could not rely on that. A lot of students would not talk because they were shy, but an online environment allows you to sit where you are most comfortable and actually have the chance to speak and say what you want to say." —Karen

Student and Teacher Feedback

"Honestly, I don't think much could have been different to help me grow as a writer in this class. I learned that being invested in your work is necessary to learn and the responsibility and focus necessary for an online class helped me to do this. The combined feedback from Prof W and my peers was really helpful. Whether it was positive or negative, it was more responsive than many other experiences that I have had with course in both high school and college. It's almost ironic that our classroom was a virtual environment, and yet, often times I felt as though we got fast and informative feedback way more than in my classes that I attend weekly." —Jennifer

Managing Workload

"Being in an all-online was harder than I thought. When it came to picking classes, the choices of English classes that were given to me were either in the early morning or this online class. I'm not a morning person and I thought to myself that having a class all-online would free up my time. I laugh at that thought now. Yet, after all the readings and postings, I would say that being in this class was definitely worth it" —Rio

Reading

"I also found that the required readings were indeed helpful and some were even quite interesting! Reading different pieces of other writers allowed me to gain familiarity with different styles of writing, different approaches, and how their message can be used in every day situations. This course definitely pushed me to do a lot more work than I was used to for last term's English, but I am definitely glad I had the chance to have this experience." —Alexa

Tech Literacy

"I think being in this class gave each student a little bit of an advantage. That advantage being that we were able to fully conquer learning and interacting in an online environment, which at first is extremely difficult to become adjusted too. Not only did I learn basic writing techniques that have to do with argument, persuasion, or common essay skills in this course but I also began to build a foundation on how to communicate appropriately via online resources such as discussion boards, and how to successfully give an online presentation. The lessons and tools I learned in this course I know will stick with me for the long-run and will help me not only with my writing but with interactions with my peers in general." —Susannah

Writing

"The discussions section showed that even though this is an online course, you can have appropriate and thought provoking arguments and discussions. I thought this online course would have a lighter work load, but I was mistaken. But the work load helped me become better at my writing. Like I said in the beginning of this course, I don't consider myself a great writer, but with the help of Prof. W. and my fellow classmates I can see that it is improving." —Artan

"I had some enjoyment from this course. It provided a pavement to say your voice. You have the time to say what you want without constraints from outer pressure. I'm timid when I talk so when online, it is easy to say what I will." —Alan

"Working online is much different than in a class, learning to clearly relay a message is very crucial when someone can't hear the tone in your voice. The techniques used within this class really do help in the real world, at least from my experiences so far." —Donald

I wondered if this thread cut into another thread, the "Review reflections" thread. Our moderator for this thread had jumped over from that other stagnant thread, and she wasn't very active, perhaps as a result of moving mid-week.

As I mentioned, students made several general nice parting comments, including Katie saying, "It was a pleasure having class with you all!" and Karen writing, "To that effect, good luck to everyone in whatever they choose to do, and good luck in learning to apply whatever comes your way in a positive manner."

Thread: Stranger

This thread was built around a Writing about Writing–type study that focused on one writer, Dave. I wrote a straightforward prompt-from-a-reading to welcome students into the conversation:

Author: Scott Warnock **Topic**: Stranger
Subject: Stranger **Date**: March 12, 11:15 AM

Hi all,

Simple question first: Why is Dave seen as a "stranger in a strange land"?

Could you relate to the experiences Dave shares? How does seeing writing as a social activity affect the study approach and results?

Perhaps you might want to think about the design of the study itself. What do you make of a careful study of one student?

Interested in your comments,
Prof. Warnock

Reply

← "Simple" opening: Let's just start the conversation.

← Then we get into it.

← If they like, they can talk about the study design itself.

Although it was Week 10 and the reading was chunky, many students contributed; I'll narrate the progression and sequence of responses here as a way of demonstrating that even though they may have been tired, they were still willing to compose at a high level on the Discussions:

- Lisa jumped in Tuesday night with a 527-word post addressing all the questions well. Interestingly, though, she responded directly to my post and then apologized in a short follow-up post, writing, "oops, I meant for this to be my primary post." Despite having gone through a whole term with the loose primary / secondary definition that I had encouraged, she, one of the strong students in the course, still thought I wouldn't be able to tease out that indeed a 527-word was a *primary post.* She reposted as a subthread.
- John replied to her, mainly answering the prompt, and I was able to reply to John, who had been in my 101 the previous term, "After having you in a hybrid 101, I must say that I think you shifted 'gears' quite effectively into the electronic discussion environment."
- Lisa's repost led to a lengthy conversation:
    - I replied to her on Tuesday morning, "There are interesting observations about not only Dave's 'stranger' status but the limits of the study design. I'm interested in seeing what others say as well."
    - Tuesday evening, Diana replied, "I found your suggestion of incorporating a social aspect to writing fascinating."
        - Drawing from parts of Diana's post, I wrote, "Can students successfully navigate between their 'formal' writing of school and profession and the 'informal' writing of social media?"
    - Lisa then wrote another long post describing a high school project in which her class was asked to make Facebook pages for characters in *The Great Gatsby.*
    - The conversation moved toward discussions of formality and social media, with the students having a good dialogue and using overt language to connect to each other's posts. Deryck found "this topic fascinating, as well"; Susannah wrote, "I also agree that this is a very interesting topic, and I have to agree with Diana's statement"; Nate wrote, "I actually find myself almost never using abbreviations when typing a text message or on social sites such as facebook"; John wrote, "I agree . . ." One student posted at the very end of this subthread, on Thursday afternoon, merely answering my prompts. As we've men-

tioned, detached posts like that tend to end the conversation, as this one did, and are out of place with the dialogue that precedes them.

- John started another good subthread, titled "Stranger." He wrote provocatively, "The author also saw writing as a social event. I think this could possibly have an effect on the outcome of this study. Writing in an English class could be seen as a lot more social event than the experience of writing in a science class. . . . From experience, I have come to learn that the feeling of writing in a science-based subject is a very lonely feeling." Susannah replied directly to John in a long post. Artan said, "I feel the same way as Dave, too" and elaborated. Donald wrote, "I agree as well." Jennifer, replying to John, said, "I think the way you explained Dave's situation is exactly right."
- Katie fell behind as the moderator, but on Friday she did try to jump in with a subthread titled "Technical writing," in which she asked, "Do any of you enjoy technical writing?"
- Jennifer, Karen and I all responded directly to Katie. Jennifer wrote, "I definitely do not enjoy technical writing" (!).
- Going into the weekend, two students posted late primary posts. While they answered my initial questions, they were out of step with the others, with the *conversation*, that week.
- At the end of the conversation, in fact, on Monday of Week 11, I wrote:

Author: Scott Warnock | **Topic**: Stranger
Subject: The loneliness of writing | **Date**: March 19, 1:51 PM

You all captured well that feeling of transitioning between different types of writing, but I was struck by what a "lonely" experience science writing can be.

I hope you take with you from this class the idea that you can (almost) always incorporate others into your process, even if it's just talking through the initial brainstorming of a project.

Take care,
ProfW

Reply

Thread: My Favorite Poster

Earlier in the term, I asked the students in a metawriting prompt to post about a favorite *post*. This week, I asked them to reflect on who was their overall favorite *poster* in the course.

Author: Scott Warnock | **Topic**: My favorite poster
Subject: My favorite poster | **Date**: March 12, 11:14 AM

Hi all,

As we did a few weeks ago, I want you to look back through the archives of our Discussion threads this term. However, this time, I want you to identify a particular person whose posts stood out for you all term. Identify a few examples by this person, and use actual quotes to demonstrate the talent of this writer and to provide evidence for your choice.

Give out some compliments,
Prof. Warnock

Reply

← I open in a low-key way.

← The directions are succinct but, I hope, clear.

As I mentioned in Week 5, I almost always use a thread like this at the end of a hybrid or online course. I like that they have to build an argument based on their perceptions of other students' writing. I like that they pay each other compliments. I like to see the students who have worked hard get the deserved kudos and confidence boost on this thread. But I mainly like that the students must circle back and review the Discussions, touching those texts yet again.

While five students received a "vote" for favorite poster, Diana was the overwhelming favorite. This post by Jennifer perhaps summed it up:

Author: Jennifer | **Topic**: My favorite poster
Subject: Re: My favorite poster | **Date**: March 16, 4:09 PM

Although everyone went on and on about how great of a writer Diana is already, I have to agree that she was my favorite poster. I thought that she exemplified exactly what it is to be a persuasive writer and give convincing arguments. She was never offensive or defensive in proving her points and overall had my favorite argument from all of the vast posts throughout our many discussions. One of my favorite posts from the whole entire course is Diana's post about Odd Girl Out. She explains how her evaluative purpose was successful driven by her use of a little engine "if we do not understand (the importance of unique style), we will not understand (the value individualism brings to society)" and explains that her solution is lacking. I feel as though in most ways she went past the questions that Prof W was asking us, and went far past everything that was required. Overall, she explained everything better than I possibly could have.

Reply

← First, Jennifer mentions other posters on the thread.

← She uses some quoted evidence from one of Diana's posts. She also connects with some other learning in the course: "a little engine."

At the risk of making Diana blush in retrospect, I think the support was more than warranted. There were other strong writers, but she certainly distinguished herself.

The students showed a great range of reasons and "research" behind their decisions: Many students did what I asked, as Jennifer did: They used evidence and often quotes from their choices. These did not strike me as casual choices. The students who were chosen wrote back with short replies thanking their fans in English 102!

Thread: One Conversation Too Many

During the week, I also started a thread with this prompt:

Author: Scott Warnock	**Topic**: Review reflections?
Subject: Review reflections?	**Date**: March 12, 11:23 AM

Hi all,

You have looked at a lot of each other's writing this term. If that process has been helpful, feel free to use this thread to post a draft of your reflection, and hopefully one or more of your colleagues will take a few minutes to provide some in-depth thoughts about what you wrote—I certainly will as well.

Best,
Prof. Warnock

Reply

Katie jumped in as moderator, but that was the only post! Perhaps, as Diana described, the students had reached a state of writing exhaustion, and that's worth thinking about when designing a week's activities in an OWC, especially toward the end of a term.

Diana: Should I Really Have Been the "Favorite"?

When I saw we were tasked with selecting our favorite contributor in the course, I immediately knew my pick would be Alan. While I was happy interacting with all of my classmates throughout the course, whenever I saw Alan's name pop up on the Discussion boards I knew the conversation would be energetic, humorous, and insightful. I wrote a lengthy post referencing memorable posts from Alan and closed with the following lines:

> Aside from Alan's knack of stimulating everyone's thinking, I admire him most for being a positive energy in the class. Of course, we all know that real classrooms experience specific moments of small bursts of fun conversation. Unfortunately, in this environment, students have the tendency to stick to material and rarely diverge from serious discussions. Alan, however, was the lighthearted energy in our class discussions that we needed.

Of course, I was excited for Alan to read this post, but I was also eager to see who the other favorites were among my peers. I had a few in mind but was looking forward to a journey down memory lane with the rest of my classmates.

By the end of the week, though, I was not comfortable with how this Discussion thread played out. Out of my thirteen classmates who participated in the thread, nine chose me as their favorite. This was a huge compliment and testament to my work in the course. I was happy to receive such overwhelming recognition from my peers, but I couldn't read through the Discussion thread without my face burning up with sheepish embarrassment. What must my other classmates be thinking? Did some of them regret joining the "Diana was the best" bandwagon after seeing the unbalanced results? Did others wish they had been recognized? Why did this happen in the first place?

I was also frustrated with the unbalanced discussion that took place. Throughout our course, ProfW repeatedly instructed us to diversify the content in our posts and vary our interactions to stimulate a fluid conversation. In the first few weeks we ran into difficulties repeating each other's words and neglecting to ask/answer new questions. By the end of the course, however, I felt we had greatly improved our abilities to foster a progressive dialogue in the Discussions. Yet, even if I was the overwhelmingly obvious choice for the best poster in the course, nine students should not have repeated one another. What happened in this thread?

Perhaps it was simply individual laziness due to the end of the term. It was Week 10, we still had several assignments to finish in the course, let alone a pile of work I'm sure we all had in other classes. It could have been that nine students *did* initially think I was their favorite poster, but when they logged onto the Discussions to see that multiple students had already picked me, they didn't care about repetition and submitted their post anyway. In the same vein, a tad bit of groupthink could be responsible for the unbalanced discussion. The very basis of groupthink discourages creativity and individuality, so when a class of students are stressed due to other responsibilities and burnt out from the course, it's not surprising that they would settle on similar responses.

If this question had been asked earlier, maybe in Week 8 or 9, my classmates might have produced a more varied dialogue. Then again, we had a tight work schedule near the end of the course, so that might not have helped the distraction of my classmates. Perhaps anonymizing the results could have varied my peers' responses. If individuals knew their names wouldn't be revealed, maybe they would have gone for a less obvious pick. I think a restructuring of the question might have created a more interesting dialogue. Simply asking for "a favorite poster" automatically limits the conversation to one answer. Yet, if this thread was set up with more variety—an "end-of-term superlatives" if you will—we could have had a lot of fun with it. Categories like "most creative writer," "best moderator," and "most active contributor" could have spread the acknowledgments around to recognize a variety of skills and contributions.

I'm acknowledging this not to diminish the recognition my peers gave me as a significant contributor to the class. Of course, I am overwhelmingly grateful that I was not only praised by my peers but was also given the opportunity to show admiration and gratitude to my classmates. I also hope I'm not diminishing the creative, harmonizing role ProfW so often played in the class. His level of engagement happens so rarely in classrooms, let alone those in higher ed. However, striving for the best conversation, the best thinking, and the best results in our Discussions is what made this class so great in the first place.

Scott: Portfolios and Reflections

Again, many FYW programs and teachers use portfolios. In using an eportfolio, I had to make sure that things were off to a good start and that, technologically, students had set me up as a reviewer; I posted a version of this announcement on Wednesday *and* Friday of Week 10:

Announcements for Friday, March 16:

- As of today, five of you still *do not have me listed as a reviewer* of your **ePortfolio.** Time is ticking down, as the portfolios **are due today**. *Please take care of this ASAP.*
- Please be sure to complete the **course evaluation** below.

I emphasized this message with a pop-up announcement that appeared when students opened the homepage. In the pop-up, I went a step further, listing students whose portfolios I *could* see.

"Gathering" the portfolios was easy: Once all students had made me a reviewer, I simply had to use my ePortfolio account. I encountered some logistical and technological glitches. By the weekend, I still had two students who did not provide me with access to their portfolios, so I emailed them. One resolved the problem quickly. Another, late afternoon on Friday, wrote:

From: Jennifer
Sent: Friday, March 16 4:47 PM
To: Scott Warnock
Subject: Portfolio

Hi Prof W,
Sorry that this is sort of last minute. I am aware that the portfolio is due today. However, I typically compose all of my assignments in word and then transfer them over to whatever medium we need to submit them in. I didn't take English last term, and I didn't see that we were supposed to email you if we didn't already create a portfolio. So, I just wanted to ask you how I go about doing that so that I can submit my assignments. Thanks a lot.
Jennifer

I replied in the "stern-but-I'm-still-your-supportive-teacher" voice:

From: Scott Warnock
Sent: Friday, March 16 5:25 PM
To: Jennifer
Subject: re: Portfolio

Hi Jennifer,
Sorry, but I've been asking you to set this up for three weeks. I've sent multiple messages and posted multiple Announcements about the process of setting up an ePortfolio account and making me a reviewer. Everything you need is either in the Projects folder or in a response I wrote to Rio on the "Questions about the course" thread. I'm a little frustrated, but I am here to help you, so if you run into obstacles, you should definitely reach out to me by phone or email.
Best,
ProfW

This exchange provided another opportunity to consider OWCs and literacy. I wasn't sitting in front of Jennifer, providing other cues to let her know that while she had not done her part, it wasn't fatal for the course. It takes hard writing by me to communicate these nuances to students—and that "writing well" will of course still be a function of if the student *sees* the writing in that way. The message I wrote to her was in that tough-to-write category: I wanted to let her know firmly that she had to be accountable for her work (a "Don't worry about it!" from me wouldn't cut it here), but I didn't want her to panic. Jennifer had done well enough in the course all term, and I did not want to see this end-of-term issue ruin her experience—and her grade.

Other students asked if they could revise their 101 portfolios (the answer: "Yes!"), how to handle the audience of the reflective analysis, and how, again, to use the software to allow me to see their portfolios (several students asked about this; I had provided directions in multiple places, and many students seemed to have procrastinated). Looking through and evaluating the portfolios was not difficult or time-consuming either, since I had read closely almost everything that was in them. Using a brief rubric as a guide, on Wednesday morning of Week 11, I evaluated the portfolios and emailed comments in the three rubric categories: Reflective Analysis; Artifacts (Evidence); Portfolio Design/Presentation. The reflective analyses were short, and many of them were effective in describing the students' work in the course. I didn't communicate the grades via email, though: They had to go to the LMS for that.

One student, in an honest email right after receiving my comments to her, which simply said, "There is nothing in your portfolio except the template materials. Right now, this assignment receives a zero. Please contact me as soon as possible so we can fix this," admitted to being busy with other finals. Via email, I wrote this in response:

Subject: Portfolio
Well, I appreciate your honesty, because you do realize that you should have known about the portfolio for several weeks? You ask about the reflective analysis, but, again, I ask if you've read the assignment and the dialogue on the Discussions over the past two weeks about it? The questions you are asking are all answered in those places.

You've done consistent work in the course, but I need to turn in grades so I'm probably going to have to give you an Incomplete until you get the portfolio done. This is not the end of the world, and we will resolve it.

I am here to help you. You can call me on my cell phone, but unfortunately I am out of town today and tomorrow.
Let me know,
Prof. Warnock

I was attending a conference, but I didn't want the portfolio to ruin her course grade, much as I felt about Jennifer's situation. After this exchange, she still had trouble making her work available to me, which is partly a function of how our ePortfolio works: Students must put material into a kind of filing cabinet in their overall account and then pull those files into specific portfolios they create. Our dialogue about this topic extended past when I submitted grades, to the Saturday of Week 11, but I did end up submitting a change-of-grade request for her not long afterward.

As in other experiences I have had with eportfolios, some students scrambled at the end. However, only one student did not complete the portfolio. Overall, portfolio grades were good.

Reflections

The cover letter for our portfolios was, in alignment with our FWP program, a "reflective analysis" that students used as the basis for their analysis of our program's outcomes. From the instructions:

> You will use the FWP Outcomes as a basis for this analysis, especially these two:
>
> 1. Students will reflect on their own and others' writing and communication processes and practices. They will learn that the term "writer" applies to themselves and their peers.
> 2. Students will use writing to embrace complexity and think about open-ended questions.

This frame gave students structure for their portfolio cover letter, and the students provided fascinating comments about the asynchronous OWC environment and Writing about Writing. They also, to be blunt, said lots of nice things about the course. As has often been the case throughout this book, particularly this chapter, it's best just to let the students speak:

- "This course has forced me to dissect my writing and identify areas that need improvement. I always knew that I needed to improve my writing, but I didn't know how. After completing this course, I now feel that I have the tools to really better myself as a writer. I feel that I am only at the beginning of this process of improvement, but there is already evidence that I have advanced my level of writing throughout this course." —Nate

- "Being aware of and writing to and for the audience that I think will be reading the paper because it can really shape the paper and direction of your writing." —Parinda
- "By taking an online class, I used discussion posts to talk to my peers and practice these skills of arguments and persuasion that I learned throughout the course." —Artan
- "If one can just get his or her two cents in, it could make all the difference in the world in the way a debate turns out. In addition to that, I believe it's worth it to note that this level of communication and interaction can't always be had in a traditional class setting. People are too nervous to speak and let themselves be heard." —Alexa
- "After going through all of my posts, all 10,304 words, and essays from this term, I think I did a decent job of using sources to back up my arguments." —Jennifer

Scott: Course Evaluations

For me, the final week of any teaching experience always brings mixed emotions. You pour so much into your courses, thinking about them constantly for months; the courses are with you throughout the day as you read the newspaper, surf the Web, talk to friends—and then abruptly it ends. Fridays during the term are a busy day, as I'm setting up the following week's work: writing and posting the Weekly Plan, grading that week's Discussions, developing the following week's prompts, getting announcements posted. So, in a way, that final Friday, with no more planning to do, is accompanied by a bit of "found time."

One specific issue in the final week of an OWC is acquiring a representative set of evaluations from students; as online learning in general has expanded, figuring out ways to incentivize students to complete evaluations remains a challenge (e.g., see Heinert and Roberts). In the spirit of constructive redundancy, I reminded them *seven* times about the course evaluations:

- I posted four reminders on the Course Announcements, which, again, greet them on the homepage every time they log into the course;
- the information was mentioned in the final Weekly Plan;
- I also, using the LMS pop-up announcement tools, created a pop-up they couldn't help but see when they logged in;
- finally, I sent them an email reminder.

That term, I also did something I don't always do: I gave a small grade for completing the evaluation, as indicated in the Weekly Plan. Overkill? Maybe. But I received all but one course evaluation. Redundancy, coupled with a minor ten-point grade, helped me achieve my purpose. Like most teachers, I couldn't wait to access those reviews, which I did a few weeks later.

I received very good, positive evaluations for this course. I had a tough decision to make about sharing the responses here, because it may appear self-promotional, even though throughout the previous nine weeks I believe both Diana and I have discussed both the ups and downs of the course.

The students seemed happy. Their multiple-choice responses demonstrated satisfaction with the course—and their experience with me. As is typical of course evaluations, the subjective questions—"Paragraph" sections in Drexel's course evaluation nomenclature—gave me further insight, and the students provided comments to specific questions I created to help me think about what future iterations of my OWCs should be like. The questions that I geared specifically to this course, to my teaching style, and to tools and approaches were the most valuable. I asked how many times per week they checked course announcements, if the Weekly Plans helped structure their course learning, if the Discussions were a valuable part of the course experience for them, and how they felt the individual and team projects connected with their learning.

The Course Readings

Keep in mind the Writing about Writing goals and approach of the course: As you have seen, I often assigned challenging composition texts (often as PDFs), so I asked them specifically in the evaluation: "Please comment on the course readings." Many students wrote that those readings were "boring" and too "long" (those were common words), although most enjoyed *The 33rd* pieces and those from our course text. A few representative comments:

- "Sometimes the PDF files given were difficult to read even for a college level student."
- "Actually, some of the readings were hard to understand right off the bat on top of being mentally tedious to read."
- "I hate the AUX readings; they are boring."

In a bit of a contradiction (course evaluations are full of contradictions!), some students also said that the readings were "interesting" and even beneficial to the course learning:

- "I truly feel that every reading that was required benefitted me in all aspects of learning, understanding, and growing as a writer."
- "They were diversified, interesting, and applicable to my learning."

A few students even found the composition readings more interesting—and challenging—than the textbook readings. The responses were a mixed bag.

Audiovisual Feedback

I had provided AV feedback to some about their drafts. In line with other research I've done about AV (or video) response (see Warnock, "Responding"), I asked them a detailed question:

> Could you please comment about the video feedback you received for Project 1. Did you find the video helpful or not? How would you compare the videos to written comments you have received about your writing? Did the videos affect how "connected" you felt to the course?

Many students liked AV response. Several did say, though, that they still preferred written feedback. A couple students commented on the novelty of receiving feedback via AV, and only one student discussed technical difficulties. Eight students said something about feeling more connected or having a better "personal" connection in the course because of video comments.

What Was Beneficial?

I asked: "What were the most beneficial aspects of this course? (Please be specific.)":

- Three students identified Discussions, and one singled out required secondary posts: "I have done english classes before where you only have to post a primary post, but having the secondary posts forced you to fight for your opinion and have conversations."
- Pacing and the time factor of online learning came up. One student liked that everyone got "to go at their own pace." Another made the enigmatic comment, "there is no time constraints in regards to getting to class. It felt less of a class is what I'm trying to convey due to the lack of a physical location and class period."

- Responsibility: "The most beneficial aspects were the responsibility that the course imposed on us. It made me a lot more accountable for my own work and a lot more responsible in keeping up with my work."

Students described aspects particular to the content of the course such as using rhetoric, citing and backing up claims with evidence, learning to write analytically, the readings, and working in groups. A few complimented my teaching, one saying a benefit was how well organized the course was and another focusing on writing feedback (from a "hard grader"—but in a good way!).

Specific Changes in the Course?

I asked: "What specific, practical changes can you recommend that might improve this course?" Students focused on readings and meeting more synchronously:

- Comments about readings (again): "manageable but meaningful amounts of readings"; "Do away completely with those AUX readings"; change course text readings; shorter readings; fewer readings; readings that didn't appear sideways as PDFs (!).
- Groups: Required meeting with instructor for groups; different grading based on performance; Skype instead of our online meeting space (although that space was generally deemed okay in the evaluations).
- Use the online meeting space for synchronous gatherings a little more, especially to explain projects. A couple students wanted more synchronous time.
- Better writing topics.
- "I feel that this course doesn't need much improvement."
- " . . . better system of reminders" and fewer Discussion requirements.

Finally: Helpful to Your Writing?

My final question was a big one: "Could you briefly comment on how this class helped, or perhaps did not help, you to improve your writing?" Nearly every student said the course benefited their writing in some way. Many comments were similar to the "most beneficial" question above. One student said, "It helped to improve my writing by forcing me to write a lot." Several students commented about rhetoric and how they might apply it in the future. A few students said the tough grading/close evaluation helped. One said instructor comments were most helpful. Another said it was not so much all the writing but the amount of analytical reading that helped. Is this not a comment you want on a course evaluation?: "I invested so much time, I feel that I truly got a wonderful experience out of this and learned a lot."

Diana: My Final Say in the Course

I now had the opportunity to give ProfW my comments. Throughout the course, he was popular for popping into Discussions to give someone a nod, stoke the fire, or push us to produce our best work. For assignments, he provided the most detailed and thoughtful reviews I've ever received from an instructor. While I disagreed with a few decisions here and there, he really was a great professor.

Even though course evaluations are always required at my university, if the professor was adequate or even decent, I would quickly fill out all the "excellent" circles and hand in my evaluation without much more. In reality, just like customers who get rude customer service and diners who are served a tasteless meal, I would only give effort in an evaluation if the professor was bad. I guess it's human nature to complain when you're angry and fall silent when things are fine, and that's especially heightened when feedback is anonymous. Yet this situation deserved detailed and thoughtful praise, because ProfW would have offered the same to me.

Scott: Into Week 11

So our course wound into finals week, or Week 11 at Drexel. I began evaluating their final work early in the week, and I posted this announcement:

Behind the Screen: Reflections in OWC

It is worth saying again: The intersection of writing studies pedagogy and education technology offers superb opportunities for teachers to teach writing more effectively. Reflection is another writing occasion through which students can demonstrate this.

In an OWC, students have this vast corpus—tens of thousands of words—from which to draw and, not insignificantly, to make some often surprising observations about their own writing. In looking back at dialogic writing instead of just at the papers they submitted for an audience of the instructor, they may identify aspects of their writing identity that they didn't expect. Patricia Webb Boyd, in "Online Discussion Boards as Identity Workspaces: Building Professional Identities in Online Writing Classes," makes this case, looking at specific assignments that teach students how to professionalize themselves by reflecting on the creation of their professional identities and by being aware of themselves as professionals through online discussions. Linda Stine, in reviewing the literature about OWI and basic writing, provides analysis of strategies, including self-reflection, that would be useful for any OWI instructor. L. Lennie Irvin, in "Reflection in the Electronic Writing Classroom," takes a broad look at how "computer networks are, indeed, hospitable mediums for reflection."

While not the focus of this course, you may also find it useful to encourage students to zero in on the technologies they write with; Kelli Cargile Cook and Keith Grant-Davie's edited collection *Online Education 2.0: Evolving, Adapting, and Reinventing Online Technical Communication* provides ways of thinking about technologically driven rhetorical reflection.

Announcements for Monday, March 19:

- I have started **grading your portfolios** today. If I can't see your portfolio, it is now late.
- Please remember to **complete the course evaluation**. Remember, it's worth 10 points.
- Your **latest grades** are available on our LMS for Discussions and other work.
- Don't hesitate to **contact me** with end-of-the-term questions. Good luck with all of your final exams and projects.

I was close to finishing evaluating and grading their work. That Tuesday evening, as I mentioned, I was heading to a conference. An online course offers an interesting convenience for teachers and students. Although I was heading out of town, that meant little for my OWC: I simply brought the course with me. I continued reading and evaluating their final work on the plane. After I landed and arrived in my hotel, I logged on and posted this final announcement:

Announcements for Tuesday, March 20:

- I will have completed all **grading** by Wednesday and will be **turning in final grades that day**. The Discussion boards are now closed. Thanks for your hard work on them all term.

On Wednesday I was on the phone from my hotel room with the one student who could not get the portfolio straightened out. We eventually did resolve it.

The end of the term had arrived. As I said, it was, for me, that bittersweet moment: The end of a teaching term, the move forward—once I returned home—to the brief break between terms that Drexel offers, and the promise of a new class and another group of students.

In Retrospect: More to College Writing Than "Papers"

We both well know that students are accustomed to writing papers for teachers. After all, they have done it all their lives. Many first-year college students have had long experience with caring, invested high school teachers. Many have used portfolios to collect and reflect on essays they have written. But while they are "screenagers" or "digital natives," most have never engaged in the level of discourse of an OWC Discussion. Their reflections about this work allow some to come to interesting discoveries, as this student perhaps exemplified: "This course helped me understand there is more to college writing than just cranking out the previously dreaded five-page paper. Online posting and group discussion boards have given me a venue to showcase and exercise my developing voice." This is the kind of "studenting" potential that an OWC represents.

The end of the Weekly Plan included some words of goodwill to these hardworking students. There would still be a few end-of-term matters, but English 102 had come to an end.

• • • •

Scott: March 21. *By Wednesday night of finals week, I had evaluated all student work and completed my grade calculations. I double-checked the numbers and provided an associated letter with each number grade. At a conference, working from a hotel, I logged into Drexel's grade system and with that solemn authority carefully entered each grade. It's always a strange experience, this ritual of final grading, especially in an OWC. There's a neatness and clarity to the grade, but I feel a vast sense of oversimplification: The lovely messiness of digital writing, the tens of thousands of words of interaction, is represented by a single numerical signifier. I came across the name "Gasiewski, Diana," and smiled as I chose "A" from the drop-down menu. She was one of several students who had worked hard over the last quarter. I thought back on these students and had a clear view of not just their writing style but their work ethic and intellectual predilections, not just who they were but how they thought. I knew them as writers.*

Diana: March 23: *Toward the end of the final week, I received an email from ProfW asking if I had a free moment to meet with him in his office to talk about my performance in the course. With excitement and a bit of horror, I told him I would be happy to. Once there, he acknowledged my success in the course and suggested I take another class with him: an intensive, peer reading preparation course. This class would comprise students who were mostly recommended by their professors to pursue rigorous training and eventually work toward becoming writing tutors at the Drexel Writing Center. At that point, I was already pursuing a change in major, applying to become a resident assistant, interested in joining the club tennis team, and taking a full load of classes next term. No way did I even think to apply to the writing center! However, after reflecting on the positive experience I had in English 102, I decided to give it a shot. And I did.*

Beyond the Final Week: The [Ongoing] Lessons of an OWC

The reach of this discipline goes much further, however, in that the practices and understandings of this particular discipline, composed knowledge, infuse and are intrinsic to successful performance in all other disciplines.

—LINDA ADLER-KASSNER AND ELIZABETH WARDLE from *Naming What We Know: Threshold Concepts of Writing Studies*

In Retrospect: Reflections about an OWC

This book presented us with an unusual opportunity to review the experience and learning of an OWC. Below, we examine briefly some discoveries we made through the process of reviewing closely and reflecting on the words, the hundreds of thousands of words, that made up this OWC.

OWI: A Dialogic Writing Experience

Return for a moment to the student who wrote this in the course evaluation:

> The most beneficial aspects were being required to do secondary posts. I have done english classes before where you only have to post a primary post, but having the secondary posts forced you to fight for your opinion and have conversations.

This student eloquently points out how the simple pedagogical mechanism of secondary posts helps students "fight" for their opinions and "have conversations." Students not only want but need more opportunities like this through which to communicate with each other, and the quasi-professional environment of a Discussion board is a good way to do it. Teachers in all modalities ask how they can have their students talk to each other more. As we described each week, we were continually struck by the work that was done on the Discussions. These were smart students with the proper technology, so access and preparation were not issues, but it was clear throughout the term that students could use Discussions to build their knowledge of the material in the course through dialogue with Scott and their fellow students.

This is no teaching wizardry, nor is it necessarily only in online learning. Instead, it is a matter of creating a structure that enables conversations to happen. Diana reflected on the problems of educational dialogue in general: She only had a few truly conversational courses in her whole career! The OWC that we described is fundamentally conversational. Building from Kenneth Bruffee's idea that writing is the internalized conversation of thought re-externalized (technologically), the many metawriting opportunities this term allowed students to talk and think about their own writing, their courses, and perhaps their whole educational experience—again, what we are calling "studenting"—to an audience of other readers and learners.

So What Have They Learned in/through an OWC?

Through course evaluations, teachers hope to gain insight into what worked and what didn't, and they often want to know if students *learned anything*. This is a hard question for education in general, and a particularly tough one for writing instruction.

Because the OWC makes so much of student process writing explicit, one could argue that we can use this method of teaching, even in the shape of digitally supported onsite instruction, to better see what students have learned and *how* that learning happened. Even the group work, especially for groups that relied on Discussions, had a transparency that might be difficult to "see" in other teaching situations. Teachers might use that transparency to drive new research about writing/composing and thinking. As Beth Hewett and Scott wrote in "The Future of OWI," the final chapter of *Foundational Practices of Online Writing Instruction*, "There are, in short, new research methods and tools that will be developed as we deal not only with the newness of these texts but also with their sheer volume and our need for ways to access and assess them" (558). Online writing teachers also have new contributions to make to distance/online learning, such as the role of volition in learning and perhaps uncovering behaviors that will contribute more to student success.

In the end, an OWC provides a great structure for writing and, more important, metabehaviors/thinking about writing. There was a temptation in this final chapter to have Diana try to express what she learned. But we didn't want

Behind the Screen: Transfer in Composition

Increasing energy in composition research is being focused on ***transfer***, or how the writing learning/instruction from one context, e.g., a first-year course, manifests itself in another context, e.g., a professional writing environment. We spend an enormous amount of time teaching students how to write and teaching them *about* writing, talking about these practices, conducting research, and writing about these practices. Moving up the education ladder, educational stakeholders are asking transfer questions about the overall education experience: *What are people learning, and how are they demonstrating that learning in other contexts?*

Such transfer is not easy to establish or identify, to say the least. As Chris Anson wrote in "Crossing Thresholds: What's to Know about Writing Across the Curriculum" in *Naming What We Know* (Adler-Kassner and Wardle), recognizing how difficult transfer is "helps faculty to realize that no amount of prior knowledge from a generalized composition course will help students to cope with new genres" (211); these genres are, and here he quotes Elizabeth Wardle, "context-specific and complex and cannot be easily or meaningfully mimicked outside their naturally occurring rhetorical situations and exigencies" (767). This is not to dishearten you. Anson and Wardle are talking about upending the role of first-year comp as a mythical training ground for "all writing."

Some foundations for thinking about transfer can be found in Mary Jo Reiff and Anis Bawarshi's "Tracing Discursive Resources: How Students Use Prior Genre Knowledge to Negotiate New Writing Contexts in First-Year Composition" and David Russell's "Activity Theory and Its Implications for Writing Instruction." Both consider transfer through *genre*. Kathleen Blake Yancey, in the chapter "Defining Reflection: The Rhetorical Nature and Qualities of Reflection," considers transfer also through the lens of reflection.

to end up with oversimplified or even treacly comments about her being a better writer after this class. She was pretty good when she came in, as you have no doubt seen. However, perhaps through Diana's specific, rich narrative and through the work of her classmates, including the course evaluations, we could argue that the "transfer" of the course need not be measured in deliverables at the next level—whatever "level" even means in this context. The transfer is in their reflective practices as writers and what they engaged in through the *experience.* (Quick comment: In puzzling out our thoughts about Diana's comments about transfer at the end here, we laughed: After all, for a FYW student, what greater transfer could you ask for than that you wrote a book with your professor?)

The Narrative Turn and Assessment

The conversations about transfer coincide and intersect with dialogue about assessment. Schools and education systems are being boxed into oversimplified structures of assessment and evaluation. Some of it is, to use an often vapid but here relevant word, unfair. This is not the place for a lengthy rant about standardized testing practices, but education is often put to unrealistic assessment standards, beyond those of any other comparable human endeavors. Scott has long wondered how it would look if people evaluated the relationships of their lives with the kind of oversimplified, standardized test-driven rubrics that schools, teachers, and students are subjected to? ("Even though it seems to be working for you, GreatMarriages.com says your marriage is a '3'"!)

OWI may present opportunities to re-approach this issue. Scott has seen on campuses how OWI has been a target of a type of "unfair" assessment thinking, with administrators sometimes asking for assessment accountability about OWCs that would not be asked for—or certainly *is* seldom asked for—in comparable onsite courses. The result can be dumbed-down programmatic assessment that benefits no one. (Edward White, Norbert Elliot, and Irvin Peckham's *Very Like a Whale* offers productive alternatives.) That being said, because of the amount of time and money that institutions, teachers, and students spend on OWCs, we should figure out if what we are doing is working. In this book, we hope to offer a view of how the path of narrative can lead us into new perspectives about course learning. Looking at the range of experiences and texts in a learning environment can perhaps best be accomplished by slowing down and taking a close look at what happened in a course and capturing and then telling that story. We did not represent our course experience/learning simply by a series of spreadsheets or an indefensible before-and-after essay writing boondoggle. Including projects, Diana wrote more than fifteen thousand words in a range of rhetorical situations. How would that work operate in the writing and, again, we can't stress this enough, the *thinking about writing* that she would engage in not just in the next FYW course but the rest of her academic, professional, and personal writing? The overall corpus of her and her colleagues' texts represented a challenge in writing the book but a tremendous opportunity overall to think about telling the *stories* of educational experiences; this approach may not replace quantifiable representations but might be more strongly considered in assessing a range of educational endeavors.

Literacy

Throughout this book, we have highlighted the substantial literacy opportunities that exist in a course like this. Students worked at literacy in various ways all term. Cynthia Selfe and Gail Hawisher in 2004 defined technological literacy as "practices involving reading, writing, and exchanging information in online environments, as well as the values associated with such practices—cultural, social, political, and educational" (678). Students working in an OWC find themselves in challenging literacy environments, and researchers are now taking an increasing look at the reading literacy that is the core of the experience for students—and teachers.

Might an OWC be an ideal environment to teach and reinforce literacy practices? We examined reading and literacy closely in Week 7, discussing the work of those such as Beth Hewett (in particular *Reading to Learn*), and June Griffin and Deborah Minter, who have examined the literacy load of an OWC. When you consider the reading, especially what we might consider the "transactional" reading, that takes place, an OWC might seem like not just a good place to teach reading but a good place to launch scholarly work that focuses on reading and literacy conceived more generally.[1]

Technologies for Writing Instruction

Diana expressed several times her critiques of the LMS and its suite of technologies. As hefty as some of them are, all LMSs have limitations, but most have particular gaps in the way they allow OWCs to be taught; they remain focused on ways of delivering content. By understanding in more depth the needs of technologically mediated writing courses, which in sheer numbers are quite large in many institutions, LMS creators might consider better ways to develop systems for managing the texts that are composed in an OWC.

As mentioned, in all modalities, we need more robust ways of facilitating student conversation in our courses, and those modes of conversation online are linked to technology development— and are also connected to avenues of OWI research.

Research in OWI

Our primary goal was to provide a narrative-driven guide for teaching OWCs. But the research opportunities are substantial and quite likely have broader implications for those invested in composition. As Beth Hewett and Scott wrote in that concluding chapter of *Foundational Practices*, "We believe that OWI will—if allowed—change how people in our profession view their work as writing teachers overall and ultimately change how outsiders view us. Good OWI should move composition—the whole structure—forward" (560). Of course, these changes, this possibility of moving "the whole structure" ahead, are connected with teaching, transfer, and assessment.

As we composed this book, tools and practices for corpus analysis were being developed and refined by composition scholars, in some cases building on the work of computational linguists: Joe Moxley and Norbert Elliot at South Florida (Dixon and Moxley), Brad Dilger and the Crow archive work (Wang et al.), and Dylan Dryer at the University of Maine. The work of the humanities in general and composition specifically has always lent itself to this type of research, and with digital texts and *tools with which to analyze them*, we have a powerful way to develop both informed practice and theory about the teaching of writing and the composing of student—and instructor—texts in instructional settings.

Again, a challenge for us was capturing succinctly and accurately the weekly Discussion dialogues. They were all so individually interesting that it was difficult not to drop into the rabbit hole of devoting significant time to each. This book demonstrates the vast corpus that is developed in every OWC; while one could say this is true of almost all first-year writing courses, the *visibility/transparency* of the texts struck us as we went through each week's work. Instructors could, or perhaps some *would* if they had the time and support, turn into researchers with material readily available to them. As we tried to show by representing the Discussions in several different ways, analysis can be simple yet still enlightening through mapping rhetorical moves, finding connections among students, looking at time stamps, etc. Seeing the connectivity of the authors and their texts might lead to generalizable ways of improving teaching, as we found specific pedagogical strategies such as student moderators, the types of readings, and the role of a teacher in a Discussion led to different outcomes in these text-driven environments.

The implications for research are apparent, and this research in writing studies might be accompanied by a shift in the politics of writing instruction—fraught territory indeed. If we establish how different digital pedagogies affect student performance, then we provide grounding for solid arguments that we need people trained in these pedagogies. Empowering these types of decisions can empower the field of writing studies as it manifests itself on the ground at institutions, where writing programs could have a more prominent place in institutional dialogue.

Students should be part of these conversations! Heidi Skurat Harris, Tawnya Lubbes, Nancy Knowles, and Jacob Harris wrote, "Because asynchronous online instruction often results in a document trail of interactions in discussion-board posts, wikis, and other forms of shared interaction, the potential exists for students not only to enact knowledge construction but also to study, use, and value that interaction" (109). We hope this book has shown strongly the value of placing students in the forefront of our representations of teaching.

Student Voices: The View of "Studenting"

Indeed, students need a more prominent place in our conversations. In our introduction, we mention how Mary Louise Pratt, in "Arts of the Contact Zone," makes this observation:

> Teacher-pupil language, for example, tends to be described almost entirely from the point of view of the teacher and teaching, not from the point of view of pupils and pupiling (the word doesn't even exist, though the thing certainly does). If a

> classroom is analyzed as a social world unified and homogenized with respect to the teacher, whatever students do other than what the teacher specifies is invisible or anomalous to the analysis. (38)

Let's linger over "If a classroom is analyzed as a social world unified and homogenized with respect to the teacher. . . ." Although most of the people involved in the endeavor that we call "education" are students, the "official" conversations about schooling and education usually don't include them. We began this project with the premise that student voices are not prominent enough in education research and assessment. That straightforward idea drove much of this book: What is a course? What happens in it? What is a school? Don't just look at numbers; try to provide platforms and venues to hear and see what the students in that school are doing.

We hope that's what we have done. This is a book about an OWC experience, but as we developed it, we felt we were creating a model for a good general way to talk more about teaching. This book provided Diana with a platform from which to speak. Teachers often have a keen interest in the topic of *accessibility*, but they often haven't thought much about what taking one of their courses is like. While writing a book is difficult—it always is!—educators must find additional ways to place students' voices more prominently, because otherwise we substitute, bluntly, the lived narrative experience of human beings with the reductive assessment, testing, and ranking culture that permeates education now.

We can do better. All stories are unique, idiosyncratic, and this one is no different. Diana was a particular student that winter, and not an average student at that. The course was its own. Scott was an experienced OWT with a certain teaching style and approach at a specific institution with its own curriculum. But, gesturing back to our introduction, where we describe our goal of depicting this educational experience through narrative, we hope that you learned more about OWI through hearing about our course than from a pile of spreadsheets that try to tell you what the course "was." And we hope that you enjoyed the story.

In the end, this course represented the opportunities of OWI. Through their intellectual work, their writing, students were able to know their teacher, know each other, work together, and learn how to be better writers. You, we hope, gained from seeing close-up how that meeting of the minds happened.

Appendix

Course Assignments

Drexel University | Dept. of English and Philosophy

Composition Project 1: The Rhetoric of Sustainability

When people can see a vision and simultaneously recognize what can be done step by step in a concrete way to achieve it, they will begin to feel encouragement and enthusiasm instead of fright.

~ Eric Fromm, *To Have or To Be*, 143

To make ours a truly great environment, we must form mutually beneficial partnerships within our surrounding neighborhoods.

~Drexel President John Frye, "A Message from the President," Nov. 5, 2010

Sustainability has been one of the major rhetorical campaigns of the late 20th and early 21st centuries: a greener earth, clean air, lasting peace between conflicting cultures and nations, a stable urban infrastructure, support for youth as future leaders, literacy education for all people, public health, a continued fostering of the arts. The *exigency* of the larger message behind sustainability seems to be this: The world is in need of repair, and it requires the steady, committed work of citizens to do it. Drexel, too, is invested in this message.

Though groups across the political, aesthetic, and spiritual arenas may subscribe to this campaign, they do so in different ways. Professional disciplines, as well as community and volunteer organizations, have found their own ways to define sustainability. Examples:

- DuPont's "JustMeans" campaign aims to create products using sustainable materials;
- The Center for Sustainable Practice in the Arts aims to connect and support smaller initiatives to create art and art curriculum about sustainability;
- Fashion giant Urban Outfitters has found a way to latch onto sustainability culture with its "Urban Renewal" campaign.

In your professional and social life, you will make decisions about the role *you* want to play in sustainability. This first project invites you to **analyze**, **evaluate**, and **develop an evidence-based argument** about a sustainability campaign that interests you.

Steps in the Process

Like any authentic research project, you'll begin with inquiry: What do I know? What don't I know? You'll use research to get to know the sustainability campaign(s) going on and emerging in a profession, field, or social or volunteer organization of your choice. Once you've done that research, you'll

1. Choose a campaign.
2. Analyze its rhetorical strategies: How it aims to convince its targeted audience.
3. Use this analysis to make an *evaluative argument* about this campaign.

As you develop this analytical argument, these guiding questions might help you:

- How is "sustainability" defined in the context I've chosen? How do I know?
- What is the *exigency*, *audience*, *purpose,* and *message* of the sustainability campaign I'm examining?

- What *rhetorical strategies* do I see going on in this campaign? Are they effective? How do I know?
- What do *I* think about this campaign? Would I get on board? How would I change it? Are there other campaigns out there that are superior?

What does a rhetorical analysis of a campaign look like? You will find useful the article "Attacking the Tobacco Industry: A Rhetorical Analysis of Advertisements by the Campaign for Tobacco-Free Kids," by Benoit and Harthcock, assigned for Week 2.

Your audience. Your instructor and your peers are part of your audience. But the message you send with this analysis may be of interest to broader audiences. Thus, you can choose a broader audience, based on your purpose, message, and context.

Form. Depending on your audience, purpose, message, and context, this composition may take a variety of forms: e.g., an opinion piece, a letter, a memo, a report, a blog.

Research and Evidence. Your project will draw on at least one form of *primary* research (see our course textbook 553-558), and at least one form of *scholarly* research. Additionally, you may draw on other sources (journals, newspapers or magazines, Websites, images, popular culture) as your audience, purpose, and message require.

Specifications:
- 1,200 words
- **Sources**: You must use at least one form of *primary* research and one form of *scholarly* research.
- Proper source documentation (see *The Purdue OWL,* http://owl.english.purdue.edu/)

As you draft and revise, utilize peer review feedback, my feedback, and The Drexel Writing Center.

Works Cited

Fromm, Erich. *To Have or To Be*. New York: Continuum, 1976.
Frye, John. "A Message from the President." Email newsletter. 5 Nov. 2010.

Composition Project 2: Collaborating to Make Change

Coming together is a beginning, staying together is progress,
and working together is success.
–Henry Ford

Though much of your academic life will be an independent journey toward professionalization, you will find that the professional world itself is abuzz with teamwork. Members of these teams use their collective energies, intellects, and creativity to solve problems and create change. In your educational careers (and possibly in your work experiences) each of you has likely participated in collaboration, in which members of a team had to work toward a common goal, responsibly and efficiently distribute the labor, keep an eye on one another's progress, and be evaluated as a collective.

This second project will help you to further cultivate those skills as you work in groups to think about a **local problem** you care about, either in Philadelphia or here at Drexel University. This local problem can be specific to your discipline, to your social lives, to your academic lives. Together, your group will **articulate the problem**, **analyze the causes and effects** of the problem, **propose a clear solution**, and **argue persuasively for your solution**. In short, you're going to put your composition and rhetoric skills to work in some *real* ways. You will work together to

1. Brainstorm and identify issues you care about in Philadelphia or here on campus
2. Uncover a problem that is most pertinent to your group's interests
3. Explore the development and effects of the problem
4. Create a feasible solution
5. Think critically about audience(s) that must see/hear your analysis and solution
6. Design a persuasive proposal directed at your intended audience(s)

Rhetorical Situation

Genre: Thinking rhetorically about purpose, audience, and context, your team will decide the form your project will take: Report, Website, blog, brochure, article for a specific publication, commercial, podcast, advertising campaign, short film, grant proposal.

Audience and Context: Your peers and I are part of your audience. But the message you send with this analysis will be of special interest to audiences involved in the problem you're trying to solve. Thus, it is up to you to decide who you want your audience to be, based on your purpose, message, and context.

Furthermore, be prepared to explain the context in which you'll be delivering this composition; how will it get to its intended audience? For example, if your group has created a commercial, how will you get that commercial on the air? Or, if your group wants to make an oral presentation to the Mayor, how will you get your foot in the door?

Research and Documentation: You and your group members will work together to gather sources and compose an **Annotated Bibliography.** Your sources list should include:

1. *Primary research*: Your project should draw on your own *primary research* of the topic. It will be informed by institutions and people related to your exploration. Primary research includes interviews, surveys, and observations that help you to find out more about your topic.
2. *Secondary research*: Your project should include at least two scholarly sources, as well as other forms of secondary research (like popular journals, newspapers, film, music).
3. *Visual:* Your project should use at least one type of *visual*, like a chart, graph, or photo.

Length: Text projects (article, blog, brochure, etc.) should be about **2000 words. Audio/visual** projects (with minimal text) should be accompanied by a 1000-word rhetorical analysis in which writers discuss in detail the purpose, message, audience, context, role of the writers in the project, and reason for the chosen format.

Summary of Project Components

Informal Writing:

1. Group Contract
2. Project reports
3. Post-mortem Reflection

Formal Components:

4. Topic Proposal and Project Plan
5. Annotated Bibliography
6. Collaborative Composition (and Rhetorical Analysis, if necessary)
7. Group Presentation

Schedule

Week 5: Form teams, group contract, topics, progress report.
Week 6: Annotated bibliography, progress report.
Week 7: Draft of project, progress report.
Week 8: Final project; progress report.
Week 9: Presentation, post-mortem.

Grading

The project is worth 250 points. The Project 2 Topic Proposal and Research Plan and the Annotated Bibliography are each worth 50.

Group Management and Evaluation

Group Contract: Once your group has formed, your first collaborative project will be to create a group contract. How will you divide responsibilities? How will you monitor the efforts of your peers? How will you make sure that all are abiding by the expectations of deadlines, proper research, and productive communication? This contract will articulate the ethical practices and commitments of your group. Specifically, your contract should address the following elements:

- •Communication
- •Effort
- •Adherence to deadlines
- •Reliability
- •Quality
- •Academic integrity

Project Report: Four times over the course of this collaborative project, individual students will email me a brief report about how the project is going thus far. These reports will reflect on how the group is working together toward their goal: Successes? Challenges? Questions? They will also help to keep me in the loop on how group dynamics are working.

Group Presentation: Once your final product is completed, we will work out a way for your group to present the project to the class. Keeping in mind that written and multimedia compositions and oral presentations can be very different rhetorical situations, your group will decide on the best format for your presentation to your peers and me.

Post-mortem Reflection: At the completion of the project (final product and presentation), members of your group will each compose a reflective analysis, in which you look back on the project, think about its many facets, and evaluate how it has impacted you, your learning, and your perspective on collaboration. You will share these reflections with one another in class.

Group suggestions/resources

This is a **team** project. You all must contribute. If someone is not contributing, tell me immediately. I don't need to tell you that team projects are challenging, but I am not handing you a team project and saying, "I'll see you in three weeks." I'm here to work with you during this project to help it run smoothly.

How do we meet? If you are all local, feel free to meet. However, this is an online course, so I don't expect you to be able to all get together in one place. I have set up a live classroom on the Course Homepage that any team can use to conduct a virtual meeting much like the one we conducted to introduce the class. More simply, and this has worked fine in the past for many teams, you can use the Discussion thread I've created for your team. You can also use tools like SharePoint or GoogleDocs to share documents, or you can get together in an "old fashioned" phone conference call. Note that if you use the Discussion threads, I can keep pace with what you are doing and help you.

Meeting progress. One way teams don't work is when there is no record of team progress. Each week I'm asking you to submit a progress report with meeting minutes so that the progress (or, in some cases, lack thereof) is apparent. I am here to help. If you have any questions, it is easy for us all to get together.

Working in a team. Take a look at chapter 15 of our course textbook. Here are two other useful links: how to run good meetings: http://www.bnet.com/article/how-to-run-an-effective-meeting/61211; how to write meeting minutes: http://www.meetingwizard.org/meetings/meeting-minutes-format.cfm

Glossary

announcement: a brief update on the course homepage.

asynchronous: not occurring at the same time; specifically in this book, communications software that does not require users to be present at the same time.

AV (audiovisual) response: providing response to student writing using short screen-capture videos.

Discussions: platforms to enable asynchronous conversations; also called message boards.

f2f: face-to-face classes; also called *onsite* throughout the book.

forum: a collection of Discussion threads/topics.

FYW: first-year writing.

hybrid course: a course that is taught both onsite and online; the amount of teaching/studenting time in each modality can vary, but a hybrid typically means that instruction happens both in the classroom and in online settings. For instance, in a hybrid course, you might meet your students for ninety minutes on Tuesday, and then on Thursday instead of meeting they would work in an online environment for the equivalent of that ninety minutes.

informal writing: writing that is low-stakes in a course; informal writing in our course was not graded as rigorously as a formal assignment for aspects of writing mechanics, and that writing was often used as a tool to help students develop their thinking about a topic or idea.

learning management system (LMS): a Web-based program to help teachers post materials, facilitate student conversations, and perform other class functions in online learning.

learning outcome: a clear, specific goal for a course.

leveraging: in the context of OWI, using texts from previous lessons or courses to reduce keystrokes and time in online teaching.

message board: see Discussions.

migration: a philosophy for teachers who are moving to online teaching in which they work from experience and convert teaching practices from onsite to online.

multimodal: communication using various media, including text, graphics, video, and audio.

OWC: online writing course.

OWI: online writing instruction.

OWT: online writing teacher.

primary post: on a message board, a longish, substantive post (see pre-chapter for exact guidelines).

project: any lengthy written essay, paper, assignment, or report.

response: the feedback you provide and dialogue you open with students about their writing; this differs from straightforward grading.

secondary post: on a message board, a shorter, response-type post (see pre-chapter for exact guidelines).

synchronous: occurring at the same time; specifically in this book, communications software that requires users to be present at the same time, such as chat software.

thread: a conversation topic within a *forum*; users can change the subject line if they like.

Weekly Plan: organizational approach that describes exactly what is due in a particular week in an online or hybrid writing course.

Writing about Writing (WaW): an approach to/philosophy of writing instruction in which students do not just approach writing as a skill but also engage in readings and learning about writing as subject matter.

Writing Studies: see Writing about Writing.

WYSIWYG: what you see is what you get.

Notes

Introduction

1. This was certainly the goal of the CCCC Committee for Effective Practices in Online Writing Instruction's publication of "A Position Statement of Principles and Example Effective Practices for Online Writing Instruction (OWI)."

2. Depending on the source, from 50 percent to 80 percent of college undergraduates change majors.

3. The above-mentioned committee's 2015-16 focus was Student Matters, and Meloncon and Harris said that "One issue that emerged from the CCCC OWI Committee surveys is the need to understand more about students' apparent readiness for online education" (413).

4. Jane Tompkins's *A Life in School* is an interesting meditation on such differences.

Pre-Chapter

1. Elizabeth Wardle and Douglas Downs created a text to support WaW approaches to FWP: *Writing about Writing: A College Reader*.

Week 1

1. For a good conversation about these approaches/modalities specifically for OWCs, see Connie Snyder Mick and Geoffrey Middlebrook's chapter "Asynchronous and Synchronous Modalities."

2. While Scott has remained an advocate of icebreakers, he facilitated a workshop, "Diversity in the Online Environment," at the 2017 CCCC Summer Conference at the University of Cincinnati Clermont College during which he and the participants used perspectives of access and diversity to critique icebreakers, including the one mentioned here.

Week 2

1. For more about moderating, see *Teaching Writing Online*, pp. 74–78.

2. An excellent review of the latest research can be found in the CompPile bibliography "Teaching Grammar-in-Context in College Writing Instruction: An Update on the Research Literature" by Zak Lancaster and Andrea R. Olinger.

Week 3

1. Scott has talked with Jeff through the years, and we both have been puzzled that more teachers don't use voice response, if for no other reason than it makes responding so much less onerous.

Week 4

1. Of course, this does not just apply to peer review. As Beth Hewett and Scott say in the final chapter of *Foundational Practices of Online Writing Instruction*, "Perhaps that reality has changed in that the computer has become—if not a must in postsecondary institutions (as well as in most places of business)—then at least a transparent part of the cultural and communications landscape: We are one with these devices; they are part of our lives" (560–61).

Week 5

1. Tuckman conceptualized collaborative work in these four categories. Groups "initially concern themselves with orientation," what could be thought of as *forming;* the "second point in the sequence is characterized by conflict and polarization," or *storming;* in the third stage "ingroup feeling and cohesiveness develop," or *norming;* and in the final stage, *performing,* "structural issues have been resolved, and structure can now become supportive of task performance" (396).

Week 8

1. Scott presented this idea at Writing Research Across Borders in Bogota, Colombia, in February 2017.

Beyond the Final Week

1. In response to this increasing interest in and recognition of the importance of online literacy, in 2016 Scott was part of a group that founded the Global Society of Online Literacy Educators (GSOLE): www.glosole.org.

Works Cited

Adler-Kassner, Linda, and Elizabeth Wardle. *Naming What We Know: Threshold Concepts of Writing Studies*. Logan: Utah State UP, 2015. Print.

Allen, I. Elaine, and Jeff Seaman. "Conflicted: Faculty and Online Education, 2012." *Babson Survey Research Group*. Babson Park, MA: Babson College, 2012. Web.

Allen, I. Elaine, and Jeff Seaman, with Russell Poulin and Terri Taylor Straut. "Online Report Card: Tracking Online Education in the United States." *Babson Survey Research Group*. Babson Park, MA: Babson College, 2016. Web.

American Psychological Association. "Publication Practices & Responsible Authorship." Web.

Angelino, Lorraine M., Frankie Keels Williams, and Deborah Natvig. "Strategies to Engage Online Students and Reduce Attrition Rates." *Journal of Educators Online* 4.2 (2007): n. pag. Web.

Anon. RateMyProfessor. 7 Mar. 2007. Web.

Anson, Chris. "Talking about Text: The Use of Recorded Commentary in Response to Student Writing." *A Sourcebook for Responding to Student Writing*. Ed. Richard Straub. Cresskill, NJ: Hampton Press, 1999. 165–74. Print.

Atkins, Anthony T. "Collaborating Online: Digital Strategies for Group Work." *Writing Spaces: Readings on Writing* 1 (2010): 235–48. Print.

Atkinson, J. Maxwell, and John Heritage. "Jefferson's Transcript Notation." *The Discourse Reader.* (2nd ed.) Ed. Adam Jaworski and Nikolas Coupland. New York: Routledge, 2006. 158–65. Print.

Bacon, Donald R., Kim A. Stewart, and William S. Silver. "Lessons from the Best and Worst Student Team Experiences: How a Teacher Can Make the Difference." *Journal of Management Education* 23.5 (1999): 467–88. Print.

Barber, John F. "Effective Teaching in the Online Classroom: Thoughts and Recommendations." *The Online Writing Classroom*. Ed. Susanmarie Harrington, Rebecca Rickly, and Michael Day. Cresskill, NJ: Hampton, 2000. 243–64. Print.

Barrett, Edward. "Collaboration in the Electronic Classroom." *Technology Review* 96.2 (1993): 50–55. Web.

Barton, Matt, and Karl Klint. "A Student's Guide to Collaborative Writing Technologies." *Writing Spaces: Readings on Writing* 2 (2011): 320–32. Web.

Benington, John, and Jean Hartley. "Co-Research: Insider/Outsider Teams for Organizational Research." *Essential Guide to Qualitative Methods in Organizational Research.* Ed. Catherine Cassell and Gillian Symon. London: SAGE Publications, 2004. 361–71. Print.

Berlin, James A. *Rhetoric and Reality: Writing Instruction in American Colleges, 1900–1985.* Carbondale: Southern Illinois UP, 1987. Print.

Blair, Leslie. "Teaching Composition Online: No Longer the Second-Best Choice." *Kairos* 8.2 (2003). Web.

Booth, Alan. "Learning History in University: Student Views on Teaching and Assessment." *Studies in Higher Education* 18.2 (1993): 227–35. Web.

Bower, Matt, and John G. Hedberg. "A Quantitative Multimodal Discourse Analysis of Teaching and Learning in a Web-Conferencing Environment—The Efficacy of Student-Centered Learning Designs." *Computers & Education* 54.2 (2010): 462–78. Web.

Bowles-Terry, Melissa, Erin Davis, and Wendy Holliday. "'Writing Information Literacy' Revisited: Application of Theory to Practice in the Classroom." *Reference & User Services Quarterly* 49.3 (2010): 225–30. Web.

Boyd, Patricia Webb. "Online Discussion Boards as Identity Workspaces: Building Professional Identities in Online Writing Classes." *Journal of Interactive Technology and Pedagogy* 4 (2013). Web.

Boylorn, Robin M. "Participants as Co-Researchers." *The SAGE Encyclopedia of Qualitative Research Methods*. Ed. Lisa M. Given. Thousand Oaks, CA: SAGE Publications, 2008. 600–602. Print.

Bridwell-Bowles, Lillian, Parker Johnson, and Steven Brehe. "Composing and Computers: Case Studies of Experienced Writers." *Writing in Real Time: Modeling Production Process*. Ed. Ann Matsuhashi. London: Longman, 1987. 81–107. Print.

Britton, James, A. Burgess, Nancy Martin, Alex McLeod, and Harold Rosen. "The Development of Writing Abilities (11–18). [Schools Council Project on Written Language of 11–18 year olds.]" (1975). Print.

Brooks, Charles M., and Janice L. Ammons. "Free Riding in Group Projects and the Effects of Timing, Frequency, and Specificity of Criteria in Peer Assessments." *Journal of Education for Business* 78.5 (2003): 268–72. Web.

Bruffee, Kenneth A. "Collaborative Learning and the 'Conversation of Mankind.'" *College English* 46.7 (1984): 635–52. Print.

Busker, Rebecca Lucy. "Virtual Kairos: Audience in Virtual Spaces." *Kairos* 7.3 (Fall 2002). 12 March 2005. Web.

Cambridge, Barbara L., Susan Kahn, Daniel P. Tompkins, and Kathleen Blake Yancey, eds. *Electronic Portfolios: Emerging Practices in Student, Faculty, and Institutional Learning*. Washington, DC: American Association for Higher Education, 2001. Print.

Caplan, Dean, and Rodger Graham. "The Development of Online Courses." *The Theory and Practice of Online Learning*. Ed. Terry Anderson. Alberta: Athabasca UP, 2008. 245–63. Print.

Cason, Jacqueline, and Patricia Jenkins. "Adapting Instructional Documents to an Online Course Environment." *Online Education 2.0: Evolving, Adapting, and Reinventing Online Technical Communication*. Ed. Kelli Cargile Cook and Keith Grant-Davie. Amityville, NY: Baywood Publishing, 2013. 213–36. Print.

Childers, Jeri L., R. Thomas Berner. "General Education Issues, Distance Education Practices: Building Community and Classroom Interaction through the Integration of Curriculum, Instructional Design, and Technology." *Journal of General Education* 49.1 (2000): 53–65. Web.

Cody, Jim. "Asynchronous Online Discussion Forums: Going Vibrantly beyond the Shadow of the Syllabus." *Teaching English in the Two-Year College* 30.3 (2003): 268–76. Web.

Coles, William E. *The Plural I—and After.* Portsmouth, NH: Boynton/Cook, 1988. Print.

Collison, George, Bonnie Elbaum, Sarah Haavind, and Robert Tinker. *Facilitating Online Learning: Effective Strategies for Moderators.* Madison, WI: Atwood, 2000. Print.

Conference on College Composition and Communication. "Scholarship in Composition: Guidelines for Faculty, Deans, and Department Chairs." National Council of Teachers of English, 1987. Web.

Conference on College Composition and Communication Committee for Effective Practices in Online Writing Instruction. "A Position Statement of Principles and Example Effective Practices for Online Writing Instruction (OWI)." National Council of Teachers of English, 2013. Web.

Conference on College Composition and Communication Taskforce on Best Practices in Electronic Portfolios. "Principles and Practices in Electronic Portfolios." National Council of Teachers of English, 2015. Web.

Cook, Kelli Cargile, and Keith Grant-Davie, eds. *Online Education 2.0: Evolving, Adapting, and Reinventing Online Technical Communication*. Amityville, NY: Baywood, 2012. Print.

Cyganowski, Carol Klimick. "The Computer Classroom and Collaborative Learning: The Impact on Student Writers." *Computers and Community: Teaching Composition in the Twenty-First Century.* Ed. Carolyn Handa. Portsmouth, NH: Boynton/Cook, 1990. 68–88. Print.

Dennen, Vanessa Paz. "From Message Posting to Learning Dialogues: Factors Affecting Learner Participation in Asynchronous Discussion." *Distance Education* 26.1 (2005): 127–48. Web.

DePew, Kevin Eric. "Preparing for the Rhetoricity of OWI." *Foundational Practices of Online Writing Instruction.* Ed. Beth Hewett and Kevin Eric DePew. Fort Collins, CO: The WAC Clearinghouse and Parlor Press, 2015. 439–67. Print.

Dixon, Zachary, and Joe Moxley. "Everything Is Illuminated: What Big Data Can Tell Us about Teacher Commentary." *Assessing Writing* 18.4 (2013): 241–56. Web.

Downs, Douglas, and Elizabeth Wardle. "Teaching about Writing, Righting Misconceptions: (Re)Envisioning 'First-Year Composition' as 'Introduction to Writing Studies.'" *College Composition and Communication* 58.4 (2007): 552–84. Print.

Drexel Publishing Group. "Publications." *Drexel University College of Arts and Sciences.* 2017. Web. http://drexel.edu/coas/academics/departments-centers/english-philosophy/publications/

Dryer, Dylan B. "Scaling Writing Ability: A Corpus-Driven Inquiry." *Written Communication* 30.1 (2013): 3–35. Web.

Elbow, Peter. *Writing with Power: Techniques for Mastering the Writing Process.* New York: Oxford UP, 1981. Print.

Faigley, Lester. "Subverting the Electronic Workbook: Teaching Writing Using Networked Computers." *The Writing Teacher as Researcher: Essays in the Theory and Practice of Class-Based Research.* Ed. Donald A. Daiker and Max Morenberg. Portsmouth, NH: Boynton/Cook, 1990. 290–311. Print.

Fey, Marion H., and Michael J. Sisson. "Approaching the Information Superhighway: Internet Collaboration Among Future Writing Teachers." *Computers and Composition* 13.1 (1996): 37–47. Web.

Filene, Peter. *The Joy of Teaching: A Practical Guide for New College Instructors.* Chapel Hill: U of North Carolina P, 2005. Print.

Freire, Paulo. *Pedagogy of the Oppressed.* New York: Continuum, 1992. Print.

Gannon, Kevin. "The Absolute Worst Way to Start the Semester." *ChronicleVitae.* 3 Aug. 2016. Web.

Gooblar, David. "They Haven't Done the Reading. Again." *ChronicleVitae.* 24 Sep. 2014. Web.

Gos, Michael W. "Nontraditional Student Access to OWI." *Foundational Practices of Online Writing Instruction.* Ed. Beth L. Hewett and Kevin Eric DePew. Fort Collins, CO: The WAC Clearinghouse and Parlor Press, 2015. 309–46. Print.

Griffin, June, and Deborah Minter. "The Rise of the Online Writing Classroom: Reflecting on the Material Conditions of College Composition Teaching." *College Composition and Communication* 65.1 (2013): 140–61. Print.

Grobman, Laurie, and Joyce A. Kinkead. *Undergraduate Research in English Studies.* National Council of Teachers of English, 2010. Print.

Haas, Christina. *Writing Technology: Studies on the Materiality of Literacy.* New York: Routledge, 2013. Print.

Hakim, Toufic M. "How to Develop and Administer Institutional Undergraduate Research Programs." Washington, DC. 2000. PowerPoint Presentation. Web.

Handayani, Nani Sri. "Emerging Roles in Scripted Online Collaborative Writing in Higher Education Context." *Procedia—Social and Behavioral Sciences* 67 (2012): 370–79. Web.

Hansen, Derek L., Ben Shneiderman, and Marc Smith. "Visualizing Threaded Conversation Networks: Mining Message Boards and Email Lists for Actionable Insights." *Lecture Notes in Computer Science* 6335 (2010): 47–62. Web.

Hansen, Randall S. "Benefits and Problems with Student Teams: Suggestions for Improving Team Projects." *Journal of Education for Business* 82.1 (2006): 11–19. Web.

Harris, Heidi S., Tawnya Lubbes, Nancy Knowles, and Jacob Harris. "Translation, Transformation, and 'Taking it Back': Moving between Face-to-Face and Online Writing in the Disciplines." *The WAC Journal* 25 (2014): 106–26. Print.

Harris, Joseph. *A Teaching Subject: Composition since 1966*. Upper Saddle River, NJ: Prentice Hall, 1997. Print.

Heinert, Seth, and T. Grady Roberts. "Factors Motivating Students to Respond to Online Course Evaluations in the College of Agricultural and Life Sciences at the University of Florida." *NACTA Journal* 60.2 (2016): 189–94. Web.

Herman, David. "Introduction." *The Cambridge Companion to Narrative*. Ed. David Herman. Cambridge: Cambridge UP, 2007. Print.

Hewett, Beth L. "Characteristics of Interactive Oral and Computer-Mediated Peer Group Talk and Its Influence on Revision." *Computers and Composition* 17.3 (2000): 265–88. Web.

———. "The Characteristics and Effects of Oral and Computer-Mediated Peer Group Talk on the Argumentative Writing Process." Dissertation, Catholic U of America, 1998. Web.

———. *Reading to Learn and Writing to Teach: Literacy Strategies for Online Writing Instruction*. New York: Macmillan Higher Education, 2015. Print.

Hewett, Beth L., and Charlotte Robidoux, eds. *Virtual Collaborative Writing in the Workplace: Computer-Mediated Communication Technologies and Processes*. Hershey, PA: IGI Global, 2010. Print.

Hewett, Beth L., and Scott Warnock. "The Future of OWI." *Foundational Practices of Online Writing Instruction*. Ed. Beth L. Hewett and Kevin DePew. Fort Collins, CO: The WAC Clearinghouse and Parlor Press, 2015. 553–69. Print.

Hill, Charles A., David L. Wallace, and Christina Haas. "Revising On-Line: Computer Technologies and the Revising Process." *Computers and Composition* 9.1 (1991): 83–109. Web.

"Homer Goes to College." *The Simpsons*. Episode 1F02. Fox. 14 Oct. 1993. Television.

Hoover, Eric. "The Human Variable in Teaching." *The Chronicle of Higher Education*. 21 Apr. 2014. A26–A31. Web.

Irvin, L. Lennie. "Reflection in the Electronic Writing Classroom." *Computers and Composition Online Journal* (2004). Web.

Kittle, Peter, and Troy Hicks. "Transforming the Group Paper with Collaborative Online Writing." *Pedagogy* 9.3 (2009): 525–39. Web.

Lancaster, Zak, and Andrea R. Olinger. "Teaching Grammar-in-Context in College Writing Instruction: An Update on the Research Literature." WPA-CompPile Research Bibliographies, No. 24. *WPA-CompPile Research Bibliographies*. Apr. 2014. Web.

Larson, Richard. "Portfolios in the Assessment of Writing." *Assessment of Writing: Politics, Policies, Practices*. Ed. Edward White, William Lutz, and Sandra Kamusikiri. New York: Modern Language Association of America, 1996. Print.

Levi, Daniel, and David Cadiz. "Evaluating Team Work on Student Projects: The Use of Behaviorally Anchored Scales to Evaluate Student Performance." ERIC. Web.

Logan, Marianne, and Keith Skamp. "Engaging Students in Science Across the Primary Secondary Interface: Listening to the Students' Voice." *Research in Science Education* 38.4 (2008): 501–27. Web.

Lucas, Margarida, and António Moreira. "A Visual Representation of Online Interaction Patterns." *Journal of Universal Computer Science* 21.11 (2015): 1496–1507. Web.

Lundstrom, Kristi, and Wendy Baker. "To Give Is Better Than to Receive: The Benefits of Peer Review to the Reviewer's Own Writing." *Journal of Second Language Writing* 18.1 (2009): 30–43. Web.

McClure, Randall. "Googlepedia: Turning Information Behaviors into Research Skills." *Writing Spaces: Readings on Writing* 2 (2011): 221–41. Web.

McClure, Randall, and James P. Purdy. *The New Digital Scholar*. Medford, NJ: American Society for Information Science and Technology, 2013. Print.

Mellen, Cheryl, and Jeffrey Sommers. "Audio-Taped Response and the Two-Year-Campus Writing Classroom: The Two-Sided Desk, the 'Guy with the Ax', and the Chirping Birds." *Teaching English in the Two-Year College* 31.1 (2003): 25–39. Web.

Meloncon, Lisa, and Heidi Skurat Harris. "Preparing Students for OWI." *Foundational Practices of Online Writing Instruction*. Ed. Beth Hewett and Kevin DePew. Fort Collins, CO: The WAC Clearinghouse and Parlor Press, 2015. 411–38. Print.

Meyer, Katrina A. "Does Feedback Influence Student Postings to Online Discussions?" *Journal of Educators Online* 4.1 (2007). Web.

Mick, Connie Snyder, and Geoffrey Middlebrook. "Asynchronous and Synchronous Modalities." *Foundational Practices of Online Writing Instruction*. Ed. Beth Hewett and Kevin DePew. Fort Collins, CO: The WAC Clearinghouse and Parlor Press, 2015. 129–48. Print.

Moore, Noreen S., and Michelle L. Filling. "iFeedback: Using Video Technology for Improving Student Writing." *Journal of College Literacy & Learning* 38 (2012): 3–14. Web.

National Center for Education Statistics. "Fast Facts: How Many Students Take Distance Learning Courses at the Postsecondary Level?" Web. https://nces.ed.gov/fastfacts/display.asp?id=80

Norgaard, Rolf. "Writing Information Literacy: Contributions to a Concept." *Reference & User Services Quarterly* 43.2 (2003): 124–30. Web.

North, Stephen. *The Making of Knowledge in Composition: Portrait of an Emerging Field*. Portsmouth, NH: Boynton/Cook, 1987. Print.

Ong, Walter J. *Orality and Literacy: The Technologizing of the Word*. London: Methuen, 1982. Print.

Oswal, Sushil. "Accessible ePortfolios for Visually-Impaired Users: Interfaces, Design, & Infrastructures." *ePortfolio Performance Support Systems: Constructing, Presenting, and Assessing Portfolios*. Ed. Katherine V. Wills and Rich Rice. Anderson, SC: Parlor Press, 2013. 133–52. Print.

Parsons, Keith M. "When Students Won't Read." *The Huffington Post*. 9 Mar. 2015. Web.

Passig, David, and Gali Schwartz. "Collaborative Writing: Online versus Frontal." *International Journal on E-Learning* 6.3 (2007): 395–412. Web.

Patel, Vimal. "$3-Million Grant Puts Ph.D. Candidates in 2-Year-College Classrooms." *The Chronicle of Higher Education*. 1 Nov. 2015. Print.

———. "Training Graduate Students to Be Effective Teachers." *The Chronicle of Higher Education*. 30 July 2017. A8–A13. Print.

Pratt, Mary Louise. "Arts of the Contact Zone." *Profession* (1991): 33–40. Print.

Reiff, Mary Jo, and Anis Bawarshi. "Tracing Discursive Resources: How Students Use Prior Genre Knowledge to Negotiate New Writing Contexts in First-Year Composition." *Written Communication* 28.3 (2011): 312–37. Web.

Ripley, Amanda. "The Upwardly Mobile Barista." *The Atlantic*. May 2015. Print.

Russell, David. "Activity Theory and Its Implications for Writing Instruction." *Reconceiving Writing, Rethinking Writing Instruction*. Ed. Joseph Petraglia. Hillsdale, NJ: Erlbaum, 1995. 51–77. Print.

Selfe, Cynthia L., and Gail E. Hawisher. *Literate Lives in the Information Age: Narratives of Literacy from the United States*. Mahwah, NJ: Lawrence Erlbaum Associates, 2004. Print.

Silva, Mary Lourdes. "Can I Google That? Research Strategies of Undergraduate Students?" *The New Digital Scholar*. Ed. Randall McClure and James P. Purdy. Medford, NJ: American Society for Information Science and Technology, 2013. 161–88. Print.

Sommers, Jeff. "Response 2.0: Commentary on Student Writing for the New Millennium." *Journal of College Literacy and Learning* 39 (2013): 21–37. Web.

———. "Response Rethought . . . Again: Exploring Recorded Comments and the Teacher-Student Bond." *Journal of Writing Assessment* 5.1 (2012). Web.

Sommers, Nancy. "Responding to Student Writing." *College Composition and Communication* 33.2 (1982): 148–56. Print.

Stine, Linda J. "Teaching Basic Writing in a Web-Enhanced Environment." *Journal of Basic Writing* 29.1 (2010): 33–55. Web.

Tompkins, Jane P. *A Life in School: What the Teacher Learned*. New York: Basic Books, 1996. Print.

Tornow, Joan C. *Link/Age: Composing in the Online Classroom*. Logan: Utah State UP, 1997. Print.

Tuckman, Bruce W. "Developmental Sequence in Small Groups." *Psychological Bulletin* 63.6 (1965): 384–99. Web.

Tulley, Christine. "Migration Patterns: A Status Report on the Transition from Paper to Eportfolios and the Effect on Multimodal Composition Initiatives within First-Year Composition." *Computers and Composition* 30.2 (2013): 101–14. Web.

Ugoretz, Joseph. "'Two Roads Diverged in a Wood': Productive Digression in Asynchronous Discussion." *Innovate: Journal of Online Education* 1.3 (2005): 7–12. Web.

Wang, Terrence, Michelle McMullin, Lindsey Macdonald, Shelley Staples, and Bradley Dilger. "Boundary Work: Designing an Archive for Research and Mentoring Across Disciplines." Purdue University ~ University of Arizona ~ writecrow.org ~ info@writecrow.org. Computers and Writing 2016, Session D2 (Fri 5/20, 4:30 to 5:45 p.m.), Nursing 102. http://writecrow.org/wp-content/uploads/2016/05/crow-cw2016-handout.pdf. Web.

Wardle, Elizabeth. "'Mutt Genres' and the Goal of FYC: Can We Help Students Write the Genres of the University?" *College Composition and Communication* 60.4 (2009): 765–89. Web.

Wardle, Elizabeth, and Douglas Downs. *Writing about Writing: A College Reader*. Boston: Bedford/St. Martin's, 2014. Print.

Warner, John. "When Students Won't Do the Reading." *Inside Higher Ed*. 18 Jan. 2016. Web.

Warnock, Scott. "Diversity in the Online Environment." Workshop at the 2017 Conference on College Composition and Communication Summer Conference. University of Cincinnati Clermont College. June 2017.

———. "The Low-Stakes, Risk-Friendly Message Board Text." *Teaching with Student Texts: Essays Toward an Informed Practice*. Ed. Joseph Harris, John Miles, and Charles Paine. Logan: Utah State UP, 2010. 96–107. Print.

———. "OWI and the Fractal Nature of Teaching Writing." Presentation at Writing Research Across Borders IV. Bogota, Colombia. February 2017.

———. "The Provoker." *Online Writing Teacher*. 31 May 2015. Web.

———. "Responding to Student Writing with Audio-Visual Feedback." *Writing and the iGeneration: Composition in the Computer-Mediated Classroom*. Ed. Terry Carter, Maria A. Clayton, Allison D. Smith, and Trixie G. Smith. Southlake, TX: Fountainhead Press, 2008. 201–27. Print.

———. *Teaching Writing Online: How and Why*. Urbana, IL: National Council of Teachers of English, 2009. Print.

White, Edward M., Norbert Elliot, and Irvin Peckham. *Very Like a Whale: The Assessment of Writing Programs*. Boulder: UP of Colorado, 2015. Print.

White, Edward M., William Lutz, and Sandra Kamusikiri, eds. *Assessment of Writing: Politics, Policies, Practices*. New York: Modern Language Association of America, 1996. Print.

Wichadee, Saovapa. "Improving Students' Summary Writing Ability Through Collaboration: A Comparison Between Online Wiki Group and Conventional Face-to-Face Group." *Turkish Online Journal of Educational Technology* 12.3 (2013): 107–16. Web.

Williams, David L., John D. Beard, and Jone Rymer. "Team Projects: Achieving Their Full Potential." *Journal of Marketing Education* 13.2 (1991): 45–53. Web.

Wills, Katherine V., and Richard Aaron Rice, eds. *ePortfolio Performance Support Systems: Constructing, Presenting, and Assessing Portfolios*. Anderson, SC: Parlor Press, 2013. Web.

Yancey, Kathleen Blake. "Defining Reflection: The Rhetorical Nature and Qualities of Reflection." *A Rhetoric of Reflection*. Ed. Kathleen Blake Yancey. Boulder: UP of Colorado, 2016. 303–20. Print.

———. "Postmodernism, Palimpsest, and Portfolios: Theoretical Issues in the Representation of Student Work." *College Composition and Communication* 55.4 (2004): 738–61. Web.

Yancey, Kathleen Blake, Stephen McElroy, and Elizabeth Powers. "Composing, Networks, and Electronic Portfolios: Notes toward a Theory of Assessing ePortfolios." *Digital Writing Assessment and Evaluation*. Computers and Composition Digital Press, 2013. Web.

Zaldivar, Marc, Teggin Summers, and C. Edward Watson. "Balancing Learning and Assessment: A Study of Virginia Tech's Use of ePortfolios." *ePortfolio Performance Support Systems: Constructing, Presenting, and Assessing Portfolios*. Anderson, SC: Parlor Press, 2013. 221–39. Print.

Index